The UAW and Walter Reuther

THE UAW AND
WALTER REUTHER

BY IRVING HOWE AND B. J. WIDICK

RANDOM HOUSE · NEW YORK

To *"the architects of the future"*

ACKNOWLEDGMENTS

THE AUTHORS are grateful to the following publishers for permission to quote from books to which they hold copyright:
Rinehart and Co., *The Legend of Henry Ford,* by Keith Sward, 1948; Scribner & Sons, *The American Jitters,* Edmund Wilson, 1932; New Directions, *Journey to the End of the Night,* Louis-Ferdinand Celine, 1947; Dryden Press, *Race Riot,* Alfred McClung Lee and Norman Humphrey, 1944; Harper & Bros., *Racial Factors in American Industry,* Herman Feldman, 1931.

Parts of this book appeared, in somewhat different and condensed form, in *The Virginia Quarterly Review, Commentary* and *The Progressive.*

Contents

Preface

IN THIS COUNTRY there has arisen, in the last fifteen years, a new and significant social force that directly affects the lives of millions of people and is certain to influence the course of our future history. The rise of industrial unionism has been one of the major events of 20th-century American social history; its consequences have not yet been fully reckoned. And of all the industrial unions, the United Automobile, Aircraft and Agricultural Implement Workers of America, CIO (hereafter referred to as the UAW), is the most important and interesting.

This is a book about that union. It is, however, neither an "official" history nor a detailed chronicle; it is rather an attempt to provide a brief but comprehensive account of the rise of the UAW, its external struggles and internal life, and the problems it faces in the postwar world. We have been particularly interested in relating its development to the larger trends of recent American life.

Too many of the books written about unions are either academic studies, which, for all their values, lack the "feel" of union life, or "official" histories, which serve usually to please whichever union leadership happens to be in power. Other books on labor are written as tracts, either by professional opponents of the unions or by apologists for the current line of the Communist Party. We reject these approaches. Particularly do we reject the claim of the Stalinists to be critics of labor from the left—for if there is to be such criticism, if it is to be valuable and credible, it must have nothing in common with these colonial agents of Russian totalitarianism.

We pretend to no pseudo-objectivity. Even if that were possible in writing on such a controversial subject, it would make for intolerable ambiguity and dullness. We take sides. We support unions, believe in their necessity, rejoice in their victories. But at the same time we have tried our best to present all the relevant facts, even when those facts might run counter to our wishes or to the feelings of those individuals whose lives are intertwined with the UAW. Our criticisms are made from within the range of labor opinion; we write as friends and supporters; and where necessary we criticize those with whom we are otherwise in frequent agreement. But in most instances, the story of the UAW simply tells itself.

This book is documented, notes and bibliographical references appearing at its end. It is the product of a close and sustained collaboration, and even if an attempt were made, no demarcation of responsibility would be possible.

For the contents of this book, we alone are responsible.

I. H. and B. J. W.

May 1, 1949

Part I

SETTING

Life in the Factory City

1 ---

On the east side of Detroit there is a small area,
not much larger than two square miles, in which six large
auto plants jostle each other like parts of a badly made
jig-saw puzzle. Chrysler, Hudson, Briggs, Budd, Conti-
nental, and Motor Products—these factories employ some
75,000 men, a vast weaving stream of workers that flows
in and out twice a day. Here, in ultimate concentration,
is industrial America; from its vortex of work, as from
several others like it, the city of Detroit receives its energies and tensions. As one moves from this tangle of factories into the residential neighborhoods that lie adjacent
to it and dependent on it, one can see just how industrialism has transformed the quality of American life.

In the twenties, Detroit became the unchallenged motor capital of the world; there is still no competitor in
sight. In the thirties it was the center of a vast, perilous
labor upsurge which provoked a minor revolution in

American life. In the forties—so far the forties have been a decade in which the conflicting pressures that rend the city have worked beneath its surface, to erupt into occasional violence. Detroit—the dynamite keg, the time bomb, the center of an unsettled new social movement associated with the name of the UAW. Properly modulated, all of these phrases are true. Detroit is symbolic of industrial America; here every tendency of urban life finds its most extreme expression; a city of "racial, religious and economic unrest," [1] it contains all the possibilities, heartening and terrifying, of American social life.

By 1900 Detroit was already the second largest center for the manufacture of the horseless carriage, as well as of internal combustion engines for lake boats. It was the natural place for Henry Ford and R. E. Olds to open their factories. It lies strategically tangential to the Pittsburgh-Youngstown steel mills, the Akron rubber plants, the Messabi iron range; and the Great Lakes waterways, joined by the Detroit River from Lake Huron to Lake Erie, make possible the cheap transportation of raw materials and finished products.

In it is the center of one of America's largest unions, the United Automobile Workers Union, CIO. Our interest in this union is prompted not primarily by its size; what stimulates one's imagination is the potentiality of this union as a force molding American life.

But before we turn directly to the story of the UAW, let us glance at the city in which the core of its members lives. There are strong UAW concentrations in other cities: Cleveland, Toledo, Chicago; but in these cities its influence is diluted by the presence of other large unions and industries. There are strong UAW concentrations in satellite towns surrounding Detroit: Pontiac, Flint, Saginaw; but the life of the auto workers in these towns is in many respects a replica of that in Detroit. For Detroit is the center, and whatever happens to the industry and the workers there will sooner or later happen elsewhere.

How then do auto workers live in Detroit? How do they work, what do they think and how do they feel about their life? Where, to begin with, did they come from?

JOURNEY NORTH

Until January 5, 1914, Detroit knew the normal growth of the Midwestern city, its population then being slightly under 500,000. On that day there took place one of those symbolic events that marks a major historical transition: the Ford Motor Company announced it would pay $5 a day to all its workers. The news that startled and frightened competitors was an attractive sign of hope to hundreds of thousands of people in this and other countries.

In his autobiography Henry Ford said of the five-dollar-a-day wage that "It was to our way of thinking an act of social justice, and in the last analysis we did it for our own satisfaction of mind. There is a pleasure in feeling that you have made others happy . . ."[2] In the same book Ford also remarked that "The payment of five dollars a day for an eight-hour day was one of the finest cost-cutting moves we ever made . . ."[3]

Whatever the motives of Ford, philanthropic or commercial, one week after the announcement of the new wage scale 5,000 men lined up at 5 A.M. on a bitterly cold morning in the hope of earning $5 a day. By the time the plant opened there were 12,000 men at the employment office. This was one of those factory gate job-lines which were to become a permanent part of Detroit life; workers in the plants still recall them with undimmed bitterness. The company was not equipped to handle the applicants, and soon a riot broke out, in which police turned a water-hose on the job-seekers. "Mob of 10,000 Riot at Ford Plant Doors," ran the headline in a Detroit paper that day. "With tempers frayed by the intense cold and failure to get work, 10,000 men rioted in front of the Ford plant this morning . . . The crowd stormed the doors of the plant, hundreds forcing their way through, bricks and other missiles were hurled at the officers and building, and the rioters were dispersed only after a drenching with ice-cold water."[4]

But no fire hose could have restrained the mass of men who started moving into Detroit. From the backwoods of Arkansas the "hillbillies" came; and the Georgia "crackers," the Kentucky farmers, the Tennessee mountaineers, the Alabama cotton-pickers, all came to earn high wages and perhaps, too, to taste life in the big city. Some heard the news by word of mouth, others read advertisements in small-town papers urging men to come to Detroit.

Even today one often sees a tall young Southerner clad in blue-jeans, with his sleeves rolled up and his cardboard suitcase in hand, getting off a bus at the Washington Boulevard terminal. Sometimes one sees a whole family packed tight into an old jalopy, looking a bit like Steinbeck's Okies. The car stops at the house of a friend or relative, where the family finds temporary shelter until it can get a place of its own.

As the auto industry expanded, it reached deeper and deeper into the South in its search for cheap and docile labor. Even during the mid-thirties, when the shock of the depression had not worn off and there were nearly 250,000 people on Detroit relief, the companies eagerly sought cheap labor in the South. "For months," one reporter announced after a slight production upsurge in 1935, "the companies have been sending their labor agents to recruit hillbillies from Kentucky, Tennessee, Louisiana and Alabama."[5]

By 1948 almost half a million residents of Detroit were Southerners who had come north to find jobs. Thousands of others, alternately lonely for home and eager for good pay, shuttled back and forth between their native regions and the auto city. In this migration, a whole culture—its folkways, speech inflections, religious feelings, race prejudices—was lifted out of its soil and brought into an environment essentially alien and hostile.

Today there are several pockets of Southern migrants scattered through Detroit. Out on East Jefferson Avenue near the Chrysler plants, a concentration of Southern white workers gives the neighborhood many of the characteristics of an Alabama town. In the beer joints and restaurants you listen to hillbilly music; in the movie theaters you absorb an even higher percentage of cowboy films than in other parts of the city; and along the streets you overhear the basic Southern drawl, sometimes edged with a recently acquired barb of Northern speech. Here Southern white feeling about Negroes festers in much of its original virulence.

Further downtown, along the lower part of Third Avenue on the city's west side, there is another Southern pocket. But where the one on East Jefferson is, so to speak, pure "mill town," the Third Avenue area is a strange and unfelicitous mixture of Southern migrants and declassed urban types. Here factory workers and social flotsam and jetsam live in irritating closeness, their brawls often a favorite subject for the papers on days when the news is slack. One reporter has described this Third Avenue neighborhood with a certain vividness:

> This section runs from Grand River Avenue north to Warren Avenue and is bisected by Third Avenue. It is a rich hunting ground for those who like to observe what humanity can be like under shudder-producing circumstances.
>
> Not but that many upright citizens live in the area—people as honest and decent as those who live in any other section. But it also happens that the area has attracted large groups of poor folk, who were born and bred in the South—Kentucky and Tennessee, for instance.
>
> Most of them came from small towns and some bear the title "hillbilly," a title they do not look on with favor. This group is laced with men and women from many lands, Mexicans, a few French, a few Chinese. Many of these persons (but not all) give the district its bad name.
>
> You will find them most in evidence in the bars that teem in the area and bear fantastic romantic names, for instance, "Sweetheart Bar." They drink, fight, curse, weep, are homesick, boastful, aggressive and sullen.[6]

From the Third Avenue area, where the line of separation between worker and "lumpen" is sometimes blurred, has come the bulk of the supporters of the fascist and quasi-fascist groups that periodically flourish in Detroit. Here Gerald L. K. Smith has found followers. Here the Ku Klux Klan (estimated to have had 18,000 members in Detroit in 1942, the last year for which an estimate is available) is still strong, perhaps not organizationally but certainly ideologically. Its brutal offshoot, the Black Legion, which claimed 200,000 members in Michigan in 1936 and was held responsible by the police for over fifty murders in the late thirties, found this area receptive to its propaganda.[7] Such movements feed on and aggravate the spiritual malaise of people who have abandoned the seat of one culture and have not succeeded in finding sustenance in another.

For many of these people racial and religious prejudice provides a means of objectifying their vague, half-conscious resentments into some external symbol of enmity. This symbol is presumed powerful and malicious enough to cause them troubles, but is yet weak enough for them to victimize with impunity. Social pressures thus result in irrational discharges of energy. Against this accumulation of traditional prejudices, deeply rooted in a people's folkways and nourished by economic deprivation and psychological improverishment, mere rational persuasion often proves ineffective. Appeal to the top of the mind of a factory worker who came to Detroit ten years ago from Alabama and you may, if you are skillful and persistent, make a scratch; but how shallow that scratch seems when compared to the deep pools of prejudice that well up in his unconscious and, to a large extent, his conscious emotions.

Yet there is another side to this matter of prejudice. Often the fanaticism of the Southern migrants, though once the root of KKK feeling, can become or be made into an asset for the union. Some of the best UAW members are Southerners who throw into their union loyalty something like the fundamentalist feeling that might, under other circumstances, be elicited by a Baptist church. There is nothing more satisfying, more likely to bolster one's faith in the possibilities of human development, than to hear, as one occasionally does, a union-educated Southern white worker argue in a thick Alabama accent in behalf of Negro rights. This doesn't happen very often, but it does happen. And those few Southern white workers who have been shaken in their prejudice by the UAW's patient educational work can sometimes establish a feeling of fraternity with Negro workers that Northerners, for all their theoretical lack of prejudice, cannot. It is an encouraging experience to attend the UAW's summer school, held yearly near Port Huron, Michigan, and watch white and Negro workers learn to eat, talk, study and live together; one can see there democratic habits beginning to grow and flourish.

But, in truth, this is the exception. The vast bulk of Southerners in Detroit has not found a sense of security. In Detroit there is a sharp and unmediated clash between two divergent cultural patterns: Southern folkways, uprooted from a natural context, run head-on against a mechanical, depersonalized urbanism. The most poverty-stricken strands of both cultures establish contact and come into conflict, while their more attractive features tend to be dissipated. Southern ways without the soil, the industrial city without much cosmopolitan culture—it is not a happy mixture.

In later sections of this book we shall have a great deal to say about Detroit's Negroes. Here we would only record the fact that along with the Southern whites came Southern Negroes—Ford's $5 a day appealed to both.* Ford, which made its racial quota into a claim to justice, took on many Negroes during the First World War, always punctiliously hiring 10 percent of its working force from among them. From 5,741 in 1910 to 40,838 in 1920, Detroit's Negro population grew in response to calls for unskilled labor at the Ford plant.

* "I was 12 years old when Pat Brooks heard about the money Ford was paying. He went up first, and then brought us up to Detroit. We moved in with some of our kin in MacComb Street. It was kind of crowded there, but the house had toilets indoors and electric light. Down in Alabama we had outhouses and kerosene lamps. My stepfather got a job with Ford, and we got a place of our own in a frame tenement in Catherine Street."—Joe Louis[8]

It is easy enough to surmise the motives of Southern Negroes: better pay, escape from the sharecropping and tenant-farming systems, the prospects of the Northern city where Jim Crow is, at least, not official. Steadily the great migration continued through the twenties and thirties; in 1938 over 150,000 Negroes were jammed into Detroit's dreadful slums. During the recent war the trek northward was accelerated as the need for war workers dissolved some of the more blatant aspects of job discrimination. Over 60,000 Negroes came to Detroit from 1940 to 1942. The heart of the Negro residential area, called with rare sarcasm "Paradise Valley," is in the downtown East Side of Detroit. It is "one of the most intensely crowded urban districts in the United States. Filthy, smelly, dive-ridden, whore-infested Hastings Street is as crowded as Coney Island on a Sunday."[9] But there are no words adequate to describe "Paradise Valley," with its weary shacks and rotting houses; perhaps the only comparable Negro slum is the one that lies, unnoticed and uncelebrated, on the flank of the nation's capitol.

JOURNEY WEST

While Southerners were moving north, immigrants from Europe were coming west. In 1940, after twenty years of drastically reduced immigration, there were 320,000 persons of foreign birth in Detroit, a figure that has probably not been changed very much since then. Some of these immigrants—the 14 percent from Britain and Ireland and the 23 percent from Canada—have found it fairly easy to adjust to American patterns of living. Among Detroit's small labor aristocracy, the tool-and-die makers, there is a large percentage of English workers; the English union tradition still strong in their blood, they are among the most effective, if least demonstrative, members of the UAW.

The least assimilated group in Detroit is the 350,000 Poles of first- or second-generation stock who cling strongly to the cultural tradition of the old country. In many parts of Hamtramck, an independent political unit within Detroit, Polish enjoys at least equal status with English as the community language. Store signs are bi-lingual, restaurants feature Polish dishes; and Polish nationalist feeling, desperately intense since the division of Poland by Hitler and Stalin, is a major political force.

Between the Poles and the Southerners there has been constant though little-noticed friction. The religious issue, inflamed by demagogues on both sides, becomes the pretext or occasion for factory conflicts. It is a revealing sidelight on the problem of race and color prejudice that before the large-scale influx of Southerners, the Poles in Hamtramck showed little anti-Negro prejudice—they had first to be educated in American ways. In fact, "Before the masses of Polish immigrants had become naturalized, the Negroes, as native-born citizens, considerably influenced Hamtramck politics. A Negro was elected to the city's first common council, and Negroes have been appointed since to various administrative posts . . ."[10] This is no longer true today. Among the Hamtramck Poles, anti-Negro, as well as anti-Semitic, feeling is strong. In part, they have "learned" from Southerners; in part, they have turned against the Negroes because the latter are a social group conveniently below the Poles in Detroit's scale of ethnic snobbery.

Until the unionization of the auto industry, Hamtramck remained an island in Detroit's ethnic sea: self-contained, suspicious, proud, provincial. During the mid-thirties Father Coughlin's movement found strong support in Hamtramck, and similar movements are likely to find considerable support there again. Even the UAW, the bulk of whose leaders has always considered Coughlin a demagogue dangerous to the labor movement, found it expedient to invite him to speak at the union's first convention in 1936 in order to attract Polish and Irish workers from the Dodge and Chrysler plants. Though the UAW has succeeded in penetrating its perimeters to some extent, Hamtramck remains a remarkably insular community.

The only other white grouping that requires notice here is the Italian, consisting of 8 percent of the foreign-born population. In many UAW locals there is a strong tendency for some Italian workers to form "blocs" which have no legitimate basis in union issues or needs but which inject an extraneous racial solidarity—and thereby provoke extraneous racial antagonisms. One of the extremely difficult problems in this regard is that Italian home-owners, often living in neighborhoods very close to Negro areas, fear a lowering of real-estate values if the Negroes succeed in bursting out of their ghettoes and into the Italian neighborhoods. For individual home-owners this may be something of a problem, but in many instances unscrupulous landlords have taken advantage of it by buying Italian homes cheaply and selling or renting to the expanding Negroes dearly. This is one of those problems resulting from group hatreds that, if taken in isolation, is quite insoluble.

Though there are more than 100,000 Jews in Detroit, most of them earn their livings at middle-class occupations; few work in the shops. To many of the factory workers the Jews seem an alien group, slightly exotic, slightly sinister. Anti-Semitic incidents are not so frequent as anti-Negro incidents, but they do occur in milder forms. A few illustrations may show how difficult and complex this problem can be.

An acquaintance of the writers, a young man working in one of the shops and an active unionist, bears a name that is racially "neutral." After some years in his plant, he mentioned casually that he is a Jew. Many of the men, genuinely fond of him, refused to believe him—how could a Jew work in the shop—a Jew opens a store, becomes a doctor, even a union official, but the assembly line!

Another incident: a Jewish UAW official participated in recent wage negotiations with noticeable brilliance. When, a few weeks later, his work was reported to a local union meeting, one member was overheard saying to another: "Well, it's good we have a few of the smart ones on our side, too." And it should be added that this remark, for all its inner prejudice, was made with admiration and conscious good feeling.

These racial and color groupings and antagonisms play an important part, not merely in the life of the city, but also in the life of its most important institution: the UAW. The leadership must face the existence of racial prejudice. When slates for local leadership are made up, it is often necessary to think in terms of the Polish or Italian or Southern vote. Of course, for long periods of time Detroit seems—and is—quite peaceful; otherwise life would be completely intolerable. But the deep antagonisms simmer and are available in all crises. No one in the leadership of the union is happy about this situation, but it is one of those difficult and not readily solved problems that can neither be evaded nor talked out of existence.

LIFE IS HARD AND FAST

These racial prejudices are explicable only if seen as an accompaniment of a very difficult process of adjustment which groups of non-urban people have had to make

to the most heavily industrialized city in the world. Detroit's proletarianization was based less on changes in
the status of its own residents than on the migration of
culturally backward peoples from the South and from
Europe. These were precisely the peoples least ready to
withstand the pressures of industrial life.

"Detroiters work hard. The bulk of them have little
time for culture, for the theatre, the night clubs or the
erudite lecture."[11] But of course it isn't only a matter of
time; the whole rhythm of the factory city's life hinders
cultural expression. The fundamental prerequisites for
sustained cultural activity—sufficient leisure, continuous
education, at least partial economic security, an environment encouraging sensitivity and expressiveness—are not
available to workers in a factory city.

For most auto workers the family is the focal point of
their non-working life. In a recent survey of union members who did not know they were being polled by the
union, almost 30 percent acknowledged family worries.[12]
In shop conversations one hears frequent complaints about
having insufficient time to spend with families. Behind
these complaints (for the mere quantity of time cannot
be the entire problem) is something the auto worker finds
difficult to articulate. The irritation caused by poor living
quarters, the accumulated tension produced by the factory and the city, the worries about the future of children
who, with luck, may not end up as factory workers, makes
the family the symbol of the whole life-situation of the
auto worker. To cite one instance: Detroit papers break
into a periodic rash over the "juvenile delinquency" problem. In October, 1948, a midnight curfew was imposed
on minors of seventeen years or under. But such bursts
of publicity or restrictive measures do not answer the
questions that bother the auto worker: what shall his

children do? go into the factory or try to go to college? how can they be supported in the meantime?

But of course people do live and enjoy themselves as much as they can. Detroiters will make such extreme sacrifices to buy an auto that ownership of one is not at all a reliable index of income status. In a city where streetcars and buses are completely inadequate, cars are a transportation necessity, but even more important, they are the only means the auto worker has of escaping his usual conditions of life. A drive to the country, to Belle Isle on Sundays . . . The auto worker is caught between two competing psychological pulls—to and from the factory—and the pull away from it moves on wheels.

There are other things: Detroit has an enormous number of bars and churches. Baseball arouses passions for a few summer months. Almost 10 percent of the UAW members participate in bowling leagues. Each Labor Day week end, hundreds of thousands of Detroiters line the banks of the Detroit river to watch the motor-boat races.

But recreation for a small minority and cultural activity for a far smaller one hardly fill the gaps in the auto workers' life. In the shops there is a large amount of gambling on sports events, horse racing, football and baseball pools. A conservative estimate would be that of the $75,-000,000 yearly gambling "take" in Detroit about $20,000,-000 comes directly from the auto plants.[13] In the monotony of assembly-line work, gambling provides the relief of excitement and variety, and perhaps even that miraculous lucky break.

For the desire to get out of the shop is very strong among auto workers, and is a frequent subject of conversation, especially among the younger, less resigned men. It is not unusual, however, to see a man with ten years of seniority suddenly take a leave of absence and try his hand at some little business which he can "work on my own." One is often impressed with the depth of this desire—even a lifetime of factory routine and discipline cannot dissolve it in the minds of the more intelligent workers. The union often faces the problem that precisely the men who are most alert and serious and hence most likely to be active unionists, are also usually most eager to get out of the plants. A tiny stratum of these has succeeded in becoming union officials, but the others who should be the union's backbone of secondary leaders sometimes suddenly light out of both the shop and the union. Nor can many people blame them.

Among younger workers the resistance to factory work takes the form of an extremely high turnover in employment. Company figures on this turnover are not available, but it is possible to guess its vast extent by checking the shifts from union local to local. Hundreds of transfers take place during each three- or four-month period. A conservative estimate of the yearly turnover in many UAW locals in Detroit would probably run as high as 30–35 percent.[14] "The hell with it, I quit," is a phrase one hears frequently from younger workers. The older men, fearing another depression, guard their seniority, and they know, too, that from plant to plant there's not very much difference.

Though superior to the early and mid-thirties when the union had not yet established its power, living conditions in Detroit are still hard. As a 1948 survey puts it:

1. Most families in Detroit are dependent upon the earnings of one worker.

2. The average weekly earnings in manufacturing in Detroit are barely adequate to support a family of four at a modest but adequate standard, even if the family-head enjoys uninterrupted work for 52 weeks in the year.

3. In addition to wages being barely adequate when employment is continuous, it is seen that many hazards interfere with the continuous flow of wages (unemployment, old age, disability, death) making wages even less effective in providing economic security.[15]

These difficulties are aggravated by one of the worst housing situations in the country. The 1940 Detroit census showed that 34 percent of the dwelling units occupied by Negroes were substandard. "Substandard housing included attic, basement, garage and store front quarters, housing lacking bath facilities, cooking facilities, infested with rats and vermin, no inside toilets, no running water." By 1944, "The situation has become much worse. A reasonable estimate would indicate that for every three Negro families, at least two are living in substandard homes." More generally, reported the Detroit Housing Commission, which cannot be accused of wishing to exaggerate the problem, "One-fifth of the residential area in Detroit is so badly blighted that it is in need of complete rehabilitation and rebuilding. Over 90,000 families of our population are living in substandard living quarters."[16] By early 1946 the Housing Commission reported that:

Of the forty-two square miles of residential land in Detroit, there are approximately sixteen square miles of slum area, or 10,240 acres that are in need of eventual rebuilding. There are also an additional seventeen square miles or 10,880 acres, in need of rehabilitation. Over one-fourth of the population of Detroit lives in these highly blighted sections. . . .

In Detroit residential construction in the thirties averaged about 4,400 dwelling units a year. In contrast, in the preceding years from 1922–1929 there were 15,000 to 25,000 dwelling units built a year. The decade of the twenties furnished about 9,500 dwelling units for rental a year, but building fell down to only 298 rental dwelling units a year in the thirties. What new building took place from 1940 through 1945 was building offered for sale only.[17]

By 1948 the situation had become worse than ever. Testifying before a Congressional Committee, George Edwards, president of Detroit's City Council, said that, "Much of the heart of the city is a rotting slum . . . 70,000 families were living doubled up, 37,000 married veterans were holed up in rooms, cabins, shacks, trailer camps, or poaching on friends or in-laws."[18] In view of these facts, who could reasonably expect the people of Detroit not occasionally to erupt in discharges of violence of which the symptoms seemed to have slight relationship to the causes?

FIGHTING THE LINE

Yet it is not the city, with its turbulent racial and color antagonisms, its wretched housing and social tensions, that determines the fundamental quality of the workers' lives; it is the factory. The factory is the center of Detroit life; the factory is the cause of its weariness and the source of its energy; the factory determines the city.

Pride in work is a usual characteristic of the skilled worker. In the auto industry this pride is restricted to the tool-and-die makers, a few similar categories of workers, and a very few production workers whose native ingenuity overcomes the drabness of their work. Along the winding assembly lines, where the bulk of the workers do their job, skill and pride are neither present nor necessary, for the rationalization of mass production has taken both out of work. As a rule, there are few jobs in which a man cannot be taught how to "break in and make out" within three days. No one, not even an infantry private, is more easily replaceable than an assembly-line worker.

Yet the almost total absence of skill does not altogether destroy the desire of many workers to do something that, in no matter how small a way, is theirs rather than the line's. The lowliest cleanup man at the end of the assembly line wants to get on "production" work. The man on the assembly line wants to become at least a trimmer—that is, a worker who puts the head-lining into the car, and, being slightly more skilled, gets higher pay and has a better standing in the shop than the ordinary assembly-line man. Among production workers as a whole there is frequently a desire to get into the machine shop. It would be naive to believe that their only motive is the need to do more meaningful work, but it would be correspondingly insensitive to assume that their only motive is the wish to make more money or not do the work usually assigned to Negroes. Finer work, higher pay, getting off the line—these are the immediate desires of the production worker.

The whole point of assembly-line production can be summarized in one word: rationalization. If, for example, there are 100 operations to be performed, ten men trained to perform ten operations each can do the job in, say, x units of time. But if 100 men are available they can each be trained to do one simplified operation, with the result that their speed is increased and the total unit of time for doing the job may be cut to three-fourths, say, of the time it took before. Though simplified, this example does illustrate the way rationalization of production and the division of labor works out. In terms of production: efficiency; in terms of the human being: depersonalization, robotization, and a sense of alienation from the total productive process.

As an illustration, let us take the trim or body assembly line, on which one of the authors of this book works. The bare steel bodies are put on the line, two rails along which the body-rests are driven by a conveyor-belt. The assembly line may stretch for 100 to 400 yards, and along it there may be as many as 300 men working. Some crews put on the glass; others tack on the head-lining; some put in the seats and still others attach chrome moldings. The bodies move along at a rate of forty to sixty an hour.

In another part of the plant the chassis line operates. From a skeleton chassis frame to an imposing foundation with motor installed there is a process of accumulation in which the work is minutely rationalized. One man may, for example, hold six bolts for another man to tighten on each car as it moves by. That may mean roughly 250 bolts an hour; 2,000 bolts a day; 500,000 a year. How does this affect a man's life if he keeps at it year after year?

The inexorable flow of the bodies or motors along the assembly lines gives the workers a sense of constant preoccupation which makes relaxation almost impossible. One feels oneself becoming a function of an impersonal apparatus—and do not think that simply because most workers are unable to articulate this feeling that they do not have it! They may just say "it's driving me nuts," but in those four simple words is a profound psychological problem reaching the very heart of industrial civilization.

Sometimes the men on the line try to get time for "a break" by moving "up the line." This means that they work very quickly so as to move ahead to future units of work before the momentum of the assembly line would require them to. In this way they may gain five or ten minutes for a smoke. But soon enough the line catches up with you (it never seems to get tired) and you have to fulfill its demands. Sometimes you may fall behind and bang a hammer on a piece of steel or shout for the "utility man" in order to get some help. But move "up the line" or fall behind it, the assembly-line worker is deprived of one precious privilege that the skilled worker still enjoys: that of setting, within any small unit of time, his own pace of work even though he may consequently have to work harder later on.

Soon the auto worker gets the feeling the men in the plants sometimes call "fighting the line," which might best be described as a mixture of punch-drunk and city-tense. Implicitly rejecting the idea that he is merely a function of a mechanical process, the worker tries to rebel against it; but not only doesn't the assembly line recognize his rebellion, it even refuses to recognize his separate identity. The psychological result is that the worker's aggression against the line can be released only against himself or other workers.

Intermittent attempts have been made to apologize for the dehumanizing aspects of the assembly line. It removed the need for heavy labor—true enough, but it replaced heavy labor with a monotony and an enforced rapidity of motion that result in at least as much fatigue. It was, said Henry Ford, a "boon" for factory workers who have "no brains."[19] In 1941, Ford was to gain a rather different impression of the mental powers of his workers, but even before then it might have occurred to him that mental stupefaction among auto workers was partly due to the assembly line. Only, said W. J. Cameron, Ford's Sunday-hour spokesman, "writers" and "the pale, inactive critic . . . out of touch with his times"[20] make a fuss about the assembly line. But couldn't, in turn, this description of the critics be turned around to apply as well to the apologists? No one had ever seen W. J. Cameron, the man in touch with his times, rush into River Rouge to put in a few refreshing hours at the line.

Quite apart from the form of society, industrialism has produced extremely serious problems for modern living: the loss of skill and pride, the mechanization of the worker, his transformation into a function of a process. A society more attuned to human values than our present one might find ways of relieving this situation, but nothing less than a fundamental reorganization of factory work, very careful factory planning, decentralization of industrial communities so as to bring them into closer proximity to the country, and ultimately a remodeled relationship between intellectual and manual work could remove the fundamental strains of factory life.

Such considerations are, at the moment, ultimate. Not many factory workers are concerned with them, for they have recently been worried about a more pressing matter: the speedup. No detailed scientific studies of the speedup in the factories are publicly available, though the UAW has recently begun to instruct its stewards in time-study procedures. The rate of labor productivity is a secret zealously guarded by the corporations. But by now recognition of the speedup has so thoroughly permeated American consciousness that it is hardly necessary to describe or "prove" that it exists. For years the speedup at Ford was one of the most terrifying aspects of American life. The knowledge that he might be discarded in favor of younger, quicker hands was a constant specter of fear hanging over the head of the older worker.

It is difficult, at the moment perhaps impossible, to set norms of work speed against which to measure speedup or slowdown. That is one of the reasons why speedup not only results in hundreds of unrecorded "quickie" stop-

pages but raises some of the most complex problems encountered in union-management negotiations. Since the
unionization of the industry, it has to some extent been
controlled, though it is introduced in so many subtle, almost imperceptible ways that the union has not always
been able to cope with it. Abstractly, one would say that
any pace of work leaving the worker too tired for active
leisure-time recreation is a speedup, though such a human-
ized norm does not play much of a role in negotiations.
At the very least, the insistence of thousands of workers
week after week that the work pace is too fast must be
taken into consideration—and that is precisely the complaint of auto workers in the middle of 1949.

The speedup becomes a particularly acute issue when
new models are introduced. Since the new models always
require at least a few changes in the productive process,
it is often extremely difficult to use the work rate of the
previous model as a basis for comparison. On such occasions, a struggle over work rates, with the union claiming
speedup and the company slowdown, bursts into the open.
Comparisons between the recent postwar years and the
war and prewar years are also of little value. The nature
of the productive process has been so changed that there
is no way of meaningfully comparing the amount of time
put into, say, a deluxe station wagon and a prewar car.
Both sides have increasingly resorted to time-study specialists, but the statistics they assemble cannot present
with sufficient dramatic impact the human problem to
which they refer.

One group of workers does escape some of the difficulties of the line—the skilled tool-and-die makers. They
alone develop something akin to a "labor aristocracy" psychology. During negotiations, supplementary contracts
dealing exclusively with their working conditions are

drawn up. Even during the worst depression days a skilled worker could usually support himself and his family by earning from $800 to $1,200 a year. These men are one of the most stable groups in the UAW; they do not drift in and out of shops; more than anyone else in the UAW, they feel that they have a stake in the status quo.

THE RANKS REPLY

To attempt now to construct some sort of composite picture of the UAW member would be a very risky business, probably impossible. But, fortunately, we do have at our disposal a certain amount of information that helps to portray the makeup of the union. In 1948 the UAW sponsored a survey of its members, conducted by a sociologist under conditions independently established by him.[21] The union members did not know the poll was sponsored by the union. While the results have to be taken with some caution because of the smallness of the sample, they are nonetheless most interesting, verifying as they do other observations and conclusions.

Eleven percent of the UAW members in Detroit, the survey indicates, are over sixty years of age. Thirty percent are over fifty. Fifty-four percent are over forty and 75 percent over thirty. (At the Ford plants 57 percent are over forty.) These figures suggest some rather important tentative conclusions. There has been a considerable over-all stabilization of the labor force in the industry, despite numerous intra-industry transfers of employment. The expected flow away from the industry and back to rural areas and small towns did not take place after the war's end, and it seems reasonable to expect that no such flow will take place in the next five or six years. More important, the veterans of the union, those who participated in the sitdowns, are now of course in the higher age brackets. It also seems likely that the average age level of the industry's labor force has risen since the pre-unionization period. That may well mean, among other things, a certain turn to conservatism among the older workers who were once rank-and-file firebrands, a turn further accentuated by the union's stabilization and the increasing number of attractive administrative posts at its disposal.

The survey also indicates that one out of every four UAW members has been graduated from high school, though about 50 percent did attend. What the survey could not of course determine was the effect of a decade of unionism on the thinking and educational level of its members.

In 1947 the average UAW family in Detroit had an income of $2,864. One in six families had an income of less than $2,000, while one in four had an income of more than $3,500. There must, of course, be a considerable correlation between larger income and larger family.

How was the living? It was made "extra tough" by layoffs and short work weeks. Almost two out of every five UAW members in Detroit were laid off sometime during 1947, the average layoff coming to five and a half weeks. One out of every three UAW members had short work weeks during that year, averaging slightly more than four short weeks.

Although 16 percent of the UAW members interviewed declared that they never worried, the remainder showed anxiety. Most of those admitting to worries were between thirty and fifty years old; roughly three out of five in this age group were worriers. A slightly smaller percentage, 55, of workers under thirty also admitted to worries. Two problems caused the most worry: how to support their families if they couldn't work because of illness or injury; and how to support their families if they were laid off or discharged from their jobs.

While highly suggestive, such a survey cannot touch some of the incalculable factors in the life of the auto workers. What change in their emotional lives was produced by a decade of auto unionism? The survey indicates that 90 percent of the auto workers feel that the union has done something for them—and it is most important to note that the longer the men are in the union the more they feel a sense of solidarity with it. Of those who replied that they thought the union had brought them benefits, more than 50 percent mentioned better wages and working conditions. About a third replied that the union had given them a greater sense of security on the job. Two percent said something about the sense of solidarity, the feeling of "working together," that the union had brought to them. (These answers were spontaneously volunteered, not chosen from several possible suggestions.)

Offhand, it would seem that only a very small minority— no doubt, the same minority that is active in union affairs —thinks consciously of the union's repercussions on its life. But it would be most unimaginative to assume that only these 2 percent have actually had the psychological patterns of their lives changed by unionization. For the factor of job security which a third mentioned has obvious psychological repercussions, and even the simple bread-and-butter answer that the majority volunteered also has profound implications. There is no way of measuring such matters precisely, but there are a few valid indications: the large amount of talk about the union, even if some of it is "griping," that takes place in the factories; the greater sense of independence toward factory foremen and managers that is so evident today in comparison with the early thirties; the development of a small but crucial layer of union militants who speak for the less articulate workers. Then, too, one must remember that the survey was taken on the level of verbal articulation, that is of conscious awareness; the response was in terms of what the worker believed he thought and of what he could express of that belief.

No matter how partially or insufficiently, the UAW has begun to fill a large gap in the life of the auto workers. It has given them something of their own, an institution in which, with no matter how many reservations, they take pride. It has given them a means by which to express themselves. Or perhaps more accurately, they have made these things for themselves.

During the early thirties the usual impression of visiting journalists was that the auto workers were cowed, fearful, sullen. Today that is not true at all. On the contrary, the auto workers behave as if their "big pitch" is yet to come. As one observer has remarked, "The UAW represents a revolutionary movement which is democratizing the most regimented process in industry—the mechanical synchronization of materials, tools, conveyors, skills. Auto workers are not proletarians—they earn and enjoy all the middle-class comforts. But they are not the traditional middle class, either—they are not white-collar workers and they are proud of it."[22] If by proletarian is meant the classic definition of that term (a worker who sells his labor power for wages) then the auto workers most assuredly are proletarians. But with one implication of the above denial of their "proletarian" status we can agree: the auto workers breathe a sense of confidence and liveliness, of aggressiveness and self-reliance they did not know fifteen years ago.

SCARRED MEMORY

This confidence in their combative powers is modulated by one decisive memory: the depression.

In May, 1927, the Ford Company discontinued Model-T production. Over 100,000 men, 60,000 of them in the Detroit area alone, were laid off for periods of from six months to over a year, while the company retooled for Model A. Besides the direct hardships resulting from such layoffs, auto workers in other plants were also harmed. A vast increase in the labor force seeking jobs meant an opportunity for foremen to press employed workers harder and, when any expressed dissatisfaction, to remind them of the unemployed eager to take their places. This was the first large shock of its kind suffered by Detroit's auto workers.

It still dogs their lives today. Next to speedup, the fear of unemployment is the main, almost obsessive subject of conversation in the plants. The older workers will never be able to remove the psychological scars left on them by the depression.

In 1929 slightly more than 470,000 men worked in Detroit's auto factories; by 1930 this figure had dropped to 341,000 and by 1931 to 257,000. Of these, very few worked full weeks. The job lines used to swell to the point where thousands of men would gather before employment offices each morning. Often these men knew there were no jobs to be had, but they came anyway. By 1931 there were 211,000 people on Detroit's relief rolls, and another estimated 150,000 had left the city to return to farms and towns.

The memory of those days remains vivid and frightening. At union gatherings men frequently reminisce about the depression days and remind the younger ones "what it was like before the union." John Kelly, now a UAW official, often tells a story that, in one form or another, is known throughout the city: "We used to get out to the employment gates by six in those days and we would build a fire and wait around. If you knew someone inside you stood a better chance of being called in. Foremen used to come out and pick whom they wanted, and seniority didn't mean a thing. My brother was a superintendent, so I used to get some breaks. I felt sorry for the others, but what could you do? When I started to sign fellows up in the union my superintendent warned me I'd get fired and never get another job. He said he couldn't believe I would do anything like that when I had a brother who was a superintendent. One night my brother came over to the house and begged me to quit. He was afraid of losing his job because I was a union man."

Another typical story is told by Joe Hattley, president of a Chrysler local: "One day I started to complain about a job. My foreman took me over to the window and pointed to all those guys standing outside the employment gate. 'If you don't like your job there's plenty of them outside who want it.' What could I say?"[23]

Nor are these mere isolated instances. The famous Henderson report on the auto industry, prepared for the NRA, said:

> The fear of layoff is always in their minds, even if not definitely brought there by the foremen. The speedup is thus inherent in the present situation of lack of steady work and an army of unemployed waiting outside.

The lack of seniority rules led to a practice of rehiring men on a "work ability" basis, which meant favoring the younger men and those least friendly to unionism.

The automobile industry has set a new low age for displacement of workers. Men near forty find great difficulty in securing jobs with the industry or being rehired after layoffs.

There was bitter opposition to the group piecework and the group bonus plans which were devised to drive them to excessive speed.

Of course, such employment policies and working conditions created fertile soil for unionism, and many attempts were made to organize the industry in the early depression days. In that period the auto manufacturers resorted to two major techniques for discouraging unionism: firing known union supporters and employing labor spies. For a two-and-one-half-year period, reported Henderson, General Motors paid the Pinkerton Detective Agency $419,000 and Chrysler Corporation gave $211,000 to the Corporation Auxiliaries Corporation, which also provided spies and stool pigeons. "The espionage systems which are widely existent are bitterly resented by the workers as being un-American," said Henderson with admirable restraint.

Henderson concluded: "Labor unrest exists to a degree higher than warranted by the depression. The unrest flows from insecurity, low annual earnings, inequitable hiring and rehiring methods, espionage, speedup and displacement of workers at an extremely early age . . . Unless something is done soon, they [the workers] intend to take things into their own hands to get results."[24]

Of course, the permanent establishment of the UAW as a collective-bargaining force in the industry has tremendously alleviated some of these hardships. But each turn in American economic development brings new problems and re-poses some of the old ones, which, even when themselves rather minor, arouse memories of the depression days. During the war-conversion period in 1941-42, the auto industry laid off more than 400,000 men—temporarily, to be sure, but nonetheless with resulting hardships in the lives of those laid off. On a smaller scale, this process was repeated during the postwar reconversion period.

At the moment, one can observe a certain relaxation of the fear of future unemployment. Many workers, and for that matter many UAW officials, anticipated a depression within about two years after the war. Now that it seems likely, partly because of the reorganization of American economy on a semi-war basis, that the auto industry will continue to function at high production levels, the fear of unemployment is not so acute as in the past, though it is by no means dissipated. The workers are upset by frequent layoffs, due to economic dislocations, strikes in other industries and, sometimes, poor planning. Living on a very narrow margin and straining to cope with inflationary prices, they find even brief layoffs extremely irritating.

In a sense, then, the depression has been transformed from a memory to a symbol. Many of the younger men did not experience it directly; yet, despite occasional claims to nonchalance, they worry about it almost as much as the older men. The depression has become a symbol of the overall insecurity to which auto workers still feel themselves subject. It is the one major experience which, in the minds of large numbers of people, punctured the myth of a nation uncontaminated by insecurity.

HERE ALL MEN ARE . . .

Against the background of the tensions and problems described in this chapter, it is not difficult to understand why the 285,000 Negroes of Detroit occupy such a focal position in its life. Yet as one walks along some of Detroit's more presentable and quiet streets, one may feel that the stories about its tensions have been exaggerated by writers in search of melodrama or pat political conclusions. It is possible to feel that Detriot is merely a city like other cities, quite restful in a few of the middle-class areas on the perimeter of the West Side. But keep walking . . .

In June, 1941, when the influx of war workers into Detroit had reached 350,000, the housing situation became intolerable. Single rooms in "Paradise Valley" were renting for $60 a month, sometimes more. Stirred at last to some action, the Detroit Housing Commission chose a site in the Negro neighborhood for the construction of a Negro housing project. Federal authorities, whose approval was necessary because the project was to be built as part of a national war housing program, vetoed the site and insisted on building at Nevada and Fenelon Avenues, a white neighborhood. The Detroit Housing Commission and most Negro organizations protested against the Federal decision on the grounds that it could only lead to unnecessary conflict.

In the fall of that year, after prolonged agitation by the "Seven Mile Improvement Association"—a group of whites who objected to Negro occupancy of the project—it was officially announced that the newly constructed houses, to be called Sojourner Truth, would be opened on December 15th. During January, 1942, a confused running dispute between federal authorities and Detroit officials took place over the question of using the project for whites or Negroes. On January 4th, Clark Foreman, Federal War Housing Director, wired the Detroit Housing Commission to permit Negroes to occupy the project; the next day he

wired it to "disregard previous wire." On January 20th the
Detroit commission was informed that Washington had
switched to the idea of all-white occupancy. And on January 22nd a wire from Washington informally proposed
that 300 dwelling units be built for Negroes—at another
site.

The Washington "liberals" had by now thoroughly
bungled the situation. They had insisted on locating an
all-Negro project in a white neighborhood, but had lacked
both the power and gumption to back up their decision.
The Detroit Housing Commission had acted on the
grounds of expediency: a Negro salient in a white neighborhood meant trouble. And the fundamental irony of the
whole matter was that those "Negroes and whites who
lived as neighbors did not fight one another in the Detroit
race riots."[25]

At the end of January Detroit's mayor wired Washington urging Negro occupancy of Sojourner Truth. On February 2nd Washington reversed itself and agreed to
Negro occupancy, and on February 19th the whole tragi-
comedy was climaxed by a rededication of the project to
Sojourner Truth, a Civil War heroine.

When Negro occupancy began on February 28th, the
expected and unavoided happened. The night before, a
fiery cross had been burned near the project and bands of
white men had roamed through the neighborhood inflam-
ing prejudices. When the Negroes tried to move in, they
were overwhelmed by well-organized white mobs wield-
ing bricks, rocks, clubs and knives. Many of those who had
come to find a decent place to live found themselves in
the hospital. The riot ended when an official of the Detroit
Housing Commission ran through the white mob to an-
nounce that Negro occupancy would not take place.

The incident was quickly picked up by the Axis radio and used for all it was worth. Finally, on April 30th, under the protection of 1,000 Army troops, 300 state police and 450 Detroit police, the Negro families moved into the project. For those who opposed prejudice it was a victory of a kind, but in many ways a hollow victory. For it did not dissolve racial hatred, it merely cowed temporarily those whites ready to express it most violently.[26]

No fundamental steps were taken to alleviate racial tension, not even such an elementary, insufficient step as organizing a city-wide inter-racial committee. Nothing serious was done to relieve the housing shortage, which might have been a way to prevent the violent outbursts that were yet to come. In August, 1942, *Life* published a detailed description of Detroit conditions and warned that trouble was ahead, but no one seems to have paid any attention—at least no one who had any power to do anything about it.

In the Spring of 1943 there was another sign: 20,000 white workers at Packard went on strike against the wishes of the union leaders because some Negroes had been upgraded. In that same uneasy Spring there were repeated incidents on the streets of the West Side in which Negroes were beaten. Retrospectively, it hardly seems possible that city officials could have been so blind as to ignore all of these crude signs. Or was it perhaps, as the novelist James T. Farrell has since remarked, that "In Detroit, nobody cares?"[27]

By that Spring it was already too late; Detroit had the worst race riot America has seen since the St. Louis riots of 1914. It is worth telling the story briefly, for it will help illuminate much that is to come in this book.

How did it begin? Did it begin with a fist fight between

a Negro and a white on Belle Isle, packed with thousands of war workers seeking Sunday recreation? Or was it the work of a rumor?

Rumor: a Negro baby was thrown off a bridge at Belle Isle by whites.

Rumor: a white baby was thrown off the same bridge by Negroes.

Rumor: two white women were attacked on the bridge by Negroes.

Rumor: white girls were attacked by Negroes while swimming.

But undeniable was the fact that by 10:30 that Sunday evening, June 20th, fighting had spread from the park, across the bridge and into the city, with more than 5,000 people participating.

Undeniable, and to this day never explained, was the fact that over 200 sailors from the nearby naval armory on the bank of the Detroit River fought Negroes for hours without once being brought under military control.

Undeniable was the fact that in a Paradise Valley night-club a Negro announced that a Negro woman and her baby had been killed by whites, and that enraged Negroes then stoned cars driven by whites on their way to work.

All the fears and phobias beneath the surface of civilized life came surging upwards. From midnight until early Monday morning fear-crazed Negroes roamed the streets stoning white-owned cars, breaking into white-owned stores. A few hours later white mobs began retaliatory action, mainly along Woodward Avenue, a bisector of Negro and white slums.

Negro leaders asked the mayor to call federal troops to restore order; he refused. The governor was told by federal officials that his request for troops would be granted only if he declared martial law; he refused.

The first "break" came on Monday afternoon, when R.J. Thomas, then president of the UAW, joined Negro leaders in demanding federal action to stop the rioting, and announced that all union stewards had been alerted to keep peace in the plants. The UAW proudly announced that in those plants under its control, not one fight was reported.

But the riot had reached the point where it seemed as if it could burn itself out only in a fury of bloodshed. At 8:30 Monday evening gunfire broke out in Paradise Valley. Here is the story as told by two Wayne University professors:

The police were trying to drive back a crowd surging east on Vernor, intent on doing violence to the Negro ghetto centering in Paradise Valley. The white mob had been momentarily stopped at John R., a block east of Woodward. Milling, shouting, surging back and forth across Vernor Highway, the mob presented a horror-inspiring spectacle to Negroes in a hotel a block to the east. Then shots began to ring out through the stifling evening air. They seem to have come from the Frazier hotel, a Negro hostelry . . .

Two policemen were shot, and their comrades killed the man who had fired at them. Soon more police arrived and engaged in a gun battle with the Negroes in the hotel. Tear-gas bombs, firearms, and the arrival of reinforcements ended the battle. Dozens of Negroes were taken from the hotel and other buildings and hustled either to jail or hospitals.

Violence reached a peak during this period. . . The governor finally took the necessary steps to bring in the federal troops. By midnight the U.S. Army had established an "armed truce" between Detroit's warring factions. A group of Negro soldiers at Fort Custer (140 miles west of Detroit) were arrested in an attempt to take arms and a truck to assist their families in Detroit.[28]

Of thirty-four dead, twenty-three were Negroes; of 800 injured more than 500 were Negroes; of 1,800 arrested over 1,200 were Negroes. Yet from Monday morning, when the major violence began, until the end of the rioting, the Negroes were obviously on the defensive. A few days later both the *New York Times* and the *Detroit Free Press* published a picture showing two policemen holding a Negro while a white man punched him.

Even if the Negroes had been the "aggressors"—which they were not—anyone wishing to arrive at a sound analysis would have to ask himself what it was in the life of Detroit Negroes that could provoke them to such desperate aggression. As it was, they fought with a kind of frantic hysteria. Some inconsequential incident, now forever buried in the past, had touched off the dreadful riot and all of the city's social pus had risen to its surface.

The causes were simple enough: "housing atrocities, rising Negro resentment against economic discrimination, real or fancied, increasing white resentment of the black man's invasion in the form of industrial employment."[29] Gunnar Myrdal, in his study of the American Negro, mentions another contributing factor:

> Detroit also seems to have a larger number of Southern-born policemen than most other Northern cities. In the recent clashes between the police and the Negroes, many of the police were whites from Kentucky and Tennessee.[30]

Myrdal's observation is given additional weight by the fact that of the twenty-three Negroes killed in the riot, the majority were shot by police, while of the eleven whites killed in the riot none was killed by the police.

As soon as the actual fighting was at an end, everything relapsed into the old patterns. As one observer remarked, "Since Detroit, as before Detroit, neither federal nor local government, North or South, has done anything to remove the fundamental causes for race riots or correct any of the conditions that generate them."[31]

In 1949 Detroit is still an uneasy city. Progress has been made, but the sores of 1942–43 do not heal very easily; the disease that caused them remains virulent. Fights break out day after day, most of them unreported in the press. Two thousand white men picket a Negro's home on Harrison Avenue, formerly a "restricted" area. The Negro community is stirred to bitterness by the killing of a fifteen-year-old Negro boy by two white policemen who claim that the boy was shot while trying to escape. He had, they say, been speeding.

Guilt, large pools of clogging guilt, covers the city. Discrimination remains widespread, prejudice deep. Parts of the city are as race-crazed as a town in Alabama. The UAW tries hard, but it is fighting against ingrained phobias, traditional folkways. Politicians talk of housing but do nothing. The shacks in Paradise Valley rot.

If decisive cleansing action is not taken, the terrible events of the past will repeat themselves, perhaps in even more terrible ways. In the meantime the problem persists, the ultimate shame of a people—and in Detroit the constant hurdle in the path of the UAW.

RHYTHMS OF A CITY

There are two kindred errors to which an observer can succumb while viewing the life of the auto city: the one that reduces its troubles and tensions to inflictions from

some external source of malice or to the "growing pains"
of a peaceful and healthy city; the other that reduces the
city—a place, after all, where people live—to a mere chain
of explosions and incidents to be exploited in melodramatic headlines. Both views are false: the first palpably
ignores the facts and the second, were it true, would mean
that the city would be simply uninhabitable. In reality
Detroit life is an alternation, more accurately an inter-
weaving of quiet and turbulence, peace and violence, relaxation and tension.

In a visit to Detroit some fifteen years ago, the writer
Edmund Wilson aptly remarked:

> You can see here, as it is impossible to do in a more varied
> and complex city like New York, the whole structure of an
> industrial society: almost everybody in Detroit is dependent
> on the motor industry and in more or less direct and obvious
> relations to everyone else.[32]

Wilson here noted Detroit's centralization—not merely
economically, which is obvious enough, but also in its
social and psychological life. Detroit has little of the diver-
sity of a larger cosmopolitan city. The usual cultural
activities are there—the symphony, the museums, the li-
brary—but they seem more marginal, they seem to im-
pinge less on the life of its people than is the case even in
the larger cities. One possible reason for its cultural
barrenness is that Detroit has very little of a native, tra-
dition-bred wealthy class; most of its factories are absen-
tee-controlled, by capitalists who use their money to
endow cultural activities in other cities, such as Cleveland
and New York. The dominant tone of Detroit is crude and
harsh and powerful, striking you at every point and never

letting you forget it. Even when you look into its art museum, the most powerful impression is made by Diego Rivera's mural depicting industrial life in great detail: a mass of cylinders, pistons, drills, presses, blocks, molds, wheels, cranes, chasses, conveyors. And the flimsiness of Detroit's attempt to garner something of traditional culture is ironically symbolized by the fact that Rivera's mural stands in a room patterned after an ornate Italian court . . .

Nor are there in Detroit any of the shading or veiling amenities that can be found in the larger cosmopolitan centers. Here social relationships are stripped to their crudest essence: management and union stand in flat and heavy opposition to each other, despite half-hearted attempts to construct some façade of "co-operation." Those writers still bemused by an America that passed away five or six decades ago and still claiming that this country's social relationships are fluid and unpolarized, should take a better look at Detroit. A fringe of its workers sometimes drifts back to the rural areas, a tinier fringe sometimes succeeds in escaping the plants, but by far the great majority is fated to remain auto workers. (So considerable is this polarization that even in Wayne University, the city's college, over 50 percent of the students are self-supporting workers.)

A life centered around a mass-production factory in which the worker is an auxiliary of a machine and in which only the flimsiest demands are made on his intelligence or imagination, cannot provide a genuinely satisfactory or truly creative existence. Not only does the factory take up the bulk of the auto worker's day—it must also place a heavy hand on his leisure-time thought and feeling. No more vivid description of this process of de-

personalization has been written than by Louis-Ferdinand
Céline, a French novelist who worked in Detroit for some
time:

> One was turned by force into a machine oneself, the whole of
> one's carcass quivering in this vast frenzy of noise, which
> filled you within and all around the inside of your skull and
> lower down rattled your bowels, and climbed to your eyes in
> infinite, little, quick unending strokes . . . you long to stop it
> all and be able to think about it and hear your heart beating
> clearly within you; but now it's impossible. I can't stop. Dis-
> aster is in this unfortunate steel trap, and we, we're spinning
> round in it with the machines, and with the earth itself. All
> one great whirling thing . . . The workmen bending solici-
> tously over the machines eager to keep them happy, are a
> depressing sight; one hands them the right-sized screws and
> still more screws, instead of putting a stop once and for all
> to all this smell of oil, and this vapor which burns your
> throat and your eardrums from inside . . . When at six o'clock
> everything stops, you carry the noise away in your head. I
> had a whole night's noise and smell of oil in mine, as if I'd
> been fitted with a new nose . . . my mates were mere echoes
> and whiffs of machinery like myself, flesh shaken up for
> good . . .[33]

The most deadly and deadening aspect of urban industrial society is that the rhythms of the factory tend to be
repeated in the entire life of the city. The quality of
leisure-time activity does not differ significantly from that
of the work day. Except for churchgoing, the conviviality
of the bar, the Sunday ride to the country and the easygoing camaraderie of the ball park—themselves becoming
less and less spontaneous activities—most of the auto worker's amusements are stereotyped and synthetic. In his
after-work hours, the worker seeks relaxation and diver-
sion, but the standardized products of "mass culture"—the
popular music of the radio or jukebox, the movies, the

comic strips, the newspaper features—offer him no fundamental relief from the emotional and psychological
patterns of factory routine. They do not stir him to in-
dividuality or creativity, as genuine cultural participation
can; rather they reinforce the passivity and pervasive
boredom of factory life. One writer has well described
the effects of mass culture on workers:

> Boredom has become so great that only the brightest colors
> have any chance of being lifted out of the general drabness.
> Yet it is just those violent colors which bear witness to the
> omnipotence of mechanical, industrial production . . . the
> means used to overcome reality are more humdrum than
> reality itself.
>
> To escape boredom and avoid effort is incompatible. . . .
> They seek novelty but the strain and boredom associated
> with actual work lead to avoidance of effort in leisure time . . .
> [But] that means boredom again . . .[34]

In a highly industrialized city which lacks the worthier
features of both countryside and cosmopolitan center,
these patterns of life must lead to overwhelming tensions,
to be released either in destructive irrational channels or
in constructive social activity. This tension is seen "pure"
in the explosive burst of men leaving the factory, men
rushing out as if eager to get a breath of pure air. It appears destructively in race riots and bar brawls. And it
arises more constructively in the loud voices and surprising passion with which workers sometimes speak at union
meetings.

Life in Detroit grips, pushes, batters you—and yet it is
immensely attractive and vigorous. The factory destroys
personality, but in their union the auto workers have
found one force which, all too hesitantly and inadequately
but still persistently, has begun to help them regain personality. The city is very tense—a friend of the writers has
remarked, in a flight of fancy that is not too fanciful, that

one can feel the social steam rising from its sidewalks. Yet it is not the febrile, nervous, edgy tension of New York; it is the powerful, untamed tension of a city both terrifying and fascinating in its potential. How terrible life in such a city could be if the rhythms of the factory, the barren dehumanized process of production were to determine its total quality! How fascinating it is, on the other hand, to see the potential for good living which the city's immense productivity implies, and to see the dim but present potential for good living which the union's co-operative procedures suggest!

Thus far, indeed, the only significant force modulating the industrial quality of Detroit life has been the UAW. Only the UAW has tried to grapple with the social problems outlined here. By the very nature of its existence and purpose, it has been unable to avoid them. For it faced the choice of either coming to grips with these problems or allowing them to tear it to pieces. When one measures the results of fifteen years of its work, one is astonished to see what a revolution has taken place in the lives and minds of the auto workers. Today they are far more articulate, self-reliant, and integrated into a co-operative venture than fifteen years ago. Yet, much remains to be done: the union, for example, has hardly scratched the problem of imbedding a few seeds of genuine cultural curiosity among its members—or, for that matter, among its leaders.

As one looks at Detroit one must conclude that, if by some stroke of catastrophe, the UAW were removed, life in the city would be quite intolerable for those who work in its giant plants. It alone has brought a sense of human warmth into an area dominated by robots, pistons and dollars—and that, more than anything else, is the measure of its triumph. This is the central fact to keep in mind as we now move to the story of the UAW: its history, its problems, its future.

Part II

--------------------------------- GROWTH

Early Sitdowns
and Lasting Conquests

2

S I N C E the destruction of chattel slavery and the triumph of capitalist economy in the last half of the 19th century, the most important social development in America has been the emergence of mass industrial unions. Not even the bloodiest strikes in the late nineteenth century posed the issue of "property rights" versus "labor rights" so sharply as did the sitdown strikes of 1936 and 1937. The sitdowns were the closest American workers have ever come to the modes of revolutionary action developed by European workers.

"Prior to the passage of the National Recovery Act in 1933 there were but few trade unions in the [auto] industry. Management had been thoroughly accustomed to the exercise of complete control. The industry has been conspicuous for its . . . resistance to unionism."[1] Until the 1930's, the feeble, half-serious efforts of the AFL to or-

ganize auto had never succeeded. Most auto workers
were hardly aware of its presence in the industry. But in
the early 1930's, when the depression ate into their minds
like a nagging acid, a series of spectacular strikes broke
out in the plants. In 1933 alone, more than 100 auto plants
were shut down by strikes.

There was then only one place for restive auto workers
to go: the AFL, a drowsy organization equipped neither
structurally nor intellectually to unionize mass-production
industries. When it made a few gestures toward taking in
auto workers, its locals would be suddenly besieged by
hundreds of applicants hoping for some drastic improvement of shop conditions. But what could men so antedilu-
vian in their thought and so timorous in their behavior as
William Green and Mathew Woll do with these untu-
tored, straining workers?

The AFL auto leader, William Collins, would call a
meeting for the workers of plant X, at which attendance
was usually high. Collins would then organize a "federal
local,"* appoint its officers, and try to persuade corporation X to bargain with him in order to "stabilize" labor
relations. In the meantime, these federal locals would be
left to the mercy of AFL internationals intent on carving
them into craft bailiwicks. By then, the workers, never
overly enthused about "stabilized" labor relations, would
have become disgruntled and would drift away from the
federal local. As this pattern became increasingly prevalent, the actual center of unionization shifted from the
AFL hall to the plants themselves. The actual leaders

---

* A "federal local" was a union grouping based on one plant, not part
of an AFL international, responsible only to the AFL Executive Council,
and enjoying little or no self-rule. Such locals were used by the AFL
leaders to keep unions in the mass-production industries under their
domination. Sometimes, it seemed as if they feared such unions almost as
much as the corporations.

were not the stolid AFL business agents distributing craft manna from on high, but inexperienced young men in the shops.

By 1934 the initiatory squallings of auto unionism had become loud and insistent. It was a year of tremendous labor struggles. In San Francisco a general strike erupted, with Harry Bridges assuming leadership; in Minneapolis two teamsters' strikes, led by the Trotskyist Dunne brothers, ended with violence and victory; in Toledo workers at the Auto-lite plant, reinforced by thousands of unemployed, battled national guardsmen for two days in a bitter strike. To establish a minimum of order in the industry, President Roosevelt appointed a National Automobile Labor Board on March 25, 1934. Though AFL leaders applauded this step, the men in the shops soon became cynical about the board's cumbersome procedures ("You could starve to death while the board prepared to hold a hearing") and its inability to cajole the corporations into collective bargaining. Legal maneuvers, while necessary, were clearly insufficient.

DANGLING UNIONS

In June, 1934, 157 delegates from seventy-seven auto locals met in Detroit under the half-hostile guidance of the AFL. They returned the hostility with interest by demanding the exclusion of AFL representatives from floor discussions. Formally they accomplished little, but actually they sent out the first tenuous feelers to John L. Lewis, who was then preparing to launch his industrial-union campaign.

How thoroughly discredited the AFL had become among auto workers was shown by a poll held by the National Automobile Labor Board in the spring of 1935.

Over 88 percent of those voting favored "no union," while a mere 8 percent wanted the AFL. Did this mean that the auto workers were hostile to unionism? Hardly, for soon they were to be neck deep in strikes. It could only mean that they were repudiating the AFL specifically.

Tension mounted; wildcat strikes erupted in the least expected places; and the AFL leaders must have begun to wonder if the cushioned world they had come to love—the world of pleasant chats with employers, of bluff speeches to passive followers, of regular dues regularly collected—was coming to an end. By April, 1935, they had further reason to wonder: the men in the Toledo Chevrolet plant walked out. The strike spread to other GM plants—Fisher Body in Cleveland, Chevrolet in Norwood, Ohio. Soon 30,000 GM men were out.

Here was a chance for the AFL to regain the workers' confidence. But the strike was soon aborted by Francis Dillon, AFL representative, who accepted an arbitration plan that gave the strikers few concessions. Such young local leaders as George Addes opposed the settlement, but by threatening to snatch the AFL charter from the Toledo Chevrolet strikers and by ingenious parliamentary devices Dillon persuaded the strikers to accept his meager terms.[2]

A momentary defeat—but it meant the final discrediting of the AFL in auto. The local leaders, many of them influenced by revived radical movements, were gaining experience in dealing with the AFL representatives, and in a series of national caucuses they worked out a program for immediate action. The points of this program were: industrial unionism in auto; initiation of a large organizing drive; democratization of the union; and preparation for independent labor activity in politics.[3]

A consolidated auto union was finally established in August, 1935, much against the resistance of the AFL leaders; but even then its members did not have the power to elect their own officers. William Green appointed Francis Dillon president and Homer Martin, a young unionist from Kansas City, vice-president. Perplexed and directionless, the plant-level leaders asked Lewis for help. After the October, 1935, convention of the AFL Lewis resigned as vice-president and created the Committee for Industrial Organization.

Lewis now faced a curious problem. He could use his burly coal-mine organizers for the new CIO, but he sensed that for many purposes they would be insufficient; they would not be able to express the larger social motivations which were essential if the CIO was to gain the support of workers in mass-production industries. The Lewis "boys" were all right for hurly-burly and plugging, but they were a little weak on ideas and inspiration. Consequently, Lewis had to turn to a group of radical unionists whom he had previously driven out of the UMW because they had opposed his dictatorial regime and, unlike him, had always championed industrial unionism. He called in such heterodox unionists as Powers Hapgood, a militant socialist, John Brophy, Rose Pesotta, an aggressive radical loaned by the International Ladies Garment Workers, and Leo Krzycki of the Amalgamated Clothing Workers and then national chairman of the Socialist Party. At this time, it should be remembered, there was precious little glory and less comfort in organizing for the CIO. As a rule, only men moved by a conviction that unionization of mass-production industries was a step toward a larger social end were willing to take the risks that came with the job. Which is why Lewis had to use radicals on his staff, and why, again, many of the local auto-union leaders were either radicals or under their influence. Not many other people cared enough; the time-servers would buzz in later.

By May, 1936, at a convention in South Bend, Indiana, the auto unionists decisively rejected the AFL, and listened instead to people like Hapgood and Pesotta of the CIO. The union elected its own officers, men quite different from the AFL Babbitts. As president, it chose Homer Martin, one of the most eccentric figures ever to rise in the labor movement. A former Missouri Baptist minister, Martin had worked in a Kansas City auto plant for a few months and quickly became a local union leader. He spoke with other-worldly fervor; his language was colored by Biblical phrases; no other man could pierce to the hearts of Southern-born workers as he could. A gifted agitator, he made men feel that in organizing a union they were going forth to battle for righteousness and the word of God.

By contrast, the other leaders were more subdued and, happily, more hard-headed. Wyndham Mortimer, a cagey and experienced unionist charged with being associated with the CP bloc in the union, was elected vice-president. Young, tough and shrewd George Addes became secretary-treasurer. And on the executive board was a young socialist, Walter Reuther, who came from Detroit's West Side locals. Of all these men, Walter Reuther alone has been able to survive the nervous wear, the financial enticements of industry, and the factional warfare to which they were to be subjected.

So independent and radical were the delegates to the 1936 convention that they soon ran into Lewis' stone will. Prodded by socialist delegates and with the mute consent

of the CP bloc, the convention defeated a proposal to endorse Roosevelt for re-election.* When Lewis' man,
Adolph Germer, heard about this, he raged: "Communists
and socialists have taken over the convention, and are
voting not as auto workers but according to their political
views."[4] Lewis, after being prodded by a perturbed White
House, informed the delegates that unless they supported
Roosevelt, his promised $100,000 donation for organizing
would be withheld. The UAW felt that it had no choice;
$100,000 was certainly worth a formal statement which
few would credit. "In about five minutes before adjourn-
ment, the convention unanimously voted to support
Roosevelt for re-election."[5]

SITDOWN! SITDOWN!

The sitdown-strike wave began in Akron, Ohio. Large
sitdowns had occurred in Europe, and it is interesting to
note that instinctively workers in both continents reached
out for the same tactic. Yet it is doubtful if one of 100
strikers in America knew anything about the history of
sitdowns in Europe. At the Akron Goodyear plant, in November, 1935, workers simply sat down until a grievance
was settled; at the Firestone plant the same thing happened a few weeks later. Nor was this similarity of
method accidental. A modern industrial plant is so organized that its production can be disrupted when a few
strategically located men stop working. Tire builders, for

* As was to happen repeatedly, the CP found itself somewhat embar-
rassed because it was in the midst of a "change of line" toward Roosevelt.
Two years before it had called him a "social-fascist"; a half year later
it was to hail him as the leader of the "people's front." But at the moment,
it was not quite sure whether he was a fascist or a great progressive. So
it concurred in the refusal to endorse him but did not work actively for
that refusal.

example, can halt most of the production in a rubber plant. In an auto plant a work stoppage by a few assembly-line feeders cripples all production. By its very nature the sitdown is usually a more spontaneous action than most strikes; the men react directly and immediately to a grievance and, not having the patience to wait for a union meeting, simply cease working. Talk about sitdowns as conspiracies against "property rights" was usually nonsense, for there was seldom enough calculation, let alone political consciousness, among strikers to make such a possibility seem even plausible. But once the first sitdown succeeded, the new industrial unions, fighting hard for a foothold in heavy industry, saw that what had begun as a spontaneous eruption could be used as a planned method.

The sitdown has obvious advantages. For one thing, if it occurs spontaneously, no picket lines are necessary— which means less possibility of clashes with police or scabs. But the big weakness of the spontaneous sitdown is that strikers in the plant can be bottled up too easily, for it is almost impossible, in a few hours, to prepare sufficient aid on the outside. When sitdowns are planned in advance, the union usually keeps a minority of its men in the plant and uses the remainder as pickets outside. In that way, food can be passed in and communication maintained with those inside. Being confined to the limited area of the plant, the sitdown strikers can be molded into a disciplined force by their leaders, though certain chronic morale problems (gambling, boredom, family troubles, loneliness) invariably arise. In any case, it would be an error to overestimate the amount of calculation in the 1936–37 sitdowns, since most of them were simply the result of desperation.

They spread like a hungry fire. November, 1936: seven-day sitdown at Bendix plant, South Bend, Indiana. Midland Steel, Detroit: two-week sitdown. Five-day sitdown at Kelsey-Hayes, Detroit. Before the end of the year, sitdowns at Chrysler, Bendix, Briggs, Fisher Body. In each instance, substantial gains were won by the union.

The largest of all the sitdowns began on December 28, 1936, in the GM plants. On the part of the CIO, it was not a planned action; Lewis had hoped to organize steel first. Shortly after the GM sitdowns began, Lewis tried to prevent them from spreading,[6] but once he saw that was impossible, he threw all the CIO's strength into ensuring their victory. For some time UAW organizers had been hammering away at a few arguments: "The year in which GM's profits were $228,000,000, the workers' average wage was slightly over $1,100. Between January, 1934, and July, 1936, the corporation spent close to $1,000,000 for plant espionage. Speedups again and again . . ." And what incensed the workers most was the corporation's persistent refusal to negotiate with the union.

On January 4, 1937, the corporation rejected every union demand, began a back-to-work campaign and asked federal action to clear the plants of strikers. What had begun as an uncalculated skirmish became a closely marshalled war. The major front was in Flint, where 50,000 of 165,000 people worked in auto plants, most of them GM-owned. To paralyze the central Fisher Body and Chevrolet plants in Flint meant to threaten the entire GM structure. The Flint auto union had had an uneven history, its membership having dropped from 26,000 in 1934 to a mere 120 in 1936. This tattered handful had been carefully nurtured through some depressing days by Wyndham Mortimer. In 1936 the UAW sent two skilled organizers to Flint: Bob Travis and Roy Reuther, the first Reuther brother to work full time for the union. Travis had a knack for getting along with the workers; Roy

Reuther was endowed with that rarity among organizers: an overall conception of what his day-to-day activity meant.

In early January, GM obtained an injunction ordering the men to leave the plants and refrain from picketing. The judge who issued this order, Edward Black, admitted to owning $250,000 worth of GM stock—which did not help the strikers to take his injunction very seriously.[7] But the formation of the "Flint Alliance" by George Boysen, a former GM paymaster, and now a factory owner, was something that had to be taken seriously. The "Flint Alliance" began a back-to-work movement, which could, of course, lead only to a frightful clash with the men in the plants.

UAW leaders soon saw that the fate of their whole Midwest organizing campaign depended on the Flint sitdown. From Detroit, Cleveland, Toledo and Akron union activists poured into Flint; soon the city was split as if by a civil war. On January 11th, Flint police tried to stop shipments of food to the men in Fisher plant 2. Police and pickets, about 150 of each, fought for four hours; dozens of unionists were injured and fourteen shot; but the food got through. As the fighting ebbed and flowed, the pickets' ranks were augmented by thousands of unionists who rushed to the plants.*

Fearing further violence, Governor Frank Murphy of

* A vivid statement of the strikers' version of this battle appeared the next day in *The Flint Auto Worker:*

When outside strikers came with food for the evening meal, they found the door . . . blocked. They began passing it through the windows. Then company guards attempted to prevent them from doing that. . . . A tear gas bomb went through the window of a plant. Another went into the crowd outside. . . . Then came the first shot! A striker fell. He was shot in the shoulder. . . . Bill Carney, doughty Rubber Workers' organizer, grabbed the microphone of the sound truck, which by that time had arrived on the

Michigan sent 1200 national guardsmen to Flint on January 13th, but, as a New Dealer elected with the union's help, Murphy restrained those Flint officials who wished to serve 1200 "John Does" on the strikers. Simultaneously, he tried desperately to persuade GM to negotiate with the strikers.

In the meantime, the men in Fisher Plant 2 built up their food reserves, while outside the plant massive picket lines patrolled the streets. Governor Murphy prevailed on the UAW leadership to agree to empty the plants as a prelude to negotiations, while in turn the corporation promised to refrain from operating them for fifteen days. A good many strikers viewed this arrangement with suspicion, for they had little reason to trust GM. Still, the agreement was signed and the UAW men left GM plants in Detroit and Anderson, Indiana. Shortly before the union was to vacate the Flint GM plant, a UP reporter, Bill Lawrence, accidentally discovered that GM was planning to use a loophole in the agreement in order to negotiate with the Flint Alliance. When they heard of this, the strikers refused to leave the plants, even though William Knudsen, GM president, later repudiated the telegram discovered by Lawrence.

For the next few days Flint was quiet, while Washington fretted. GM officials agreed to meet with Labor Secretary Francis Perkins but refused to see John L. Lewis.

---

scene, and excoriated [the] police. . . . The answer was another blast of gunfire. Police were firing pointblank into the crowd. . . . Union sympathizers were retaliating with the only means of defense they had— stones, lumps of coal, steel hinges, milk bottles. . . . Throughout the fight the sound truck was in the heat of the battle. Manned by Victor Reuther, organizer, the amplifiers gave forth a continuous stream of encouragement and inspiration as Carney, B. J. Widick, editor of the *United Rubber Worker*, Roy Reuther, and Walter Towner, organizers, and Henry Kraus, editor of the *Flint Auto Worker* took turns at the microphone.[8]

Angered beyond his low boiling point, Lewis issued one of his testy philippics:

> For six months during the presidential campaign the economic royalists represented by General Motors and the Du Ponts contributed their money and used their energy to drive this administration from power. The administration asked labor to help repel this attack and labor gave it. The same economic royalists now have their fangs in labor. The workers of this country expect the administration to help the strikers in every reasonable way.[9]

Good enough—but what was the "reasonable way?" No one in Washington seemed to know and as conversations there dragged, the struggle in Flint was resumed. GM secured an injunction to oust the sitdown strikers. The men in the plants were beginning to feel the strain of their long isolation, and partly because of the failure of the Washington negotiations, their morale began to crumble. One thing became clear to the strike leaders: an unusually bold and dramatic move was necessary if the strike was not to peter out. As in war, strikes sometimes require throwing all one's forces into an ultimate gamble. In Flint, the time had come for the gamble.

LET THERE BE NO MOANING . . .

Roy Reuther worked out a plan which was approved by Travis, Hapgood and the head of the Chevrolet strike committee, Kermit Johnson. It was classically simple and bold. Only a fraction of the GM plants in Flint had been shut down. In some the union was simply not strong enough to call out the men, and in others it refrained from doing so because, its resources for supporting strikers limited, it wished to concentrate its fire on a few crucial plants. Roy Reuther proposed, then, that the union "seize" Chevrolet Plant 4 in which the workers were not on strike but in which there was a core of unionists. Chevrolet 4 contained the motor-assembly division, and its inclusion among the shut-down plants would ensure the success of the strike, or at the very least, would greatly improve the strikers' morale. Since a frontal assault was impossible, Roy Reuther proposed that the unionists fake a seizure of another plant, Chevrolet 9, and then, the police having been diverted, march a picked body of men into Plant 4, where the workers would be persuaded either to join the strike or go home. To divert the stool pigeons in the union, the plan had to be presented to the strikers simply as a means of entering Plant 9.

It seems fantastic, perhaps—but it worked. Probably the very melodramatic quality of Roy Reuther's idea ensured its success. The UAW's women's auxiliary, led by a firebrand, Genora Johnson, staged a demonstration in front of Plant 9. Inside, unionists fought rough and tumble with company guards, thereby diverting the police. In the meantime, a group of union "commandos" led by a burly striker, Ed Cronk, rushed Chevrolet Plant 4 and took control. Delighted with this coup, the strikers regained their fighting spirit.

Then began the real uproar. Governor Murphy, furious and frustrated, threatened to have the National Guard drive the strikers out of Plant 4, by force if necessary. Food shipments to the men inside it were stopped. Now numbering 2,000, the men in Plant 4 were completely isolated.[10] To try to oust them would lead to incalculable bloodshed; to try to starve them out would sooner or later also provoke a battle.

At this point the local strike leaders called on John L. Lewis to assume personal command in Michigan. Grumbling because he had been awakened by a phone call at three in the morning, Lewis agreed to come. Before leaving Washington he was summoned to the White House and urged to get the strikers out of the plants. When he replied by asking when GM would start negotiating, there then developed a noticeable coolness between Lewis and his host. On boarding the train for Detroit, he said: "Let there be no moaning at the bar as I put out to sea." Lewis understood that the future of the CIO might well be decided in Flint and having, with or without the accompaniment of moaning, put out to sea, he meant to reach port.

On February 2nd a Flint judge who did not own GM stock ordered the men to vacate the Fisher Body plants under threat of imprisonment and $15,000,000 fines. Sheriff Wolcott of Genesee County read an order to the sitdowners which gave them until February 3rd to leave. In Flint, on the streets and in the union offices, there was intolerable excitement, but in the plants the men remained calm. They drew up a statement directed to Governor Murphy:

> We, the workers in the plant, are completely unarmed, and to send in the military, armed thugs and armed deputies . . . will mean a bloody massacre . . . We have carried on a stay-in strike over a month in order to make General Motors Corporation obey the law and engage in collective bargaining. . . . We have decided to stay in the plant. We have no illusions about the sacrifices this decision will entail. We fully expect that if a violent effort is made to oust us many of us will be killed, and we take this means to make it known . . . that if this result follows from the attempt to eject us, you are the one who must be held responsible for our deaths.[11]

Was this statement merely a geyser of rhetoric? Hardly, for there had been long and serious discussions among the strikers. They were convinced that the shedding of their blood was preferable to defeat, for they could not face the thought of what life in the plants would be like if the strike was lost. They were sober and not at all reckless men, but they felt that the time had come to draw a line.

Before the February 3rd deadline, thousands of unionists poured into Flint from every city in the Midwest. Walter Reuther arrived heading a flying squadron from Detroit's West Side local. Ragged armies, carrying bricks, bars, and baseball bats moved into Flint. Soon there were so many unionists that they blocked all the streets near the plants. Using sound trucks skillfully, the union leaders took over control of traffic. In the plants, windows were barricaded with steel plate and the men organized into fighting formations.

But the moral hesitations of one man forestalled a battle for which everyone was prepared. Since Governor Murphy could not bring himself to order the National Guard to move, its troop commanders waited for a wire that never came. Instead, he pressured William Knudsen to negotiate with Lewis. When Knudsen and Lewis met with Murphy, the Governor suddenly insisted that Lewis tell the men to quit the plants. Lewis replied:

> I do not doubt your ability to call out your soldiers and shoot the members of our union out of those plants, but let me say when you issue that order I shall leave this conference and I shall enter one of those plants with my people.[12]

Again Murphy had to retreat. On February 11th President Roosevelt personally wired GM requesting that its representatives meet with the union once more. An agreement was finally reached by which the UAW became bargaining agent for the workers in those seventeen GM plants closed by the strike. Injunction proceedings were to be dropped and other important concessions made to the union. For the UAW this was a turning point; in a few weeks its membership doubled from 100,000 to 200,000.

Governor Murphy was subjected to acrimonious criticism by the conservative press for his failure to "be firm" with the strikers. But most of this talk was simply thoughtless—*even from a conservative point of view*. To have attempted to force the men out of the plants—what would have been the result? General strikes in the Michigan industrial cities? Thousands of CIO workers rushing from nearby cities to reinforce the strikers? A miniature civil war in Flint? As a few intelligent conservatives understood, the time had passed when unions could be smashed by brute force. The corporations would have to recognize them, and then, if possible, defang them.

Sitdowns broke out everywhere in Michigan. Sixty thousand Chrysler workers struck on March 8th, and the union had difficulty in persuading most of them not to remain in the plant.[13] Strikes took place at Briggs and Cadillac, in the latter case accompanied by clashes between police and strikers. The UAW charged police violence and, to show its power, called a demonstration in Cadillac Square in late March, which was attended by 150,000 people. Certainly *they* could not be dispersed by the National Guard. Chrysler officials raged, but they had no alternative: on April 6th they signed with John L. Lewis.

NECESSITY AND REVOLUTION

The sitdown strikes aroused more passionate responses in this country than any other act of the UAW. To many people they seemed a dangerous revolutionary challenge to capitalist economy*—a threat to the very structure. of American society, its traditional legal pattern of private-property rights. Seldom have American editorialists "viewed with alarm" so persistently, and from their point of view, perhaps, with so much justification. As *Business Week* wrote in 1937:

> By means of sitdown strikes, the country has been put at the mercy of thoroughly irresponsible groups which in effect have no leadership, no control, no authority that can restrain them. Great industries, whose operations affect the daily welfare of millions, are confronted with demands to sign contracts with groups which, day by day and hour by hour, demonstrate that they have almost no control over their own people, no conception of the validity or the sanctity of a contract, no respect for property rights or for rights of any sort except their own.[14]

This, well put, was the conservative view. But to socialists who wished to abolish the private-property system, the sitdowns seemed a cheering portent of things to come. They saw a connection between the sitdowns in America and the pattern of sitdowns in Europe, and believed that objectively the workers were challenging the central structure of capitalism, even though hardly aware of the significance of their action. And it is probably true that if large-scale unemployment had continued in America and if the depression had not slid into a war economy, sitdown strikes might have continued in the late thirties and acquired a political complexion and significance they did not yet have.

* Long after the sitdown-strike wave subsided, the United States Supreme Court declared the use of sitdowns illegal in its decision of Feb. 27, 1939, in the Fansteel case. The majority opinion stated, "The strike was illegal in its inception and prosecution. . . . It was an illegal seizure of buildings in order to prevent their use by the employer in a lawful manner."

But it is important to distinguish sharply between the motivations of those who participated in the sitdowns and the significance retrospectively attributed to their behavior. Whatever the latter may be, it seems incontestable, as one looks back on the strikes of the mid-thirties, that the great bulk of auto workers had no conscious desire to challenge either GM's property structure or capitalist economy in general. They did not believe they were violating any laws and, in fact, hardly gave serious consideration to the legal aspects of their action.* On the part of the great mass of workers, the sitdowns were motivated by one simple desire: to win strikes and gain union recognition. Even the least politically conscious worker could not help seeing that on a strictly empirical basis they were extraordinarily effective.

There was therefore something dubious about those liberals who, while "in general" favoring unionism, yet "could not but deplore" the sitdowns. Such judicious analysts were usually people who had not known what it meant to work in an auto plant in the pre-union days; who had not known the misery and sweat that went into unionization drives; who had not known the desperation which alone could have forced workers to such dangerous and impoverishing strikes. Of the judicious critics who could not see their way to supporting sitdowns, the union and the auto workers asked one crucial question: in view of the repeated refusal of the corporations to negotiate

---

* A union veteran was recently describing his work during one sitdown to a friend of the writers. He went into great detail telling how the men had commandeered the plant for their purposes, how they had prepared barricades to halt police or strikebreakers trying to get into the plant, and how they had even thought of using its fire hose to ward off possible attackers. But, asked our friend, suppose the city turned off the water? "They couldn't have done that," the unionist heatedly replied. "That would have been against the law!"

with the union, what other way did the strikers have of forcing the corporations to bargain?* Patience had been unrewarded; government-level maneuvering had brought nothing but intrigue; the usual kinds of strike action involved the danger of large-scale strike-breaking. No, the "plague-on-both-your-houses" approach was possible only for those who knew very well that *they* had a stable house in which to keep warm and dry. Under the circumstances of 1936–37, the sitdowns were neither a revolutionary calculation nor an outburst of spite; they were, for the men in the shops, an unavoidable necessity. If today GM officials receive UAW negotiators with at least ostensible politeness, if today the GM division of the UAW bargains for hundreds of thousands of workers, if today the UAW as a whole has become a powerful and secure institution in one of America's major industries, if today the mere threat of a strike is often enough to gain the union's demands— all this is possible only because twelve years ago men risked jobs and necks to sit down.

* At the 1937 convention of the UAW, a resolution defending the sitdowns was passed which, in part, said:

The stay-in strike was beyond a doubt the only method by which the workers in the automobile industry could have forced the employers, who were determined to disregard the law of the land, into entering into real collective bargaining relationships. The stay-in strike was not only significant because it brought about collective bargaining in the automobile industry without loss of life, but it was also significant because of its singular effectiveness in stopping the very heart of the industry. The stay-in strike will remain an effective weapon against employers who refuse to recognize the moral and legal rights of workers in collective bargaining . . . it will remain labor's most effective weapon against the autocracy of industry.[15]

Homer Martin:
Friction and Faction

3 --

ANYONE who thought recognition of the UAW
by GM and Chrysler would lead to peace in the industry
was quickly disillusioned. From 1937 until America's
entry into the war, the industry was racked by numerous
brief strikes and plant-level disputes. Having recognized
the UAW simply because they could see no workable alternative, the corporations would not grant the union any
concession unless specifically required by the contract. In
practice, however, many day-to-day problems must always arise which cannot possibly be foreseen in contracts.
How well these problems are solved is a major test of collective bargaining. In the late 1930's they were solved,
from the union's point of view, badly or not at all.

For about the first half year after the sitdowns, the auto

workers were on the offensive. Passions released by the sitdowns could not simply evaporate the moment the men returned to work. In the immediate post-sitdown days many workers came back to the plants not with chips but logs on their shoulders. For the first time, they felt, they were in a position to "talk back" to foremen. Those workers who had been leaders in the sitdowns usually became shop stewards; their natural desire to maintain their prestige as militant leaders made them irascible plant negotiators. In turn, the foremen resented the loss of their old powers, since never again, it seemed, would they be able to fire men at will, run departments without check from below, and manipulate workers by doling out favors.

By the fall of 1937 a change of mood could be seen in the plants. After the CIO was defeated in the Little Steel strike of May, 1937, the auto corporations, hoping again to rid themselves of the union, began a drive against the stewards' powers. A sudden increase in unemployment during the second half of 1937 aroused serious job fears among all auto workers. Since workers are usually less aggressive when layoffs are in sight, the corporations felt safe in nibbling at union privileges.

Management and the union exchanged guerilla stabs over the shop-steward system. For an industrial union, the steward system is an indispensable foundation. If the corporations recognize the right of stewards to negotiate plant grievances, the union's power can be constantly exerted; if not, the union sooner or later disintegrates. From 1937 to 1940 the corporations frequently tried to avoid dealing with the stewards. The union was left with only one practical way to buttress the steward system: "quickie" strikes, not lengthy enough to involve it in an undesired test of strength, but sharp enough to wrench minor concessions from management. In the General Motors plants alone there were, from February to June, 1937, 170 stoppages lasting from five minutes to several days.[1]

Most of the time, the UAW did not quite know how to handle these quickies. Its president, Homer Martin, threatened to discipline workers who participated in them, even while he charged that the corporations were provoking them. (In that case, asked his intra-union opponents, why threaten to punish the workers?) Actually, the quickies were too numerous to be ascribed to one or another isolated cause. As late as 1949, wildcat strikes still continued. (At the Ford plants, there were 164 in 1942, 259 in 1943 and 225 in 1944).[2] But a few general causes for quickies can be noted: the cockiness of the victorious sit-down strikers and their need to let off steam accumulated during years of factory regimentation; management's unwillingness to accept the shop-steward system; and the inexperience of both in the daily process of collective bargaining.

AUTONOMY AND DISCIPLINE

Prompted by John L. Lewis, Homer Martin wrote to General Motors in August, 1937, conceding it the right to fire wildcat strikers and asking in turn for several concessions, such as exclusive bargaining rights and improved working conditions. Martin's gesture was appreciated neither by GM nor most of its workers. The corporation was in no mood to grant concessions, while a national conference of shop delegates from GM locals repudiated Martin's clumsy letter. Martin himself soon withdrew his suggestion that GM be allowed to fire wildcat strikers.

One young UAW leader devised a way to persuade the

corporations to deal with stewards. The president of the
Detroit West Side UAW local, Walter Reuther, wrote:

> It looks very much as though General Motors does not want
> an agreement with the UAW. Now let's see what it would
> mean if the union decided to call off negotiations. The
> workers would then be free to demand a lot of conditions
> and wages that are due them, and they could sit down every
> time these were denied . . . There would be a lot of strikes if
> there were no agreement.[3]

This hint that large-scale sitdowns might be resumed if
GM refused to accept the steward system was closer to
the temper of the workers than Martin's letter to GM.

Again prompted by Lewis, Martin sought to strengthen
his powers by curtailing the autonomy of the locals. To
Lewis, a contract pledging a union not to strike for a year
or two was "sacred"—but then the power of his union
in the coal fields made it easy for him to feel that way.
In 1937 Lewis had the CIO pledge to adhere to contracts
and to discipline those units that did not. Which was all
very well—except that it did not come to serious grips
with the problem in the auto plants.

To the younger, more radical UAW leaders, Martin's
attempts to centralize the union's structure and crack
down on wildcats seemed not unlike the kind of bureaucratic unionism they had recently opposed in the AFL.
Nor was the Lewis dictatorship inside the United Mine
Workers any more attractive. The idea of letting Martin,
a far less gifted man than Lewis, establish a similar regime
in the UAW could only elicit icy reactions.

At the Milwaukee, August, 1937, UAW convention, the
disputes over wildcat strikes and union centralization were
heatedly reviewed. In two years, the union had mush-
roomed from 30,000 to 350,000 members. Such expansion
could have occurred without serious friction only if it

were directed by an organizational genius—which was hardly the way to describe Homer Martin. His lush oratory had been useful in the union's hectic early days; he had been a colorful public leader as long as some one else was at hand to tell him what to say; but now he proved a wretched administrator, inexperienced, inept, and worst of all, capricious. As one of his supporters despairingly said, "He always says yes to the last man who talks to him."

The national CIO office sent Ora Gassaway, a Lewis lieutenant, to Detroit to help Martin draft constitutional changes granting him greater authority. As part of his attempt to centralize power, Martin fired several organizers, among them Roy and Victor Reuther, and charged that "an outside organization [is] trying to seize control of the union."[4] He was referring, of course, to the Communist Party.

In the UAW's days of birth, radicals of various hues, while few in numbers, had played an important role, for they had been self-sacrificing and idealistic as few routine union leaders could be. But once the union was established, they found it far more difficult to work within it. In the days of strike struggle, inter-radical disputes had receded to the background. Now that power was being consolidated, these disputes were unavoidably refracted, sometimes in weird shapes, within the union. Simultaneously, the non-radical leaders of the union became impatient with the "politicals." They wished to institutionalize the UAW, to integrate it into capitalist economy, and to begin enjoying the usual administrative advantages of a successful union.

The union now split into two main groups, each more or less subdivided. Martin was supported by the majority

of the UAW top leadership, which naturally favored centralization of power, and by most of the more conservative
secondary UAW leaders. Servicing him with ideas was the
tiny but effectively placed "Lovestone group,"* a dissident communist sect bitterly opposed to the official Stalinist party. In the anti-Martin coalition, the tightly knit
and extremely powerful CP faction was the strongest
force. Much smaller was the socialist group led by Walter Reuther which, while increasingly uneasy about its
Stalinist partner, still felt that Martin represented the
main danger in the UAW. Also supporting the anti-Martin coalition was a stratum of active members who viewed
with suspicion any leader seeking to concentrate power
in his person. In the anti-Martin coalition, Wyndham
Mortimer was the most influential leader.**

The 1937 UAW convention was a noisy affair, often
degenerating into personal attacks and several times verg-
ing on a free-for-all. Splitting the union were issues of
first importance, and certainly an objective debate would

* This group, known first as the Communist Party Opposition and then
as the Independent Labor League, was composed of supporters of Jay
Lovestone who had been expelled from the CP leadership in 1929 for
"rightist deviations" and for political sympathy with the point of view of
Nikolai Bukharin in Russia. Rejecting the CP "dual union" policy of the
early 1930's, the Lovestonites favored working in the established trade
unions. Their inclination was usually to establish intimate relationships
with union leaders in order to influence them privately. Shortly after the
outbreak of the Second World War, the group dissolved because of its
inability to establish a common point of view toward the war. Since then
Lovestone has become a confidential adviser to David Dubinsky of the
International Ladies Garment Workers Union.

** Formally, the Martin group called itself "the Progressives," while
his opponents were known as the "Unity group." Such labels, habitually
employed by union factions, seldom mean anything. In this book, they
are seldom used; we attempt to give a more realistic characterization of
union factions.

have been useful. But by the time job-eager politicians had finished maneuvering for posts and wild discussions about "outside political groups" had subsided, the central issues facing the union were thoroughly lost. Intervening personally to establish a façade of unity, Lewis worked out a "compromise" by which both sides were represented on the union board, with Martin enjoying a majority.

The union had now to face the problem of "outside political groups," that is, radical parties. When the UAW was first formed, it had been taken for granted that left-wing "politicals" could freely express their views. That such left-wing unionists were motivated by ideas beyond the intellectual horizon of the average auto worker had not seemed a serious difficulty, if only because most UAW members were then more concerned with external strug-gle than internal power relations. Now, however, the prob-lem of defining the status of radical groups functioning in the UAW—whether it was any different from the status of other members—became important.

Martin denounced his opponents as being dominated by the CP, a charge not entirely accurate. Unquestionably, the CP was the most influential political force in the anti-Martin coalition, but it was hardly, as he claimed, its un-disputed master. What held that coalition together was not any positive agreement on union or political matters, but a distaste for Martin's high-handed ways. It can be granted that many of those opposed to Martin, especially the Stalinists, were just as ready as he to engage in power maneuvers. No retrospective judgment of this faction fight should therefore present it as unqualified righteous-ness arrayed against unqualified evil. The situation was far too complex for an apologia, either way.

When Martin labeled his opposition Communist, he

rubbed a good many unionists the wrong way. It must be remembered that, rightly or wrongly, in the mid-thirties the Communist Party was not viewed with as much distrust as it later roused in the labor movement. It was thought of primarily as a radical party rather than a totalitarian annex of the Russian dictatorship, and even the dissident Marxist groups still considered it part of the radical community. It would be several years yet before this attitude toward the CP changed. Furthermore, the CP people had worked hard and often skilfully to build the UAW—a fact many union members remembered. They also remembered that in the AFL any critic had been denounced as a Communist and that during the sitdown strikes *all* the UAW leaders had been called "reds." For such reasons, the ranks did not take as kindly to Martin's attacks on the CP as they were to take to Reuther's ten years later. What finally rendered absurd Martin's accusations of "outside" influences, was that he himself was working closely with the Lovestone group, as "outside" or "inside" as any other.

In general, Martin's cries had dangerous overtones for the union's internal life. All too often talk in unions about "outside influence" is demagogic; what matters is not whether people are "outside" or "inside" but whether they are right or wrong, honest or dishonest, intelligent or stupid. The UAW had taken pride in its free internal life, and now its most conscious members uneasily sensed that Martin seemed to be itching for something close to ideological conformity. His attacks, while often accurately describing Communist politics, were so intemperate and his actions so high-handed that many unionists not sympathetic to the CP began to doubt his loyalty to democratic values.

THE ROAD TO SUICIDE

The erratic Martin rode high for a while, firing dissident organizers and trying to censor critical local papers. But he was the sort of man whose momentary victories could only lead to ultimate defeat. Each time he flourished because of the help of others he grew less willing to accept their further advice.

Martin's greatest blunder was his failure to take advantage of the noticeable coolness that arose in early 1938 between the Stalinists and Reuther. Back in November, 1937, when it had become apparent that Reuther could not be sucked into the Stalinist movement,* the CP had tried to split his main base of strength, the large UAW local in West Side Detroit, into several smaller ones. Had Martin been sufficiently alert and intelligent, he would then have seen that the alliance between the CP and Reuther was beginning to crack and could not, in any case, long continue. But he was so blinded by his own rhetoric that he thought of the Reuthers as nothing but Communist accomplices and therefore made no serious overtures to them.

Though the Reuther group felt it had to oppose Martin's dictatorial inclinations, it grew increasingly uneasy about

* In 1935–37 the Communist Party had pursued a policy of befriending those socialists who, like Walter Reuther, were believed to be sympathetic to Russia. Reuther was approached by several CP leaders, among them Louis Budenz, to join the party; but when they told him he would have to submit to its discipline, especially on foreign affairs, he refused. Inside the Socialist Party Reuther was subjected to severe criticism by those who thought his relations with the CP in the anti-Martin coalition too intimate.

Since then, Reuther has been viciously attacked by the Communist Party, but even as late as February, 1949, the *Daily Worker* rather plaintively wrote: "There was a time when Reuther didn't red-bait. That was in the days of 1936 and 1937 when Reuther was in alliance with the Communists. . . ."[5]

its Stalinist allies. At an April, 1938, Michigan CIO convention, Victor Reuther was defeated for a high office
because the CP deserted him. From here on in, the
Reuthers would have to tack and veer, supporting the anti-
Martin coalition but alert to the danger that they might
be crushed during a wild exchange of factional blows.

By mid-1938 the faction struggle degenerated into a cat-
and-dog affair, which it would be wearisome to describe
in detail. The union was completely torn by intrigues,
maneuvers and denunciations. In June, 1938, Martin suspended five dissident UAW officers (how he loved to
suspend people!), among them Addes, Mortimer and
Richard Frankensteen. (Until April, 1938, Frankensteen
had been Martin's first lieutenant, but now, for reasons
that soon became clear, he switched sides.) Presumably,
Martin acted under loosely defined powers granted him
by the constitution which Lewis had generously supplied
the UAW in 1937. Now alarmed by Martin's instability
and hysteria, Lewis no doubt had occasion to reflect that
not everyone could play the high-handed boss so effi-
ciently as he.

When Frankensteen admitted to Louis Stark, *New York
Times* labor writer, that he had conferred with William
Z. Foster and other CP leaders ("I'll talk to anyone about
the union"),[6] Martin quickly charged that the CP meant
to capture the union with Frankensteen's expert aid. In
turn, the officers whom Martin had suspended and later
expelled, portentously declared that, "The conspiracy that
actually existed... was a conspiracy between Homer Martin and an irresponsible, disruptive political adventurer
and meddler, Jay Lovestone."[7] They released private letters written by Lovestone that purportedly showed Lovestone to be Martin's political mentor.

Martin claimed the Stalinists were using Machiavellian

methods to capture the union; his opponents said the same about the Lovestoneites. (There was truth in both charges.) Then Jay Lovestone protested that the letters from which Addes and Frankensteen quoted had been stolen from his files by a Russian GPU agent. How Addes and Frankensteen did manage to get the letters never was satisfactorily explained.

Martin now proceeded to commit a series of extraordinary blunders. In August, 1938, the expelled officers, who claimed that their trial by Martin had been a farce, appealed for help to the national CIO. Before Lewis rendered any decision, Martin denounced him for presuming to have the right to interfere in the UAW. "I will not," he blustered, "turn over the international UAW to John L. Lewis."[8] Since he was hardly in a position to combat Lewis, Martin's braggadocio could only drive Lewis into supporting his opponents. The UAW ranks, thoroughly sick of a faction fight they could seldom fathom, hoped that Lewis would establish order in the union. As a result Martin soon had to retreat, with a thin shred of dignity, by accepting a Lewis "compromise." A CIO receivership was appointed over the UAW and Martin was stripped of part of his power. Philip Murray and Sidney Hillman, the "receivers" appointed by Lewis, discharged several of Martin's supporters and reinstated the officers he had expelled.

Hoping to revive his prestige in the UAW, Martin had entered into dubious negotiations with the Ford Company in October, 1938. He worked on the theory—either incredibly ignorant or naive—that Henry Ford didn't know the truth about labor conditions in his own plant and that, if once informed, would agree to recognize the union.[9] In January, 1939, Martin even had the UAW board approve his conferences with Ford. But soon these negotiations collapsed amid accusations, never adequately proved or disproved, that he had been preparing to make a "secret deal" with Henry Ford.[10]

In January, 1939, Martin suffered another blow when one of his lieutenants, R. J. Thomas, deserted him and charged that he, Thomas, had been present at meetings at which Martin and an official of the Ford Company had discussed ways of getting the UAW to leave the CIO.[11] Whatever the UAW ranks might have thought of this or the other leader, they were intensely loyal to the CIO as a whole. For any UAW leader to be associated with a proposal to join the detested AFL meant the end of his career.

Increasingly desperate and hysterical, Martin suspended fifteen of the union's twenty-four executive board members in January, 1939, when they voted to call for a convention of the union. Surrounded by bodyguards, completely inaccessible to shop delegations that came to see him, and unable to recognize the simple fact that he had been outmaneuvered to the point where he no longer had most of his once considerable support, Martin took a final plunge. He decided to call a convention of his own—that is, to leave the CIO.

In March, 1939, two conventions were held. In Detroit the Martin supporters, representing at most 60,000 UAW members, met in an atmosphere of sickening adulation of their leader. When Martin stepped to the rostrum, he received an hour-long ovation. His rump union soon joined the AFL and slid into insignificance.

The bulk of the UAW locals sent delegates to the anti-Martin convention in Cleveland. But even with Martin gone, there was no peace—far from it. The Communist Party had helped defeat Martin, but who was now to prevent *it* from taking control of the UAW? Its delegates suggested a slate for UAW office headed by Addes and Frankensteen. (Now it was clear why Frankensteen had abandoned Martin.) At Cleveland the CP controlled the strongest bloc of delegates. Opposing it was only a small socialist group led by Reuther and some run-of-the-mill unionists whose views were expressed by R. J. Thomas. The CIO sent Philip Murray and Sidney Hillman to the convention to prevent its seizure by the CP. At off-the-record convention sessions Murray and Hillman bluntly told the Stalinists to refrain from using their votes; the CP quickly retreated. A "compromise" candidate for UAW president, R. J. Thomas, was proposed by the CIO and accepted by the convention. Though at first unhappy, the CP later had little reason to regret Thomas' election.

Taking advantage of the weakness of the UAW, of Martin's appearance as a rival claimant for recognition, and of the frequent physical clashes between the two, GM announced in the spring of 1939 that it was suspending collective bargaining. Several strikes, obviously tests of strength, broke out in the industry, the longest and first important one, at Briggs, being won by the UAW. In July, GM asked the NLRB to hold an election to determine whether the UAW or Martin's AFL rump represented its workers. Martin tried to squeeze in edgewise by calling a strike at a GM plant in Flint, but the workers' response was negligible. To help clear up GM's convenient confusion on who represented its workers, the UAW called a "strategy strike" based on a clever scheme devised by Walter Reuther.

His "strategy" consisted of two parts: first, to shut down GM at the peak of the summer retooling season, so that its new models would be delayed; and second, to have only the skilled tool-and-die workers strike, so that the "non-striking" production workers could draw unemployment insurance.

In early August, 1939, there was violence at Cleveland and Detroit GM plants, but it soon became clear that, whatever else, the bulk of the auto workers would never accept the AFL. In plant after plant Martin was defeated and soon all he had left was his gilded AFL charter. Somewhat later he went to work for the Ford Company. Homer Martin had begun as a theological student at the freshwater William Jewel College, had become pastor of the Baptist Church at Leeds, Missouri, and because of his sympathies for the workers in his parish had been fired. He then had taken a job as an auto worker in Kansas City, become convinced of the need for unionism, and worked as a union organizer. He had fought hard for the union and could never understand why the workers who had once applauded him later rejected him. And now he was retreating to the protection of Ford, the most bitter enemy of auto unionism. As a labor leader, he had committed suicide.[12]

With Martin out of the way, the differences of opinion in the UAW leadership quickly came to a boil. Despite moments of calm, the union entered another period of factionalism, which continued until 1947, when Reuther decisively defeated the Stalinists.

The 1940 UAW convention passed a resolution condemning the "brutal dictatorship" of Russia in the same terms as the Hitler and Mussolini regimes. It failed, however, to say anything about Stalinism in the union, even though the CP was then behaving in the wildest manner because of the Hitler-Stalin pact. CP-led UAW locals called precipitous and ill-managed strikes: a seventy-day walkout at Allis Chalmers in Wisconsin and another at North American Aircraft at Englewood, California. Once, however, Hitler invaded Russia, the CP shifted from indiscriminate strike calls to the most insistent opposition to all strikes. In 1941 the Reuther group, feeling that the time had come to move against the Stalinists in the UAW, introduced a resolution to bar them and fascists from union office. "No matter how often the Communist Party line may change," said Reuther, "we shall have no part of a policy of appeasment either with the agents of Stalin or Hitler."[13]

The Stalinists tried to counter Reuther's resolution by introducing a motion to bar socialists as well as communists from UAW office, but this silly maneuver failed. Actually, their motion was a stupid blunder. Immediately after accusing Reuther of "red-baiting" them, they did the same to him. (In those days, it should be remembered, the Communist Party accused socialists of being ultra-radical.) By countering the possible anti-democratic implications of Reuther's proposal with an even less democratic motion, they simply proved that Reuther's characterization of them had been accurate.

THE PRICE OF FACTIONS

The Homer Martin episode is the least appetizing part of UAW history, but its consequences have been deep and continuous. To some extent, the fight between Martin and his opponents was an unavoidable part of the union's "growing pains." Since it had been built in years of severe struggle, the UAW's internal life could not be stabilized (or, if you will, bureaucratized) by mere whim. The consolidation of so immense a union was bound to result in a struggle between those who wished to centralize power in the top leadership and those who wished to preserve local autonomy. It was bound to result in a wild, undignified scramble for the new posts that were tempting secondary leaders. This process of stratification and of the elimination of anachronistic leaders was inevitable.

Homer Martin was an agitator able to translate simple ideas into dramatic slogans and close enough to the workers' level of thought to articulate those slogans in their language. But once the movement for which he spoke had triumphed, he unavoidably mismanaged its attempt to consolidate power. Being little more than a sensitized mouthpiece, he allowed his mass popularity to turn his head. As soon as he deluded himself into believing that the words he spoke came from *his* mind, he was doomed.

Part of the responsibility, however, for the internal UAW debacle must be placed on the radical groups. Many of the radicals who had done yeoman service in the union's early days were now, whatever their intentions, of dubious use to the union. Some of them were inexperienced in practical unionism; others often exaggerated, out of wishful thinking, the CIO's "revolutionary potential" and hence acted rashly; still others attempted to "capture" the union by maneuvers with opportunist leaders, even though the sensible thing for them would have been to accept minority status; and, not least important, many radicals became intellectually disoriented in the late thirties because of the disintegration of the anti-Stalinist left.

If factions are based on program rather than only on a quest for power, they can be a means for defining differences of opinion and pursuing a vigorous democratic life. But in a trade union it is almost impossible to keep separate program and power, ideas and ambitions. As a consequence, the leaders' powers must be limited if democracy is to continue. This was the central lesson the UAW active members learned from the Martin episode. Delegates to future UAW conventions would repeatedly vote in such a way that rival factions found themselves more or less evenly balanced in power. At least in part, their motivation was a feeling that, having badly burned themselves with Martin, they would not soon let another leader or group concentrate too much power. In retrospect, this seems a lesson well worth learning, even if at so heavy a price. It is also worth remembering.

The Fall of Ford

4

UNTIL he was nearly forty, Henry Ford was a business failure. A pioneer in building a saleable auto, he had worked for several companies as a production man, had experimented with new models on his own, had raced his cars in public, and had even been threatened on the streets of Detroit by teamsters whose paths he crossed. But he had not achieved financial success. When the Ford Motor Co. was formed in 1902 with a total cash capital of $28,000, Henry Ford was only a minority stockholder.

In one of the most revolutionary steps in American business history, the new Ford Co. set out to build a car within reach of moderate-income groups; its first one sold for $850. This car was an immediate success, and through a series of lucky accidents and his own perseverance Ford became the major stockholder in the company.

In 1908 he built another car that was light but sturdy, high-slung, narrow-wheeled and homely. Counting every last nut, it had only 5,000 parts, and these parts were so

83

standardized that replacements could be bought in any of the Ford-servicing garages. In 1909 Ford turned out over 10,000 of these cars. A major factor in the industrialization of this country, they had a name easy to remember: Model T.

By 1912, 7,000 dealers were selling Model T's and Ford was doing 40 percent of U. S. automobile business. In two years sales of Model T doubled; in five years sales multiplied by about twenty times. The Model T brought the farm close to the town for, unlike any other car then produced, it could get across almost any road, no matter how rocky or muddy. In a few years Ford announced a dividend of 1,000 percent.

As orders for the Model T rocketed, Ford was unable to produce the cars fast enough. In 1910, when the company moved its plant to Highland Park to gain more space, Ford made a second major contribution to American industry by beginning to use mass-production methods. The old all-round mechanic soon disappeared, and workers were restricted to several simple operations. By 1913 the idea of the "moving assembly" had been worked out in practice, and by 1914 the automatic moving belt, which lifted the assembly off the floor, was introduced. In these early days Ford often fraternized with his men, especially the important mechanics and inventors, and as a result morale at the plant was high. The workers felt that all might yet share in a big killing.

But by 1914 it was already possible to see the beginnings of what has since become the Ford system. Rigorous supervision of work pace, increasingly monotonous jobs, a terribly cramped and crowded plant, fewer breaks for rest—these were the characteristics of Ford life. Since there were others jobs to be had, men began to quit. The I.W.W., then at the peak of its power, tried to organize

the Ford workers and distributed handbills attacking Ford
as a "speed-up king."

Ford countered with a brilliant managerial idea: the $5
day. With this step he stabilized his labor force and ended
the wasteful turnover of 40 to 60 percent per month.
He drove or bought out his partners and began to sketch
the pattern of his subsequent autocratic control of the
company. In 1919, in a deal involving $105,000,000, Ford
gained complete control of the company. Once or twice
he was on the rocks. In 1921 he narrowly escaped bank-
ruptcy by unloading cars on reluctant dealers. But his
company survived for good economic reasons. In an expanding industrial economy it answered fundamental
needs, used sure-fire methods. From its rationalization of
production to its increasingly rigid supervision of labor,
it was a model for and precursor of the American industrial age.

MAN OF WISDOM

Henry Ford was unlike his industrialist peers in one
important respect: he became a folk sage whose voice
expressed the ideas by which millions of his fellow citizens lived. Had they been able to preserve him in machine
oil, the World Fair savants who buried the most characteristic products of our age should have put Ford into
one of their capsules.

To the man in the street, Henry Ford seemed proof
that a poor boy could get ahead and that riches need not
spoil a man's character. For Henry Ford was, he always
insisted, a man like other Midwesterners, with moderate
wants and moderate passions, living by the code of ab-
stinence. He seemed to represent the rugged virtues, the
persevering independence and stubbornness, which the

Michigan farmer or Ohio gas-station attendant could admire. He was self-made.

As early as the First World War, Henry Ford began his career as practical sociologist. He set up a "Sociology Department" in his plant, headed by Rev. Samuel Marquis, Dean of the Episcopal Cathedral of Detroit. Representatives of this department visited Ford employees, keeping charts of their moral steadfastness and helping immigrant workers "Americanize" themselves. Marquis' men tried to prevent workers from taking in male boarders ("an evil custom," said Ford) and spending evenings "unwisely." Drinking and divorce were unwise. When a Ford worker was found to be "living unworthily,"[1] his wages were cut. The private affairs and morals of his workers were Ford's business.

Ford became a publisher, a "Chronicler [he said] of the Neglected Truth." In *The Dearborn Independent* he printed articles railing at capitalists and bankers ("a lot of Jews sitting around smoking cigars as long as that chimney"[2]), and crusaded for churchgoing, early rising and staying on the farm. Denouncing both "Jewish Wall Street" and the orgies of Hollywood, his paper spoke the language of the crackerbarrel philosopher and the Bible Belt evangelist. For, despite the fact that he helped revolutionize the quality of American life more than any other single individual, Ford still longed for the good old days. Despite his millions, Ford suspected that somewhere in our society something had gone wrong—and was this not a conviction shared by millions of other Americans?

When the First World War began, Ford was a bitter pacifist. He did not believe in getting mixed up in foreign affairs; the war was the work of New York bankers and British magnates. When Rosika Schwimmer asked him to lead a peace mission to Europe, Henry Ford, the Michigan farm-boy who had once declared his conviction that "history is bunk," felt the call of history ringing in his ears, and with grave awareness of his immense responsibility sailed on the peace ship. On the morning before the Christmas on which he was to "get the boys out of the trenches," Ford abandoned the expedition.

Like other Midwestern fundamentalists, Ford hated the "capitalists," and certainly never thought of himself as one. The capitalists, he had once said, were unproductive, dishonest and caused wars. Had Ford been a poetry-reading sort of man, he might have enjoyed Ezra Pound's diatribes against usury.

For Ford, capitalists often meant Jews. In 1920 the *Dearborn Independent* ran a series of anti-Semitic articles in which Jews were called "the conscious enemies of all that Anglo-Saxons mean by civilization."[3] Benedict Arnold had been their tool and so had Queen Isabella when she sent Columbus on his journey. The *Dearborn Independent* picked up the infamous fabricated *Protocols of Zion* and reprinted them, together with emendations by its editors, in hundreds of thousands of copies. Ford established a private detective agency in New York City which, at great expense, was to uncover incriminating material about the Jews.

When in 1927, Aaron Sapiro, a Jewish lawyer, sued Ford for a million dollars, the auto magnate allowed his ghost writer, W. J. Cameron, to take full responsibility. Fearing cross-examination on the witness stand, Ford finally came to a private settlement with Sapiro and honored him with a personal apology. He had not known, said Ford, about the anti-Semitic articles in the *Dearborn Independent*! But Ford never quite abandoned anti-Semitism. In the

late 30's his man Cameron became president of the anti-
Semitic, quasi-fascist Anglo-Saxon Federation. The Ford-
printed *Protocols of Zion* appeared again. And in the summer of 1938, after the anti-Jewish terror in Germany, Ford
accepted the "Award of the Grand Cross of the German
Eagle" from the Hitler government.

There was hardly an aspect of human life on which
Ford failed to comment. He told a reporter for *The Manchester Guardian* that he "had entertained his mind with
ideas of having lived before."[4] He became a devotee of
old-fashioned dancing and published a booklet called:
*Good Morning: After a Lapse of 25 Years, Old-Fashioned
Dancing is Being Revived by Mr. and Mrs. Henry Ford.*
(Long before, he had denounced "Jewish Jazz.") These
dances, which Ford said helped to prevent nervous
trouble, were dug up by agents who toured the country
to look for them. Ford hired a private orchestra (dulci-
mer, cymbalo, violin and sousaphone) to accompany him.[5]
In Greenfield Village, near Dearborn, he collected thousands of relics of an age he had helped to destroy. He pur-
chased the courthouse where Lincoln started practising
law, the Menlo Park workshop where Edison had made
the electric-light bulb, and the little frame building where
Mary (of *Mary's Little Lamb*) had gone to school.

Of course, Ford felt that the bankers and Jews kept
persecuting him. When he sued the *Chicago Tribune* for
calling him, of all things, an "anarchist," he was rewarded
six cents by the court but had to undergo the public
humiliation of telling the *Tribune's* lawyer that the American Revolution took place in 1812 and that Benedict
Arnold was a "writing fellow." But still he remained a
highly respected figure as the economist of simplicity who
could solve all financial problems with a farmer's analogy.

Championing the virtues of plain living even after 1937, when his family wealth was estimated at $624,970,000,[6] he remained a man of the people.

In a *Fortune* poll in 1940, 73 percent of those answering believed that Ford had been "helpful to labor." He topped Senator Wagner, Secretary Perkins and John L. Lewis by comfortable percentages. Except among the auto workers of Detroit and unionists and political sophisticates elsewhere, the Ford legend was not seriously damaged.

His personality was something of an enigma. On the one hand, he was seen as a rather lonely man suspicious of strangers. "One of his offices at the plant is at the top of a steep flight of iron stairs. People coming to see him always arrive a little out of breath and this in some peculiar fashion seems to gratify him."[7] He was capable of all sorts of petty spites. Once he built a wall in front of a gas station near Dearborn because its owner had refused to sell his benzol. When the station owner sued Ford, the judge awarded damages to the owner and said that, "It looked like the fence an old woman builds when she is mad with her neighbors."[8] At other times Ford was spontaneously generous; he hired more cripples, tuberculars and men with prison records than any other employer in the country. When he went on camping trips with Edison and Harvey Firestone, he insisted on doing the cooking himself so that Edison would be free to read and rest.

The good and the bad, the spiteful and the kindly, all were based on the assumption that his will was not to be denied. He took it for granted that his sociology department had the right to snoop into workers' private lives. He took it for granted that he knew what he was talking about when he ranted about the Jews and high finance and world affairs. It seemed incredible to him that any man of good will would oppose his desires, for was not everybody, or almost everybody, part of the vast machine he was directing? What then could human beings mean to him? In a sympathetic profile in the *New Yorker* in 1928, Niven Busch said that Ford's wife and his son Edsel were the only people "whose existence makes any serious difference to him."[9] Perhaps, but when one remembers how Ford allowed his satrap, Harry Bennett, to hound Edsel for years because Edsel was suspected of being "liberal," one questions even the narrow margin of feeling granted Ford by Niven Busch.

In the end Ford emerged as a personification of the emotional thinness, the intellectual provincialism and, to be fair, the organizing talent of a society passing from the frontier to the machine age. There were millions of Americans who thought like him and who accepted his word as gospel. From the reservoirs of folk wisdom, he fished up his sayings:

> If you study the history of almost any criminal you will find he is an inveterate smoker. . . .
> I do nothing because it gives me pleasure. . . .
> Reading can become a dope habit. I don't like to read books; they muss up my mind. . . .
> I give nothing for which I do not receive compensation. I do not believe in charity. . . .
> I pity the poor fellow who is so soft and flabby that he must always have "an atmosphere of good feeling" before he can do his work. . . .
> The average man won't really do a day's work unless he is caught and cannot get out of it. The very poor are recruited almost solely from the people who refuse to think. . . .[10]

These were the thoughts of the man who was the biggest employer of labor in the United States.

"LITTLE DIGNITY AND LESS SECURITY"

Henry Ford, it must be admitted, always had an eye
for men he could use to advantage. When, one day in
1916, he ran into a young clerk who impressed him, he
made him head watchman of the Rouge plant. For years
afterward Ford trained that clerk, a former Navy pugilist,
in the methods of his organization. And from Ford's point
of view, all the effort that went into teaching Harry Bennett the ropes of administration and labor supervision
were worth while.

Harry Bennett had the policeman's psychology in its
purest form. Over a period of twenty years he built up
one of the largest private armies ever employed by a man
whose avowed purpose was not to wage war. At its peak
in the late 30's, this army, the Ford Service Department,
was estimated to number nearly 3,000 men. Bennett employed ex-pugs, policemen who had been fired from their
jobs, gangsters and men released from prisons. Within
the Service Department there was semi-military discipline and Bennett's word was law. Toward the peak of his
reign, when Ford was immersed in such hobbies as Greenfield Village, Bennett was virtual dictator of the Ford
organization. He had full powers to hire and fire—and not
only lowly workers, either.

In a thorough study of Bennett's methods, John McCarten wrote in the *American Mercury* of 1940: "Practically
all the Ford employees are fearful of Bennett. They speak
of him privily as if he were a combination of Dracula,
Pearl Bergoff and J. Edgar Hoover. They are convinced
that he has as many spies in his pay as Hirohito . . . On
every assembly line and in every shop at River Rouge,
there are Service operators whose connection with the

Department is kept as quiet as possible . . ."[11] Of these operators Bennett once said: "They're a lot of tough bastards but every goddamn one of them's a gentleman."[12]

One of these gentlemen was "Legs" Laman who had a record as a rum-runner, kidnapper and squealer and who, after six years in prison, was paroled in the care of Ford Motor Co. Another gentleman picked up by Bennett was Chester LaMare, a powerful Detroit gang leader who in 1929 was granted the fruit and vegetable concession, worth $100,000 a year, at River Rouge. Still another gentleman employed by Bennett was Sam Cuva who was jailed for having shot his mother-in-law. Tough bastards but gentlemen . . .[13]

Was it any wonder, then, that, under Bennett's rule and with the Service Department prying into every corner, the Ford plants began to resemble prisons? *Fortune* described the status of the Ford worker in the following glum terms:

> The rank and file of the workmen at the Rouge are so much less important than the machines they tend that the contrast is extremely depressing . . .
>
> . . . automobile labor . . . is labor with little dignity and less security.
>
> There is no official prohibition against smoking during office hours and presumably none against drinking outside of them, but men have gone home at night and come to work in the morning to find the furniture moved out of their office as a delicate intimation that their services are no longer required.[14]

The Ford Service Department worked on the theory that an ounce of prevention is worth a pound of cure. When in 1932 the tool-and-die makers at the Rouge were considering joining an independent union, they found, after having been away from the plant for a brief inventory shutdown, that their private tool kits had been smashed to pieces. During the shutdown only maintenance men and the Service Department could get into the plant.

Workers in the Ford plant developed ingenious devices for talking out of the sides of their mouths or for pretending to be conversing about the work while really engaged in normal small-talk. They knew that in the eyes of the Service Department smiling, humming or whistling indicated laziness. In 1940 John Gallo, a worker at the Rouge, was fired for smiling, but was reinstated by a state labor referee who could find no correlation between smiling and inefficiency. The Ford Co. fought the case all the way.

In his sober study of the Ford empire, Keith Sward writes:

> For years after Bennett came to power, it was the proud, undisguised aim of the Service Department to blot out every manifestation of personality or manliness inside a Ford plant . . . Bennett's mercenaries finally mastered every tactic from the swagger of the Prussian drill sergeant to outright sadism and physical assault. On the night shift they would jolt an incoming worker out of his wits and take the starch out of his system by flashing a light in his face and shouting at him, "Where did you get that badge?" or "Who's your boss?" Another intimidating practise that came into being under Bennett's rule was the act of "shaking 'em up in the aisles." In this case a workman summoned to the employment office for any reason at all, even one that was totally unrelated to his work, would be shoved and pushed along the aisle by a pair of officious Servicemen, like a felon in the custody of the police.[15]

To readers who have not examined the evidence or who are too young to remember the reports of such incidents in the twenties and thirties, Sward's remarks may seem exaggerated. But, if anything, they are quite moderate; one need but talk to veterans of pre-union Ford to know as much.

Why then did the workers take such treatment? While unorganized, there was nothing they could do about it. Before the depression thousands would quit Ford and try to find jobs elsewhere. But once the depression came, fear of losing the job overpowered all other fears, and the men stayed.

Yet the men did rebel—again and again and again. Even during the depression there were sporadic slow-downs. At Briggs Manufacturing Company which had leased the Ford Highland Park plant to make bodies for the Ford V-8, there was a major strike in 1933. Certain Briggs workers, reported a committee appointed by Mayor Frank Murphy, had been working a fourteen-hour day for ten cents an hour. When Ford heard of the strike he said that it was "the biggest surprise of my career" and wondered why "6,000 employees of the Briggs Company had walked out without giving any particular reason."[16] Later he blamed unnamed bankers for inciting the strike.

The Briggs strike was the result of a basic policy that Ford had adopted in the depression years: leasing out work to smaller companies that paid lower wages than he did. This was one of the little-noticed crimps in the $7-a-day wage that Ford was supposed to be paying during the depression years. Actually, Ford used the $7-a-day wage to considerable advantage: first, by firing skilled and better-paid men and then rehiring them at $7 a day; second, by instituting a speedup of unskilled labor.

BITTER YEARS

The Ford workers had plenty of reason to feel discontented, and when the UAW began organizing them in 1937 they responded favorably. But most union leaders underestimated the difficulties of the job.

After having organized General Motors and Chrysler in 1937, the UAW began to move against Ford. Hundreds of workers signed up during that year. But when Ford said in April, 1937, that he would never recognize the UAW or any other union, he meant it, and he used weapons that neither GM nor Chrysler had had. The two latter corporations had been caught unawares by the union drive, for sitdowns were new and difficult to handle. But Ford could learn from his competitors' misfortunes. He also had a hard-boiled plant leadership and an efficient espionage service that the two other corporations had not had. When isolated strikes broke out in the Ford plants in the late thirties, he broke them without difficulty.

Ford was encouraged in his opposition to the UAW by some temporary defeats that the CIO met shortly before the drive to organize his plants. Little Steel had won at least a partial victory over the CIO's organization drive. The Memorial Day massacre in Chicago had led President Roosevelt to denounce both the CIO and the independent steel corporations, and the CIO had called off its strikes at Republic, Bethlehem and other companies. If getting tough worked, well . . . wasn't Henry Ford the man to get tough? And weren't Harry Bennett and his gentlemen ready for action?

On May 26, 1937, they went into action. The UAW had previously announced that, for the first time, it was going to distribute leaflets at the Rouge. Dearborn's municipal administration had granted it a permit. When the sixty union distributors, two-thirds of them women, came to the Rouge, they were set upon and severely beaten by Ford Servicemen, whose ranks had been augmented by recently employed Detroit thugs. Two of the union's officials, Walter Reuther and Richard Frankensteen, singled out for especially rough treatment, were knocked down, lifted up and knocked down again. One unionist had his skull fractured, another was sent to the hospital for two weeks. The Dearborn police stood by but did not intervene in "the battle of the overpass."

Photographers from the Detroit papers, the *New York Times* and the *Associated Press* had their cameras snatched away from them. When *Time* published a devastating account of the beating, the Ford Co. withdrew its advertising for a year and a half. One Detroit paper, the *Daily News*, did manage to salvage some pictures and these later appeared in papers throughout the country. On May 27, 1937, the *News* published two pictures. One carried the caption "The Start" and showed Servicemen approaching Reuther, Frankensteen and other union officials. The union men are smiling and the burly Servicemen walking grimly toward them. The second picture, captioned "Action," showed Frankensteen's coat and vest pulled over his head and his body being beaten by the attackers. In subsequent government hearings some of the assailants were identified as professional boxers and thugs. Among them was the president of the fascistic Knights of Dearborn, Sam Taylor, also a Ford foreman and Charles Goodman, a thug with a record of twenty-one arrests.

Three months later the UAW tried again, this time with 1,000 husky workers ready to match blow for blow. The Servicemen stood by and watched but did nothing; they did not relish combat under such conditions. Soon Ford

developed a new technique. The Dearborn City Council
passed an ordinance which prohibited distribution of literature at congested areas—namely, the approaches to the
Rouge at the times when shifts changed. In the following
months nearly 1,000 unionists were arrested for giving out
leaflets. To avoid court tests of the ordinance, those who
were arrested were jailed and then released without
charges. Thus no trials were held while distribution was
effectively curtailed.

The next three years, 1937 to 1940, were full of terror
and violence in all the Ford plants. By 1940 the National
Labor Relations Board had judged the Ford management
guilty of unfair labor practices in nine plants. The story
of the Service Department's activities in Dallas is almost
unbelievable, but it is all there, black on white, in an
NLRB report. The NLRB report describes how toughs
were armed with blackjacks, rubber hose and pistols to
intimidate union men. A liberal lawyer not connected with
the UAW, W. J. Houston, was beaten so hard he required
hospitalization. An organizer for an AFL union, George
Baer, was beaten into insensibility. A. J. Lewis, a twin
brother of a Dallas businessman who had expressed himself in favor of unions, was beaten by mistake and, on his
deathbed a few months later, charged that the beating
had led to his death. Described as "organized gangster-
ism" by the NLRB, these methods proved successful for a
few years in keeping the union out of the Ford plants.

THE BIG DRIVE

By 1940 the tide began to turn. The faction struggle
within the UAW, which had hampered the Ford drive,
was temporarily at an end. A large fund, half provided
by the national CIO and half by the UAW, was set aside

for cracking Ford. John L. Lewis, then CIO president, sent some of his toughest organizers, led by Michael Widman, to Detroit. The UAW assigned a group of able unionists to Ford, including Richard Leonard, former DeSoto worker and vice-president of the UAW, and Emil Mazey, former president of Briggs Local 212.

What probably helped most, however, was that the entire union movement of Detroit pitched in. Local unions formed volunteer organizing committees which canvassed neighborhoods and talked to Ford workers. A CIO dairy workers' union supplied the names of Ford workers living on the routes of its members. Special groups were set up to contact foreign-language workers. All the while the union kept harping on the fact that, despite decades of Ford publicity about a living wage, the average wage at Ford was five cents less than for the entire industry and more than ten cents less than at Chrysler and GM.

In the Ford plant itself the UAW supporters gradually became bolder. A rudimentary organization was created on a department and building level and each unit elected a chairman, usually a courageous man ready to risk his job. These were trying days for the rank-and-file unionists who were doing the job at Ford. One day a worker might agree to sign up, and the next day back down unaccountably, the victim of pressures from management or from a wife afraid he might lose his job by "getting mixed up with the union." The men were extraordinarily sensitive to the slightest pressures from either side, and the UAW had to calculate each step with the greatest care. A small minority was bold, a small minority contemptuous, but the bulk of the workers fluctuated, hopeful and fearful, many eager to join the union even as they wondered if this time it would be strong enough to do the job.

When the U.S. Circuit Court of Appeals upheld an

NLRB decision which had attacked Ford for unfair labor
practices and had ordered the company to rehire twenty-
two discharged union men in the Rouge plant, hundreds
of Ford workers were encouraged to join the union. When
Justice of the Peace Lila Neuenfelt of Dearborn declared
in October, 1940, that the town's ordinance prohibiting
literature distribution was unconstitutional, and her rul-
ing was reinforced by a circuit judge who issued an order
prohibiting further interference with union distributions,
UAW victory at Ford was closer. By January, 1941, the
UAW was strong enough to sign men up openly in the
Ford plants.   60753

Ford fought back. In December, 1940, the company
had fired between 300 and 400 union supporters from the
Lincoln plant alone, but such methods no longer worked.
Spontaneous walkouts and sitdowns took place in many
of the plants. On December 30, 1940, some 1,000 men in
the Rouge tool-and-die department struck over a dispute
involving rest periods. For the first time, in many of the
plants the men felt free to act as an organized body. The
Service Department could intimidate individuals, but was
helpless against organized thousands.

Early in February, 1941, when the U.S. Supreme Court
refused to review the Rouge case, the company lost its
last hope of legal delay in its struggle against the NLRB
decisions. Ford had to rehire the twenty-two discharged
workers as the NLRB had ordered, and the UAW seized
the opportunity for all it was worth. Triumphantly, the
men marched into the plant, wearing CIO buttons—and
in a few days thousands of such buttons appeared.

By February, 1941, both sides were jockeying desperately, with the UAW determined to push ahead to victory,
and the Ford Company often unable to decide whether
to meet the UAW drive head-on or try to deflect it by

gentle tactics. A major crisis developed when the union served notice to the Michigan State Mediation Board on February 26, 1941, that a strike was imminent in the Rouge, Highland Park and Lincoln plants. The atmosphere among the workers was by now simply feverish: the tension and resentment accumulated over years was about to explode.

But the company pulled back a bit and began rehiring hundreds of the men it had fired during the organization drive. It seemed that a strike would be avoided, as both James F. Dewey, the federal labor conciliator, and the union leadership wished. Hoping to win by an NLRB election, the UAW heads failed to see how unavoidable and necessary a strike was as a means of self-assertion for the workers.

Shut-down after shut-down took place in the plants during March. Most were settled on the union's terms, and each time more workers joined. The company tacitly recognized the union by agreeing to meet with its plant-wide committees, though it still refused to talk to the UAW national leaders. But in April company policy took another sharp turn. On April 1 Ford refused to meet with any union committees, and in the rolling mill, pressed steel, tire plant and B buildings UAW committeemen were discharged. What was the company's strategy? To provoke a hasty, poorly organized strike? To wear down the union? Or was it just tacking and veering without any overall purpose, in the hope of hitting on some improvised way of defeating the union?

SHUT-DOWN

No one gave any orders; no directives came from the union. On April 1 the men just quit working and waited for the company to rehire the committeemen it had discharged. In the rolling-mill plant, where 6,000 had stopped working, tempers flared after 110 Dearborn police were rushed in. But when thousands of Ford men from other buildings moved toward the rolling-mill plant the police prudently withdrew.

The strike spread from building to building, until the huge Rouge plant was uncannily still. Begun late in the afternoon, the shut-down was completed in the evening. UAW officials didn't know what had happened, for the strike had not been planned and they had no way of communicating with the plant. But the report, which Detroit still thought was unbelievable and impossible, spread through the city like a licking flame: Ford is shut down!

Union officials quickly held a conference, and even though some had been against a strike they endorsed the one that had developed spontaneously. In a strike-conscious union it is always possible to move quickly into an unexpected strike action, and that is what happened in the UAW. Inside the plants the men waited for word from the union. Sharp discussions flared, tempers were short. Local leaders worried about the 17,000 Negroes employed by Ford: would they follow Don Marshall, Ford's Negro agent, or would they come along with the union? At 12:15 A.M. on April 2nd the union officially called a strike at Ford. In the dead of night a parade of shouting men formed at the plant and marched to the union hall a mile away.

What took place that night near the union hall is surely one of the most extraordinary events in American labor history. All night long men talked—loudly and plainly, with hardly a trace of fear or anxiety. The union kept an all-night meeting going at which leaders spoke, but simultaneously and probably more important, groups of men

milled around talking the whole thing over, estimating
their chances, enjoying the sheer sensation of expressing
themselves freely. A soup kitchen was organized, a union
hospital set up, flying squadrons instructed. The union
had learned a lot in the GM and Chrysler strikes and now
it worked with skill and dispatch. The men watched and
were impressed. They had found themselves and the
union; they had begun to respect both.

Most of those who stayed in the hall through that night
had been up since the morning, but no one thought of
sleep. They enjoyed watching their spontaneous action
transformed into the detailed organization of an expertly
run strike. In the corners, in the back of the hall, outside
of the hall men just milled around, talking, laughing,
worrying. For years they had accumulated the steam of
repression, and now they were ready to let it loose. They
were, finally, on their own.

Emil Mazey, who chaired the all-night session at which
spoke every important union leader (Widman, Reuther,
Addes, Thomas, Leonard and many others), remembers
that night as "among the most exciting in our whole experience in the labor movement. It was like seeing men
who had been half-dead suddenly come to life. And did
they come to life! It was hard to keep things going, hard
to organize, so eager were they just to mill around and
talk and let some steam go. That night you really understood what the union could mean to men."

The first big test came early the next morning. Harry
Bennett had inserted ads in the Detroit papers urging
workers to report at the plant "as usual." There were still
many hundreds of Negro workers left in the plant who
were terrified of both the union and the company, uncertain which way to turn and fearing punishment no matter
which way they went.

The Ford plant is like an island surrounded by an ocean of roads. Inside this island Ford Servicemen were concentrated at the gates, ready for action and bristling with arms. For pickets to have approached the gates or to have tried to penetrate beyond the huge walls that surround the plants would have meant to expose themselves to attack by the Servicemen. Instead, the union chose a clever strategy. Barricades of automobiles were set up at all the incoming roads: at Eagle Pass and Wyoming Avenue, at Miller Road and Airport Drive, at Schaefer Road and Dix Road. These barricades prevented anyone from getting in or out of the plant without the pickets' approval. Later they even took control of the Dearborn drawbridge and prevented delivery of supplies by water on the River Rouge. As 6 A.M. approached the Servicemen were waiting at the gates of the plant; they waited and waited but nobody came.

An hour later the first fighting broke out. "Iron bolts and nuts flew through the air in a wholesale barrage from the factory roof, while several hundred Negroes with steel bars and knives charged out of the main gate, No. 4, of the Rouge plant in two assaults on the UAW-CIO picket lines there."[17] Thirty-six unionists were hurt and treated at the union's hospital. The pickets had not expected this attack and their lines were broken.

Picket lines were soon reformed and at 9 A.M. another assault took place from within the factory. This time the pickets were ready and slugged it out with baseball bats, fists and sticks. The battle was brief, bloody and decisive for the lines held and, casualties aside, the union had shown it could close the plant. Thousands of automobile workers and curious spectators who drove out to the Ford plant helped choke up the roads. The Servicemen did not move for there were just too many unionists, many of them ex-Ford workers, ready to give as well as take. By now the mood of the strikers had changed from gaiety to grimness. They had watched the Dearborn police stand idly by while their lines were attacked. At a mass meeting on April 2nd, Emil Mazey said that, "If we need a labor holiday to win this strike, we'll have one," which, as everyone understood, meant a general strike in Detroit.

The Ford company fought hard. It issued statements denouncing the strike as a communist conspiracy. It obtained an injunction ordering the pickets to clear the roads leading to the Rouge plant. It began to organize a back-to-work movement and on the second night of the strike arranged a meeting in Detroit's Negro neighborhood at which Homer Martin, now representing himself as an AFL organizer, urged 3,000 Negroes to "march back in a body."[18] This was more than a "back to work" move—it could very likely mean a race riot. And finally, the company demanded that the federal and state governments send troops to Dearborn.

Of all these counter-moves, only the one concerning the Negroes represented an immediately serious threat to the union. A group of Negro leaders* mobilized public sentiment in the Negro neighborhoods for the UAW and caused the "back to work" movement to collapse. Detroit's AFL unions repudiated Homer Martin as a strikebreaker.

But at the plant the problem of the Negroes remained acute. There were some 800 inside it, some of them Ford workers and others newly hired Southern Negroes brought up by Harry Bennett. Using loudspeakers, Walter White and other Negro leaders urged the Negroes in the plant

* Among them were Walter White, leader of the National Association for the Advancement of Colored People; Rev. Horace White, pastor of the Plymouth Congregational Church; Dr. J. J. McClendon, president of the Michigan NAACP; Louis Martin, editor of the Negro paper, *Michigan Chronicle;* Rev. Charles Hill and Rev. Father Malcolm Dade.

to leave, and about a third did. But most stayed in, cowed by the Servicemen. Though their ranks had been augmented by 250 special deputies, most of them former Ford Servicemen and gate guards, the Dearborn police did nothing. Finally, with a promise of safe conduct from the UAW in his pocket, federal conciliator James Dewey persuaded the remaining Negroes to leave.

When Michigan Governor Van Wagner proposed a compromise settlement, the UAW quickly accepted, even though the terms were not wholly satisfactory to it. Reluctantly and "with reservations," Ford accepted too. On April 10th the strike ended. The union was still wary since Ford had sent an extraordinary mission to the first peace conference: a group of plant detectives and prize-fighters employed by the Service Department!

In late May an NLRB election was held and the UAW received 58,000 out of 80,000 votes cast. The AFL union, which had suddenly poked its nose in, received about a quarter of the votes and "no union" received less than three percent. Harry Bennett, who felt that he had been betrayed, said the election was "a great victory for the Communist Party, Governor Van Wagner and the National Labor Relations Board."[19]

At this point the Ford Company made the most complete about-face in labor relations in U.S. history. Negotiating with Philip Murray, Harry Bennett agreed to a union shop, dues checkoff, grievance machinery, seniority, time and a half for overtime, premium pay for night workers and two hours' pay for employees called in but not given work. After the agreement was signed, the UAW negotiated wage agreements which gave Ford employees an additional fifty-two millions in wages within a year. Why did Ford suddenly shift policy? Was it, as some observers felt, a move dictated by the simple business consideration that it might be cheaper to work with the union than to fight it? Was it a maneuver to gain time for a later fight? Or was it, as Emil Mazey believes, based on the hope that "the company might be able to take over the Ford local from the inside?"[20]

For the entire CIO and for the UAW in particular, the organization of Ford marked the end of a period. The "last citadel of open shopism," the most intrepid and frank enemy of unionism, had been defeated. As long as Ford remained unorganized, the unions could never feel quite safe. With Ford signed up, the UAW was clearly here to stay.

Ford Local 600 soon became the largest local union in the world, the owner of a building valued at $200,000 and the scene of a turbulent intra-union fight. For a few years it was controlled by pro-Stalinist officials, but since the victory of the Reuther group in the union that is no longer the case.

The decisive footnote to the story of the campaign to organize Ford was provided by an NLRB election in 1948 in which the Ford workers, under the provisions of the Taft-Hartley Act, voted on whether they wanted the union shop to continue. Although the election was held outside the plant and was inconvenient for most Ford workers, their participation was remarkable. Of 98,989 eligible workers, 90,157 cast ballots; 88,943 voted to continue the UAW shop.

"Labor union organizers," Henry Ford had once said, *"are the worst thing that ever struck the earth."*

Wartime Mavericks

5 --

ROLAND J. Thomas became president of the UAW at a time when Europe pressed itself most insistently on America. His position was that of a man who has been offered a blind date with history, yet does his best not to keep it. For not even his most loyal friends would have claimed that he had penetrated to the meaning of the world events which were molding the lives of the auto workers.

In many ways, Thomas was the epitome of a certain kind of union man. Husky and easygoing, he loved to chew tobacco and play poker, and if a rank and filer asked him to stop for a drink at a Jefferson Avenue bar he would seldom refuse the invitation. He found more meaning and pleasure in a straight flush than in a chart on industrial productivity. Between him and the more intellectual union leaders there was a natural, unavoidable distance. For, unlike them, he never had to give a thought to "adjusting" himself to the ranks; he came from them and had both their virtues and limitations. R. J. Thomas was an honest man who believed in unions, sometimes risked his career to defend Negro workers, but simply could not grasp the increasingly complex position of a trade union in modern economy. In almost any other union, at almost any other time, he would have been the perfect official, taking good care of complaints and honestly collecting dues, but it was his misfortune to assume leadership precisely at the time when "pork chop unionism" was least adequate. Was that his fault? Why did history keep nagging at him, why couldn't it let him alone?

Even within the narrow union compass, Thomas never advanced new ideas; he contented himself with repeating popular old ones. In 1940, he was saying, "We do not want the blood of one automobile worker to flow across the seas."[1] By 1941 he was asking for guns and butter, automobile production and war production. His hope that a large-scale war could be fought without crimping civilian economy was then shared by many Americans. Nor did he have any idea how the butter could be provided as the number of guns mounted.

Walter Reuther, however, did have a worked-out approach to the question of labor's role in wartime. In 1940 he had publicized a plan to utilize idle auto manufacturing capacity for plane production. The industry's excess capacity, he claimed, could be used to produce 500 engine-equipped planes daily. The discussions that followed tended to overemphasize the 500 planes-a-day figure and neglect the plan's social implications. A sympathetic analyst wrote that "the 500 planes-a-day figure was ridiculous on the face of it, for certain key machine tools and skills that are necessary to plane production just did not exist in Detroit in late 1940 . . ."[2] The same writer, however, felt that the fundamental idea behind the plan was sound. Briefly, it proposed the conversion of idle auto plants to war production, the pooling of equipment and manpower into a central organization, and the right of labor to participate jointly with management and government in the executive organs of this production set-up.

At first Reuther's proposal was warmly received in Washington, being noted by President Roosevelt as an example of needed ingenuity. But soon it became clear that the Office of Production Management, headed by former GM president William Knudsen, would not seriously consider it. As Henry Morgenthau, Secretary of the Treasury, bitingly remarked: "There is only one thing wrong with the [Reuther] program, it comes from the 'wrong source.' "[3] The industry stubbornly resisted any proposals that labor participate in planning. "If you are interested in production," said C. E. Wilson, GM president, to Reuther, "I'll give you a job with us."[4]

When William Knudsen argued that the pooling of equipment and the exchange of production ideas were socialistic devices, Reuther replied that what the auto corporations really opposed was having their plants "drafted" as men were having their lives drafted. They feared, Reuther claimed, that competitive profits would no longer be a dominant production motive or result. The slowness of the auto corporations in converting to war production seemed to substantiate Reuther's charges. Actually, if the auto corporations did fear that war production would result in lower profits than civilian production, they were betraying a certain lack of imagination. Had they yet considered the lush possibilities of "cost-plus" contracts?[5]

In practice, the auto industry was forced to adopt a diluted version of the Reuther plan, for large-scale war production would have been impossible in an industry still oriented to internal competition. But while grudgingly consenting to limits on corporate freedom, the industry leaders resisted to the end any attempt by labor to help determine the nature and conditions of war production. In a sense, they showed themselves more "class conscious" and less ready to sacrifice for the war program than the UAW leaders.

For labor itself, it should be noted, the Reuther plan was not without certain dangers. The more closely integrated into wartime production schemes the unions would become, the less could they fulfill their traditional role as free bargaining agencies. But as it happened, the corporations never gave them an opportunity to succumb to this danger. So obsessed were the corporations with the provision of the Reuther plan that would have given labor rights in production planning, that they failed to see how their opposition to the plan strengthened the hand of the more militant, less collaborative elements in the union.

Within the UAW, the plan helped dramatize the basic difference of approach between leaders like Thomas and Reuther. Thomas was an old-style unionist who believed in simple economic demands and was ready in wartime to refrain from pressing even for those demands—which meant that in wartime the union *as a union* would have no role to play. Reuther, while also desiring to accommodate himself to the war program, saw an opportunity for labor to widen its potential bargaining claims by wedging into the arena of economic planning from which it had always been excluded.

"EQUALITY OF SACRIFICE"

Directly after Pearl Harbor the union executive board formally pledged total support to the U.S. war effort.[6] Though expressing the views of the great bulk of UAW members, this statement hardly began to solve the prob-

lems which the war created for the UAW. How should a
union behave in wartime? Should it postpone all its demands and surrender many of its gains in the name of the
war effort? Could it devote itself both to the war program
and the defense of its members' interests? Should it consider its primary purpose, war effort notwithstanding, the
defense of workers' rights? These questions were debated
in the UAW from the day after Pearl Harbor until V-J
day. It was a remarkable debate, a full-blown democratic
discussion at a time when hysteria might have been expected and did, in fact, arise in other unions.

In early 1942 "conversion unemployment" irritated
thousands of auto workers. The UAW published large advertisements needling the Office of Production Management for its failure to adopt the Reuther plan and for
allowing the corporations to continue on a "business-as-
usual" basis. In April the union called an emergency conference to discuss the leadership's proposals that strikes be
banned for the duration of the war and that premium pay
for Saturdays, Sundays and holidays be suspended. The
ranks were not overwhelmed by enthusiasm for these proposals. Whether because they did not adequately see that
support of the war necessarily involved certain unpleasant
restraints, or because they felt that most of the sacrificing
was being done by labor and very little by business, the
delegates furiously debated the leaders' unanimous proposals for six hours. But in the end, the proposal to ban
strikes and suspend premium pay for overtime was accepted by most of the delegates.

It is important to note that for the first time in its history the UAW officials were united in support of this proposal, while opposition to it came from men in the shops.
The workers were the ones who would have to make the
sacrifices, and many of them were not convinced that they

should. The conference debate vividly illustrated how both full-time union leaders and plant militants thought. Thomas, Frankensteen, Reuther and Nat Ganley, the CP leader in the UAW, joined in support of the leaders' proposals. Frankensteen asked the men from the shops: "Are you going to tell the President of the United States to go to hell?" Ganley insisted that, "What we need is more and greater national unity." Victor Reuther argued that, "Labor will not rise to its responsibilities unless it can lift itself up from its own immediate problems."

The dissidents spoke another language. John McGill, from the Flint Buick local, said: "We are not convinced that giving up double time is vital to winning the war. Labor is making sacrifices everywhere. We gave up the right to strike. Our brothers and sons are dying in the trenches. Can anyone show any sign that the men who sign checks have made any sacrifices?"[7]

What helped the leadership persuade the majority of the men from the plants to accept the no-strike pledge and the loss of premium pay was an "Equality of Sacrifice" program* it brought to the conference. This program appealed both to the union ranks and to many other Americans by harping on big business' "cost-plus" profits. The desirability of increasing war production was taken for granted by the UAW, and both leaders and workers were proud of the industry's production records. What bothered the workers was the problem of how many union rights *had* to be sacrificed because of the war and how many

---

* The "Equality of Sacrifice" program: end all war profits; no luxuries in wartime and no war millionaires; stop rising costs and halt inflation; ration all food, clothing, housing and other necessities; adjust wages to meet increased living costs; provide security allowances for dependents of men and women in the armed forces; declare a moratorium on debts; permit labor to participate in production planning; begin postwar planning; pay all wages for more than forty hours in non-negotiable war bonds.

were needlessly being sacrificed in the name of the war.

In some ways, the UAW progressed during the early war months. It organized many aircraft plants and increased its membership to nearly one million. But the fact that for once no auto worker had to fear unemployment made the men in the shops especially impatient with the union's restraint.

In August, 1942, when the UAW held its next convention, the delegates repeatedly rejected recommendations by the top leaders, but their rebellion was without clear motivation and hence came to little concrete result. When William Mazey of the Detroit Hudson plant shouted that, "We haven't had collective bargaining since we gave up the right to strike,"[8] the other delegates applauded heavily. But their resentment could find no organized expression. On the union's top, all was harmony. Union veterans might stare in astonishment as Victor Reuther introduced a resolution for a second front in Europe and Nat Ganley rushed to second it, as Walter Reuther praised George Addes and Addes returned the courtesy.

In the ranks there was considerable dissatisfaction. What especially irritated the UAW militants was that in July the union had lost an NLRB election at the large Curtiss aviation plant in Buffalo. For the 20,000 Curtiss employees to accept the UAW would have meant voting themselves a wage cut, since the AFL had not surrendered premium pay for overtime. Naturally, they voted for the AFL.

One observant reporter wrote in mid-1942:

Actually, union officials in the war industries are working overtime to keep their men from striking. The AFL and CIO in the war industries at least couldn't be more tractable and more cooperative if they were company unions. . . .

Walter P. Reuther ... told C. E. Wilson of General Motors in Washington recently that if the disgruntlement continued another six months the auto industry would find itself "with the biggest strike on your hands you ever saw."

Reuther is reported to have added, "We can't hold the men down much longer." [9]

THE NEW PATRIOTS

The strange spirit of brotherliness at the union's summit might have continued indefinitely had not the Communist Party decided in early 1943 to show that when Stalin made a bargain it was ready to be plucked, cleaned and packaged. Its people in the UAW came forward with the unpopular proposal that the union adopt piecework and other forms of "incentive pay,"* both leading to self-

---

* "Incentive pay" is an all-embracing term for various piece-work systems. In his *Modern Economic Society,* Professor Sumner Slichter gives a good explanation of the way this system has traditionally worked. A standard time is set for a certain job. If a worker does it in less time, the time saved is divided between him and the company, usually on a 50-50 basis. Suppose the standard for a certain job is two pieces for an eight-hour day and the pay for this is $8. At piecework, if the man did four pieces he would receive $16. But under the incentive-pay plan he would divide the extra money with the employer, thus receiving $12. If he did two pieces, he would earn $4 per piece; if he did four pieces he would earn $3 per piece. Thus, while his total pay would increase, *it would not increase in proportion to his increased productivity.*[10]

The War Production Board plan was a refinement of this refinement. As *Business Week* described it: "Whenever a plant's output per man rises by a given percent, the pay, but not the wage rate, of everyone in the plant, from sweeper to president, will be increased by the same percent."[11] This scheme, of course, must lead to an especially vicious speedup since it entices faster workers to drive slower ones. From a union point of view, it is a sure-fire way of creating dissension among workers and destroying their sense of solidarity.

A bizarre twist was given to the wartime discussion by the claim of super-patrioteer Earl Browder that "incentive pay" would "force better profits on unwilling employers."[12]

imposed speedups. Earl Browder, late CP leader, wrote: "It is patriotic to demand increased earnings based on increased production."[13] There was the signal, and, as if by telepathic response, George Addes urged the acceptance of piecework at a UAW executive board meeting. His proposal was defeated. Frankensteen, merrily zigzagging between UAW factions, made the same motion a few months later. It was again defeated. In an advertisement in Detroit papers Browder accused Walter Reuther of "wrecking in the automobile and airplane industry"[14]— that is, the sort of "crime" for which people in Russia are shot.

By raising the "incentive pay" scheme, the CP could appear as a champion of increased war production. Since the scheme would, in some instances, increase the *total* pay of workers, the CP could also appear as a champion of higher wages. But to unionists the proposal was reprehensible both because it did not involve increases in hourly pay and would result in competitive speedups in the plants.

In leading the opposition to the Stalinist proposal, Reuther estimated the union situation accurately. He knew that the proposal was certain to arouse bitter enmity in the plants and that whoever was identified with it was doomed to political defeat in the union. He probably also saw that by opposing the CP on these issues he would be able to soften some of the pressure being applied by dissatisfied members on *him*. And while he believed that the labor movement had to make certain sacrifices during wartime, Reuther, unlike the CP, did not think it should give up its reason for existence.

How the workers themselves felt might have been divined by anyone who looked closely at the strikes that broke out in May, 1943, at the Kelsey-Hayes plant and the five Chrysler plants in Detroit. Rather than agree to re-treat to piecework, they insisted that rising living costs were forcing them to ask for more pay. In simplest terms, they would say: "The big guys are getting theirs, why can't we even get enough to live on?" To this question, the CP advocacy of piecework at home and a second front abroad was hardly a convincing answer.

By mid-1943 John L. Lewis' demand for a flat $2-a-day increase for the coal miners found much support in UAW ranks. The latter hoped that someone would break through the "Little Steel" formula, set up by the War Labor Board in July, 1942, which restricted wage increases to 15 per-cent of the pay rates of January 1, 1941, regardless of how high the cost of living soared subsequently. (An exception was made for "sub-standard" wages.) To the more aggres-sive unionists, and eventually to the entire labor move-ment, the formula became hateful; constant demands arose from union ranks that the CIO representatives resign from the WLB.

Another indication of the restlessness of UAW members was a severe debate at the May, 1943, convention of the Michigan CIO. A group of secondary UAW leaders rose in revolt and, to the consternation of the national CIO offi-cers, obtained the passage of resolutions calling for the rescinding of the no-strike pledge, for opposition to in-centive pay, for the formation of a labor party in America and, only after much pleading by the top UAW leaders, for the re-election of President Roosevelt. These young union rebels, who wanted to make the UAW "Equality of Sacrifice" program a reality, included Emil Mazey, pres-ident of the 26,000-member Briggs Local 212, and Ed Carey, president of the 14,000-member Chrysler Local 7.

"As of today," wrote one labor observer in May, 1943, "Reuther is the fair-haired boy of the [UAW] rank and file . . . because of the militant stand he is taking against the recent freezing of wages and manpower by the Government, his withdrawal from the War Manpower Commission . . . *but principally for his stand against the introduction of the incentive pay system in the automobile industry.*"[15] (Our emphasis—B.J.W. & I.H.)

DEMOCRACY AT WORK

It is a pity that the 1943 UAW convention, held in Buffalo, has not been studied by those writers who specialize in attacking the labor movement. They might have seen an exercise of democracy hardly matched in any other large organization. It is just as much of a pity that it has not been studied by those writers who specialize in apologies for labor leaders. They might have seen how the men from the shops spoke up for themselves when, in their eyes, the leaders proved inadequate. Here, in the midst of the war, at a time when critical thought was hardly fashionable, hundreds of auto workers came to Buffalo to debate, with free-wheeling zest but also with essential dignity, the issues facing them. The debate streamed through the veins of the convention, it overflowed into halls and hotel rooms, it rose to heights of passion and sunk to depths of demagogy—*but it took place.* It was the kind of convention that could be held by no other union in America during the war years.

The first major dispute was over piecework. A Toledo UAW leader, Richard Gosser, said: "We fought nine years to eliminate piecework and haven't been able to do it yet. You put it up now and, by God, our children's children won't eliminate it." Delegate Krebs from the Brewster airplane factory in New York spoke up: "I think it might increase pay for a small majority of them when it is first introduced . . . Our own bitter experience with it taught us [that] as we increase our earnings . . . management starts chopping down the standards to get our pay down again." A barrage of similar speeches forced the Addes-Frankensteen group to retreat to a clever "democratic" defense. Addes said: "The motion which I read to you . . . instructs me as an officer of your International Union not to go out to the local unions and sell incentive pay, but it instructs me to participate, if you please, with local unions who have voted, the rank and file voting, for the incentive plan."

Walter Reuther then attacked this "democracy" argument: "It is fine to talk about democracy. Supposing a local union wanted to sign a wage agreement working twelve hours a day without overtime. Would you say that was interfering with local autonomy if it were stopped?" The debate continued for two sessions, and in the end Reuther's resolution against piecework and "incentive pay" carried. For the CP fraction it was a bitter defeat, not made any more palatable by the *Daily Worker's* criticism of the Addes-CP group: "Its fight on the incentive-pay issue . . . was retarded by confusion and by hesitancy to come to grips with the basic aspects of the question."[16]

On the second important issue before the convention, the no-strike pledge, the Reuther and Addes groups were not sharply divided. Both opposed resolutions submitted by several UAW locals calling for the revocation of the pledge. Addes asked the UAW to reaffirm "its pledge for uninterrupted production of arms required for the speedy defeat of the Axis powers." More sensitive to the union membership's feelings and unwilling to give management a blank check, Reuther declared: "In those plants where management is not bargaining in good faith and is taking advantage of the war situation and labor's no-strike pledge

to destroy collective bargaining, the international executive board shall urge government operation of such
plants."

Speaking against both views was Emil Mazey, one of
the rising young men in the UAW, and a socialist of long
standing. He poked fun at Reuther's compromise, characterized the Stalinists as motivated by non-union interests, and ended by saying: "In order to regain collective
bargaining it is necessary to put that club [the strike]
back in our hands." Another speaker against the no-strike
pledge was Thomas Burke, of a Toledo UAW local, who
in 1948 was to be elected to Congress by a PAC campaign.
Burke put his view bluntly: "I believe that when we made
our no-strike pledge we held out our hands with palms
out and set out our chins and said to the employers, 'Hit
it,' and they did."[17]

At its end, the convention supported the no-strike
pledge by a large majority. But within the next two years
its action found less and less support in the ranks. What
happened in 1943 and 1944 was unwittingly described in
a UAW educational handbook on the shop-steward system which, while referring to English unions during the
First World War, pointedly described the situation in
America during the second war:

> With the many vital problems brought about by the war,
> these shop stewards rose to a new importance in their unions.
> Because some union officers had got too far away from the
> rank and file members, the workers turned to the stewards
> to handle their grievances . . .
> These shop stewards were much more militant and aggres-
> sive than the national leaders . . . By the end of the war, the
> shop stewards were recognized as being truly more represen-
> tative of the workers than the union officials.[18]

VOICE FROM THE RANKS

By 1944 discontent in the shops reached its peak. In February Philip Murray, CIO president, argued heatedly with President Roosevelt over the government's wartime labor policy.* The cost of living since January, 1941, claimed the CIO, had risen by 45 percent. Wages, corseted by the "Little Steel" formula, had not kept pace. In May the men at Chrysler walked off the job. When both George Addes and Walter Reuther tried to persuade them to return, they were violently booed. After the strike was over, the UAW top leadership removed the president of

---

* Victor Riesel, labor editor of the *N.Y. Post*, wrote in February 1944:

"A bitter feud between President Roosevelt and CIO leader Philip Murray is embarrassing Sidney Hillman, CIO political boss, and his new left-wing allies. "Murray's fight with the President began the morning after Mr. Roosevelt called for a labor draft law. William Green, AFL head, and Murray were in the President's study listening to him complain vehemently about labor's attitude toward the national service proposal.

"The President, according to reports, sharply attacked Murray for calling the proposal 'quack medicine,' an obvious reference to the President's use of the term 'Dr. Win-the-War.'

"Murray then asked Mr. Roosevelt: 'Do you expect to get a realistic tax program?'

"The President said no.

" 'Do you expect to get a good subsidy program?'

"Mr. Roosevelt said no.

" 'In such a case,' Murray asked, 'would you sign a national service bill if Congress passed it?'

"The President said he would sign it.

"Murray grew red-faced while Bill Green fidgeted.

"Suppose Congress were to pass a severe Smith anti-strike bill instead of a national service law. . . ." Murray queried.

"The President said he would sign that, too.

"Murray then said he would tour the country and speak in opposition to the President's proposal. Mr. Roosevelt declared that Murray did not speak for the CIO. The President then waved a telegram which endorsed his views.

"It was signed by a prominent left-wing CIO leader. Murray saw red in more ways than one—and left shortly after." [19]

Chrysler Local 490, Bill Jenkins, from office and appointed a highly unpopular official, Leo Lamotte, as administrator of the local. To show their resentment against the international's intervention, the members of Local 490 overwhelmingly re-elected Jenkins as their president. Other altercations between the top leadership and restive locals took place in the early part of 1944.

It soon became inevitable that a new faction would arise in the UAW. The Addes-Stalinist faction was the most conservative, bluntly subordinating all the workers' demands to the war program; the Reuther leadership tried to walk a precarious tightrope between the two. Sooner or later the locals that opposed the no-strike pledge and favored a more militant stand, regardless of the war or what they considered rather the false intrusion of the war issue, would begin to work together. In July a group of secondary UAW leaders, many of them local presidents or shop committeemen, formed a "Rank and File Caucus."* Its program was simple: rescind the no-strike pledge; press for independent political action by labor; elect UAW leaders pledged to these views.

What were the motives of the men who led this group? For some, the fight against the no-strike pledge was conducted from a strictly union point of view. Seeing no contradiction between their support of the war and their opposition to the no-strike pledge, they felt that the fight

* A major weakness of the "Rank and File Caucus" was that, with one exception, it lacked nationally known leaders. The exception was Larry Yost, a colorful and handsome union maverick from Ford Local 600. It did have, however, some extremely active secondary union leaders such as John McGill of Flint Buick, John Zupan of Ford Willow Run, Bill Jenkins of Chrysler, Bert Boone and F. J. Palmer of Flint Chevrolet, Robert Carter of Flint AC Sparkplug, Ben Garrison of Ford Local 400, Tom De Lorenzo of New York Brewster, and Max Weinrib of Chicago Electromatic. Most of the leaders of the "Rank and File Caucus" were politically independent.

for democracy had to be conducted on two fronts and that at home the right to strike was an important part of that fight. Other militant supporters of the "Rank and File Caucus" did not even bother about reconciling their support of the war effort with their demands for more militancy; they simply knew that it was a union's job to fight for "more and better." On the other hand, some UAW supporters of the caucus were motivated by radical political views; a few of the secondary UAW leaders were adherents of small revolutionary socialist groups. (The most active of such groups in encourging the formation of "Rank and File Caucus" was the Workers Party, a small Marxist organization which counterposed socialism to capitalism, Stalinism and fascism.) These latter unionists believed that even in wartime the rights of labor were the union's primary concern and that any attempt to nibble away at such rights was a step toward the kind of totalitarianism purportedly being destroyed abroad. Finally, it should be added that one of the major reasons for the support the "Rank and File Caucus" won in the union ranks was that it raised its opposition to the no-strike pledge after V-E Day, when many workers felt that the pressure of the war had decreased. The major argument for the no-strike pledge—that it was necessary to win the war—no longer seemed very convincing at a time when war production was being deliberately decreased by the government.

The "Rank and File Caucus" found most of its support in a number of maverick locals, which made life in the UAW lively throughout the war. A typical maverick local was the one at the Brewster airplane plant in New York City, the first, together with the Buick local in Flint, to start a campaign against the no-strike pledge. The Brewster local was constantly at odds with the plant's manage-

ment and in June, 1944, conducted a brief sitdown strike
when the Navy cancelled orders for Brewster planes. During the 1943 UAW convention it had distributed its own
paper, advocating a policy similar to that of the "Rank
and File Caucus."

The last big wartime debate in the UAW took place at
its September, 1944, convention at Grand Rapids. Here
the Addes group more or less maintained its strength, but
Reuther lost heavily to the new caucus. How deep the
ranks' resentment went was hardly understood by the top
officers. R. J. Thomas threatened that if the no-strike
pledge were rescinded, he would not run again for UAW
president—for which he was roundly booed. Had Thomas
been a bit more self-perceptive, he might have realized
that what he meant as a threat could also be taken as a
promise. When any of the top union leaders, especially
those identified with the CP, made patriotic appeals as a
means of settling, or evading, union issues, they were
greeted by the Briggs local delegation with concerted
waving of tiny American flags.

Three proposals on the no-strike pledge lay before the
convention: unconditional retention, championed by Nat
Ganley, CP whip, and Norman Mathews, a conservative
leader; retention only in those plants engaged in war production, proposed by the Reuthers; outright repeal, advocated by the third group.

On the first roll call, the last proposal received 37 percent of the vote, which the "Rank and File Caucus" considered a moral victory. The Reuther resolution was badly
defeated in a voice vote, and the Ganley-Mathews view
failed to gain a majority.

When a shrewd spokesman for the "Rank and File
Caucus" asked if this meant that the UAW now had *no*
policy on wartime strikes (which would have meant each

local could do as it pleased), the top leaders were left in dismay. They called for a simple vote to reaffirm the union's no-strike pledge, to be followed by a referendum among the members. Now supported by Reuther, the no-strike pledge was reaffirmed by a majority. The Stalinists tried to wriggle out of the referendum, but were prevented from doing so by Reuther.

Two months later, 35 percent of those UAW members who voted in the referendum supported the proposal to junk the no-strike pledge. Considering its youth and inexperience, and the massed attacks by Stalinists and conservatives to which it had been subjected, one must grant that this vote was a very considerable achievement for the "Rank and File Caucus." Truly, as R. J. Thomas said to his friends, "The rank and file is getting out of hand."

Soon the "Rank and File Caucus" disintegrated. Once the war was over its major plank became irrelevant, and most of its people went back to the Reuther camp. After the war the union again became, in the GM strike of 1946, an aggressive agency of struggle against the corporations. The energies that had been consumed in internal fights during the war were now directed outward in an attempt to catch up with the rising cost of living.

But it would be an error to see the significance of the "Rank and File Caucus" merely in terms of the vote it won against the no-strike pledge. For what was really at stake in the wartime discussions within the UAW was the question of what role the unions should play in a war for which they were called upon to make sacrifices but from the control and direction of which they were rigorously excluded. By the war's end, the few posts that labor representatives had been given in Washington were either dissolved or rendered insignificant. It was clear that the war's economic program had been controlled exclusively

by professional government experts and dollar-a-year industrialists.[20] Under these circumstances, the debates in
the UAW reflected an implicit, seldom formulated but still
strong conviction on the part of many unionists that the
labor movement could no longer function effectively if it
limited itself to mere dollars-and-hours issues. Even those
in the UAW who favored a conservative or restrained wartime course had to admit (except, of course, the Stalinists) that the debate had been a remarkable demonstration of rank-and-file participation in the union's life.

After the War Is Over...

6

As soon as the war in Europe was ended, the auto industry began to think of reconversion to civilian production. Whichever corporation reconverted most quickly would get the largest share of the postwar auto sales. Both the population at large and many businessmen and economists seemed to expect that, after a sharp inflationary upsurge in which consumer-goods industries would enjoy an orgy of sales, there would follow a serious depression. For despite much whistling in the war's twilight and brave talk about postwar plenty, the nation's psychology was heavily drenched with expectations of depression. (Had not the armament program and the Marshall Plan intervened to prop up American economy, that expectation might have been realized.) While the war's end meant for the auto corporations a wild scramble to take advantage of accumulated consumer demand, to the auto workers it brought renewed feelings of insecurity and anxiety.

By mid-1945 most auto workers found their take-home

126

pay substantially decreased. Overtime was sharply cut; jobs were down-graded and lower wage scales established in civilian production; bonuses were no longer given. Yet the cost of living remained as high as during the war. The Bureau of Labor Statistics (whose figures the then Labor Secretary Schwellenbach publicly described as "not realistic" and privately admitted to be "lousy"[1]) found that the cost of living had risen by 30 percent since January 1, 1941. These figures were seriously disputed by CIO and AFL economists, who claimed that it had actually risen by 45 percent. In either case, it was obvious that the rise in the cost of living had quite outstripped the rise in wage rates, which, according to the Little Steel Formula, could go only 15 percent above those of January, 1941. Nor could the labor movement accept the argument that this inequity was partly compensated for by the workers' ability to increase their total take-home pay through overtime. What was crucial was the failure of wage rates to rise in proportion to prices or labor productivity or profits.

Simultaneously, the BLS index for June, 1945, indicated that food costs at retail prices had risen 51 percent above those of August 15, 1939. The War Production Board released a report which showed that the price of clothing for working-class families rose 18 percent rather than the 5 percent listed in the BLS index. The difference between the two figures was due to the fact that the Bureau of Labor Statistics had failed to consider the hidden price increases resulting from the disappearance of those low-cost items which form the bulk of the workers' clothing purchases.

In July, 1945, the Gallup Poll reported that a majority of American wage earners had not saved enough to tide them over a sustained period of unemployment. Though the auto unionists were by then among the better-paid workers, there is no reason to suppose that most of them had managed to put aside any substantial savings. When Walter Reuther quoted the "astronomical" profit figures of the GM corporation ($510,836,000 in 1941, which meant that for every hour a GM employee worked he produced $1.07 for his family and $1.09 for GM), the UAW members were easily convinced that equality of wartime sacrifice had been more slogan than reality. For while many of them had succeeded in paying off debts accumulated in the prewar years and some had saved money to buy needed but unavailable consumer goods, few had reached a status that might yet be described as secure.

A further cause of irritation to the auto workers was the flood of newspaper propaganda which had accused the unions of hindering war production by constant strikes. Actually, the auto workers felt they had kept their shoulders to the war wheel pretty consistently, and sometimes under considerable provocation. The Senate War Investigating Committee reported that only .0006 of one percent of time was lost during the war because of strikes in GM plants. By contrast, the *Automobile Worker* reported that "man hours lost in GM plants during the July 4th weekend shutdown ordered by the corporation in 1944 was more than ten times greater than the total number of man hours lost through all strikes and stoppages in GM plants from January, 1943, to March, 1945."[2]

In July, 1945, a meeting of eighty-seven local UAW presidents from the Detroit area exploded with the resentments accumulated during the war years. Matt Hammond, head of the crucial tool-and-die local 157, was cheered when he said :"Our international officers have failed us to the extent that at least they could have fought and kept fighting for our economic demands. Instead they sat back and let everything drift along."[3] The eighty-seven local heads voted to ask the UAW top officials to address a special gathering of union leaders in order to explain their "do-nothing" record. If the union was to avoid a severe blow-up, drastic action would have to be taken—quickly.

It is a remarkable indication of how stultified a trade union's leadership can become after a few years of comparative comfort that only one major UAW leader responded to this crisis with any degree of imagination. Of all the UAW leaders, Walter Reuther alone sensed that if the union was to thrive in the postwar period some bold idea that lifted the auto union's sights far above the usual picket line, would be necessary. Business unionism, with its penny give-and-take and its provincial outlook, would be completely insufficient. For Reuther this was a crucial opportunity to surge ahead of his colleagues and competitors.

Scarcely anyone paid attention to the economic brief Reuther submitted on June 30, 1945, to the Office of War Mobilization and Reconversion, the War Labor Board and the Office of Price Administration. Certainly, the local union presidents clamoring for more action did not give it much notice. At best, it seemed another of Reuther's "brainstorms" and was dismissed as such in most labor circles.

Reuther's central idea was simple. "Labor contends that the economic facts of life prove that wages can be increased without increasing prices. Increased production must be supported by increased consumption, and increased consumption will be possible only through increased wages. The basic question . . . is: where will American labor's improved wage status come from?" The answer: "industry [can] pay higher wages out of the high profits it is making. It will not have to charge higher prices."[4]

Reuther claimed to have hit on a way of solving what seemed to most unionists an insoluble problem: how to raise wages without correspondingly raising prices. Workers had gone on strike, won wage increases and then seen them quickly cancelled by price increases. Union members found this demoralizing, and some even began to feel that it was hardly worth fighting for higher wages. The union's leaders could, of course, simply point out that wage increases were necessary to meet the price rises that had *already* taken place and were not to be viewed as *necessarily* leading to new ones. For wage increases, the union could claim, were justified by increased labor productivity and as a means of effecting a more just distribution of wealth. Nonetheless, the wage-price spiral of the wartime and postwar inflation helped dramatize the insufficiency of business unionism. Reuther's "GM strike program" became a dramatic and vivid way of suggesting to the union's members how the vicious wage-price spiral might be broken.

For a little while Reuther's economic brief seemed an academic matter, but two days after the surrender of Japan it became a very vital and unacademic one. On August 16, 1945, President Truman announced through his Executive Order 9599 a new government policy of permitting wage increases on condition they do not result in price increases. This order, intended as an anti-inflationary device, immediately gave Reuther his opportunity. On August 18th he submitted a preliminary brief to General Motors asking for a 30 percent wage increase *without any increase in the price of cars*. The UAW made similar demands on Ford and Chrysler, but it was obvious that the showdown was to be with GM.

At a special union executive board meeting on September 22nd Reuther won support for his "one at a time" strike strategy. Though later attacked by his intra-union opponents, Reuther's "one at a time" proposal was so obviously sound that it had to be adopted. Since the auto industry is internally competitive and since, it seemed, the postwar situation would lead to a sharpening of this competition, Reuther's proposal to concentrate on GM put the corporation in an extremely vulnerable position. In case of a long strike, GM would have to see its postwar markets won by competitors. From an immediate financial point of view, the corporation was of course in a very strong position to fight a strike, for it enjoyed an immense capital reserve and could look forward to tax rebates under favorable provisions of the excess-profits law. But from the overall point of view of again establishing itself in the civilian car market, a strike would be a severe blow. Reuther understood that a strike was, in the circumstances, unavoidable, and he was ready to take the lead in the postwar economic struggle. Lacking his foresight and boldness, the other UAW leaders preferred to wait for Philip Murray and the steel workers to set the pattern of wage demands. Had their inclinations prevailed, they might have had a good long wait.

The preliminary skirmishes between GM and Reuther were of the usual sort. Under the provisions of the Smith-Connally Act, the UAW took a strike vote. On October 3rd, Charles Wilson, president of GM, rejected Reuther's demand as "unreasonable" and asked instead that Reuther join him in urging Congress to institute a 45-hour week. If the fundamental dispute had not been so serious, Wilson's letter might have provoked a bit of laughter among the auto workers.

THE BIG DEBATE

When actual negotiations between GM and the UAW began, Reuther suggested that they be open to the press and the public. It was a shrewd move, to which the corporation replied, with some justice, that Reuther had opposed public negotiations in 1942. In any case, on October 19th, when a negotiation session was scheduled to begin, Frank Winn, Reuther's publicity director, invited reporters to come into the conference room. After GM refused to negotiate in the presence of reporters, Reuther asked them to leave, but he managed to gain publicity by releasing to the public transcripts of the negotiations, as well as the union's briefs. Since these negotiations involved the most fundamental questions of American social life, they make, for all their roughness of speech, valuable reading. The debate between GM and Reuther was acrimonious, personal, sometimes vulgar; but behind the bluster and heat lurked the still unsettled questions— what are the rights of a labor union? How far may or should it intervene in industrial life?

These questions were raised by the UAW's demands: *wage increases without price increases* and *open the corporation's books* to prove that it is able to pay wage increases without having to raise prices. From October 19th to November 19th, the debate continued through eleven negotiating sessions. Excerpts from the transcript provide vivid illustrations of both views.

What Does the UAW Want?

REUTHER: We have said to the corporation, and I repeat, that if we can't prove, based upon the facts, or if the corporation can disprove our facts that we can get a 30 percent wage increase without price increases, we don't want 30 percent.

ANDERSON: [Harry Anderson, GM vice-president in charge of personnel] Who are you going to prove it to, Walter?

REUTHER: Harry, bring out the facts.

ANDERSON: Who are you going to prove it to? . . .

REUTHER: We will prove it to anybody. We will prove it.

ANDERSON: So what?

REUTHER: The point is if we prove it to you, will you give it to us?

ANDERSON: If you can prove it. Like George Romney's talk; George Romney asked you the question point blank, could you settle your demands for less than 30 percent? What was your answer?

REUTHER: I will answer that. Let me give you the answer now on the record. We are prepared to settle this demand for less than 30 percent, providing you can disprove our contention that wages can be increased 30 percent without increasing prices and you can still make a profit. If you can prove we can't get 30 percent, hold prices, and still make a nice profit, we will settle for less than 30 percent . . .

Who Has Social Power in America?

ANDERSON: Walter, you must want a strike.

REUTHER: Harry, Goddamn it, the way you are going about it, you are forcing us to strike.

ANDERSON: I will tell you why you want to make a strike out of it.

REUTHER: Tell us.

ANDERSON: Because you have got the boys pretty well stirred up that you want a strike. In addition to that, before you had the first meeting with us, you petitioned the National Labor Relations Board for a strike vote, before you were even in the room.

REUTHER: Harry, that is the damn law you had passed.

ANDERSON: That we had passed?

REUTHER: Sure.

ANDERSON: Horse manure.

REUTHER: For God's sake, every Congressman, every Senator on Capitol Hill who goes along with the CIO or labor's general legislative program voted against the Smith-Connally Bill. And the people in your corner . . .

ANDERSON: Our boys?

REUTHER: Sure, they are your boys. Look at the record. They come to your defense every time some issue comes up. Don't tell us Howard Smith comes to my defense. They passed this law, and now you don't like it because we are complying with it.

What Are a Union's Rights?

ANDERSON: That is really up to us to decide, Walter, whether we are willing to pay it or not.

REUTHER: Your position is that your ability to pay is not a factor?

ANDERSON: That is right.

Is the UAW Fighting the World's Fight?

COEN: [Harry Coen, GM Assistant Director of Personnel] There is nothing sincere in your approach. There hasn't been yet, so far as requesting a public meeting. It is just another chance for you to get up on the soap-box before more people. You know we are all worn out on this thing. It is no news to your people. And you just get a few more people in here to listen to it.

REUTHER: Harry, if it was . . .

COEN: Keep quiet, will you? You are all wound up. Relax. I have been away hunting for a week. I am in good shape. I can look at this thing in its true perspective and I know it is all horseshit. . . .

COEN: Is the UAW fighting the fight of the whole world?

REUTHER: We have been fighting to hold prices and increase purchasing power. We are making our little contribution in that respect.

COEN: Why don't you get down to your size and get down to

the type of job you are supposed to be doing as a trade-union leader, and talk about money you would like to have for your people and let the labor statesmanship go to hell for a while.

REUTHER: Translate it so that I can know what you mean.

COEN: If you come to us and say, "We want X cents an hour," and we can talk to you about whether we can give you X cents, or half an X or quarter of X, or something like that. Instead of that you get off in your socialistic dreams, these Alice-in-Wonderland things of yours, and finally you get off to where you don't even understand yourself. Then you say we can't raise prices, and if we say we have to raise prices you don't want 30 percent but you are going to have the 30 percent or else. . . .

Should Prices Be Discussed in Collective Bargaining?

CORBIN: [Elwin Corbin, UAW official] Do you mean if we came in here with a 30 percent wage demand and offered to join with you in going before OPA for a 30 percent increase in the price of your cars, you would talk business?

COEN: We don't ask you to join with us on the price of cars. It is none of your damned business what OPA does about prices.

CORBIN: The hell it isn't. I intend to buy a car.

How Should Labor Leaders Act?

REUTHER: But don't you think it is constructive for us to relate our wage question to prices?

COEN: Nobody else is doing that but you. You are the fellow that wants to get the publicity out of this whole thing. You want to enhance your personal political position. That is what the whole show is about. . . .

REUTHER: For you to say that the fight we are making—if I came in here and said we want 30 percent and we don't care about prices, we don't care about profits, that is your business . . . then you would say Reuther is being a trade unionist and not trying to build himself up politically. But when Reuther comes and there is what you say is an attempt to be a statesman, you think that is bad. I think if I didn't do it that way, it would be bad. I think if we came in here on a selfish basis and said, "We want ours and the world be damned," then you should take our pants off.

COEN: You put a lot of things in my mouth that I haven't said, and you shade the things I have said in the direction of your thinking. None of the other labor leaders have taken the position you are taking. I am on sound ground there.

REUTHER: What do you mean when you say that?

COEN: They are asking for a $2 a day increase. That is what the others are asking.

REUTHER: They don't care what happens to prices?

COEN: I don't know whether they care or not. They haven't coupled it up with their demand. And I think they are a damn sight smarter than you are in this instance . . .

Should the Union Be Allowed to Look into the Corporation's Books?

COEN: I don't think the people out on the picket lines care anything about wage theories, too . . . Carrying a sign . . . What does he care about GM books?

REUTHER: He doesn't care anything about GM books providing you make a satisfactory adjustment, give him a satisfactory wage increase.

COEN: That is right.

REUTHER: But if you say, "No dice, we can't give you a wage increase," he says, "Let's see your books to see why you can't."[5]

THE FIRST ROUND

At the climax of the negotiations GM offered a 10 percent wage increase, which was tied to a formula to obtain higher price levels from OPA. A national conference of GM unionists rejected the offer. Reuther then proposed that the dispute be submitted to arbitration with both sides agreeing to open all books, and that wage increases not be used as an occasion to raise car prices. Charging that the UAW wished "GM [to] relinquish its rights to manage its business,"[6] the corporation rejected the offer. On November 21st some 200,000 GM workers in ninety-six plants downed tools to begin their historic 113-day strike. This was the first major postwar strike and came at a time when 100,000 telephone workers, 640,000 steel workers and 75,000 retail clerks were also preparing to strike. The "first round" of the postwar wage fight had begun.

The strike itself was peaceful. Although the company obtained a few injunctions, it did not try to run its plants with strikebreakers, and the workers picketed mainly for precautionary, publicity and morale purposes. The real conflict took place not on picket lines, but in a furious exchange of public statements.

GM published numerous advertisements charging that the UAW's "open-the-books" demand was "interference with prerogatives of management." It asked: "Is the Union Seeking Facts of New Economic Power?" Does it want "A Look at the Books, or a Finger in the Pie?"[7] By developing these formulations, GM improved on the ineptness and rude bluster of its negotiators in their tiffs with Reuther. Having found its "line", GM expressed it with some skill. In one of its pamphlets, it developed this theme:

> A "look at the books" is a clever catch phrase intended as an opening wedge whereby unions hope to pry their way into the whole field of management.
>
> The fact is that the UAW-CIO is reaching for power . . .
>
> It leads surely towards the day when union bosses, under the threat of strike, will seek to tell us what we can make, when we can make it, where we can make it, and how much we can charge . . .[8]

Testifying before a government fact-finding board, Walter Reuther offered his generalized explanation of the union's position:

> We have made the fight, Mr. Chairman, to get the company's books and records not because we want to indulge in the pleasure of going through their books . . . But the company wouldn't take up the challenge and wouldn't argue the facts, so the only way we could meet that problem is to say, "Open the books," because we knew that if they did open the books the figures and the arithmetic would confirm the union's economic conclusions . . .[9]

Any hope the UAW may have had that the Truman administration would come to its rescue was quickly dismissed when President Truman told the GM strikers to "return to work immediately" and said the strike was a "major obstacle holding up our reconversion program."[10] A few days later an emergency meeting of GM union delegates turned down Truman's demand as "ill-advised and undeserved."[11] In a nationwide radio speech, Philip Murray bluntly declared: "The CIO is . . . opposed to the basic policies pursued by the administration."[12]

The UAW appealed to prominent public figures to study the record of negotiations and prepare an advisory report on the issues behind the strike. Leon Henderson, Bishop William Scarlett, Professor John Hanna, Professor Harry Overstreet, Dr. Henry Hitt Crane of the Central Methodist Church of Detroit, and other prominent figures held public hearings, in which GM refused to participate. They upheld the UAW point of view.

President Truman again intervened—this time, less clumsily. He appointed a fact-finding board to hold hearings on the strike. Lloyd Garrison of the University of Washington, Milton Eisenhower of Kansas State College, and North Carolina Supreme Court Justice Walter P. Lacey composed the board. GM announced that if the board was going to consider "ability to pay" within its jurisdiction, it would refuse to appear before it. Lloyd Garrison asked President Truman to define the board's jurisdiction, and on December 28th the President wrote that "ability to pay" *was* a legitimate matter for its investigation. GM, through its attorney, Walter Gordon Merritt, immediately withdrew from the hearings. Merritt put the GM position bluntly. "It [GM] does not plead inability to pay as a reason for rejecting any wage consideration." GM was compelled to approach the union's objective "in making prices and ability to pay its prime issue with due regard to the radical ideology which the union has expounded in support of its argument . . ."[13]

When President Truman announced the board's findings on January 10, 1946, they represented a clear victory for the auto workers, even though the board's specific wage proposal was lower than that of the UAW. The board said that GM could pay a 19½-cent hourly wage increase *without raising the price of its cars.* The UAW accepted this recommendation with a warning that it would revert to its original demands if GM refused to compromise. GM refused.

The corporation's intransigeance incensed the UAW's ranks and resulted in increased support to the strikers. A united labor committee, including four AFL and four CIO presidents, was formed. The steel workers sent $100,-000, as did the Amalgamated Clothing Workers and the International Ladies Garment Workers. All of this was to be expected. What was particularly cheering to the strikers was that 300 farmers from Montana sent several carloads of wheat and other farmers' organizations contributed food. A national committee, ranging from Mrs. Eleanor Roosevelt to Henry Luce, from Harold Ickes to Henry Morgenthau, raised funds to help the strikers.

Soon the GM strike became a symbolic postwar struggle between labor and capital. In January, 1946, over 1,650,000 industrial workers were marching on picket lines. Steel, packinghouse, electrical and other industries were shut down. In Washington steel-industry leaders put tremendous pressure on OPA to permit price increases together with wage increases; that is, to repudiate the principles outlined in the report of the President's fact-finding board. More was involved than a few pennies per hour—the strikes had become a test of strength. Unable or unwilling to stand up for its own decision, the Truman administration reversed the position of its fact-finding board. Through the OPA, it indicated that a rise in steel prices would be approved after the industry settled with the CIO. Shortly after this news became known, the less militant unions abandoned the Reuther formula and signed contracts for 18½ cents hourly wage increases—with nothing said about prices.

To the GM strikers, however, the most treacherous blow came on February 12th when the United Electrical Workers, CIO, signed a contract with GM for the 30,000 workers under its jurisdiction, in which a wage rise of 18½ cents an hour was accepted. In the UAW, reactions to the UE settlement at a figure below the fact-finding board's recommendation were violent. The UAW Detroit strike committee, through its chairman John Anderson, denounced the settlement as a "double-cross."[14] The strikers were particularly incensed by the fact that James Matles, UE leader, had never even informed the UAW leaders that he was secretly negotiating with GM officials in Detroit. This, UAW leaders felt, was clearly sabotage of the GM strike. That Matles was known in the labor movement as a follower of the CP line (the kind who if not a member was "cheating the party of dues") made plausible the theory that the UE settlement was made with at least one eye to leaving Reuther out on a limb with a lost strike. If that was the intention of the party-liners, they did not succeed.

The GM strikers were now in a difficult position. Most of the other CIO unions had accepted the 18½-cent provision and had not concerned themselves with prices. It was an open secret that Philip Murray disliked Reuther's strike program, and that at a private meeting in Pittsburgh on December 1st they had sharply disagreed on the question. According to *The Wage Earner*, organ of the Association of Catholic Trade Unionists and usually friendly to Murray, the CIO president had urged Reuther to drop his anti-inflation program.[15] The heads of the two other major UAW divisions, Mathews in Chrysler and Leonard in Ford, followed Murray's line and ignored both prices and "ability to pay." As a consequence, the strike suffered and the morale of the men was weakened. One labor correspondent wrote:

> Many of the men at Chevrolet were exceedingly bitter about what one striker termed Murray's "stab in the back." "I woudn't mind losing to GM," said one of the pickets, "nearly so much as I mind being slapped in the face by the president of the CIO."[16]

On February 12th GM officials made the 18½-cent-an-hour proposal to the UAW, but the infuriated union leaders walked out of the conference. Yet it soon became apparent that the dominant pattern for settling the rash of 1946 strikes would have to be that set by the UE in its dubious agreement with GM. After the steel workers accepted 18½ cents, U. S. Steel was granted a price increase of approximately $5 a ton by OPA—which led to a further overall price increase. Those unionists who understood the full implications of the UAW "GM strike program" could not help but conclude that a major reason for their defeat was the sabotage of the Stalinist-led UE and the ineptness and lack of foresight of the old-line business unions. The GM strike was by no means a total loss, but its failure to reach its full objective was partly the fault of those union leaders who lacked the imagination to grasp the importance of the Reuther program.

TOUCHSTONE FOR OPINION

As ten years before, when the UAW engaged in the sitdown strikes, the union's program for the GM strike raised the most fundamental and passionate responses among various social groups in the U.S. A student of American postwar life could conveniently use the "GM strike program" as a touchstone for social opinion.

The corporation, as the largest single unit of American business, made its position perfectly plain. In a message to GM stockholders, Alfred P. Sloan Jr. wrote: "Until the UAW-CIO had been forced by circumstances to abandon its extreme theories and until a new national economic policy with regard to wages and prices had taken definite form, any settlement was impossible."[17] In cruder form, the corporation asked in public advertisements: "Is American business to be based on free competition or is it to become socialized, with all activities controlled and regimented?"[18] The question was stacked and, with regard to the immediate issues of the strike, a bit beside the point; yet it did touch on some of the strike program's implications. For the truth is that unlike most strikes in America this one did involve basic property relationships; this one, at least in terms of ultimate consequences few workers understood, did raise the question of class power.

The conservative press found in Reuther's program cause for anger and alarm. The *New York Times* wrote a number of learned editorials attacking Reuther's program as a threat to "free enterprise." Other big papers came to much the same conclusion, though in less erudite language.

The reaction of those government officials concerned with the country's economic life was characteristically two-sided. A number of leading administration officials had issued statements which, in economic terms, could only result in support for the strikers. A few months before the strike, William H. Davis, Director of Economic Stabilization, had reported that, in the years to come, industry would be able to increase wages 40 to 50 percent without increasing prices. Reconversion Director John W. Snyder declared that because of decreased production costs, "Many industries should be able to grant wage increases without price increases."[19] The Commerce Department, then headed by Henry Wallace, released a report declaring that the auto industry could, after reaching full production, pay an increase of 25 percent in wages without raising prices. Yet, after all these statements laying the foundation for Reuther's case, the Truman administration did not try to enforce its original position as expressed in Executive Order 9599, but instead submitted to the pressure of the steel industry by allowing it price increases.

These reactions were predictable and quite natural. But what was most depressing from a labor point of view was the confusion and sheer stupidity Reuther's programmatic innovation evoked in the American labor leadership. The AFL leadership, as might be expected, hadn't the foggiest notion of what was going on. John L. Lewis, who cannot be accused of being unintelligent, told a Con-

gressional committee that the government could settle
the strike in ten days if it would allow the manufacturers
a price which would permit them a "fair profit." He termed
the company's position "dishonest" and the UAW program "stupid."[20] When, at the next negotiating session
between GM and the UAW, the corporation's representatives threw Lewis' statement into Reuther's face, Reuther
pointedly replied: "We don't agree with John L. Lewis'
wage-price theory. His theory [is that] we will soak the
public a dollar more per ton of coal, and you get fifty
cents of it, and the operator fifty cents. We don't think
that is the way to increase purchasing power. We want
to increase purchasing power by holding down prices and
raising wages so that people can buy more things."[21]

The routine CIO leaders resented Reuther's innovation,
but did not venture into print. Murray confined his dispute with Reuther to their secret meeting in Pittsburgh
on December 1st and (it should in fairness be mentioned)
helped the strikers considerably with public statements
of support. A year after the GM strike, a CIO convention
adopted the "wage increase without price increases" program, but by then it had little practical meaning. By the
very nature of their seldom formulated dollars-and-cents
outlook, the old-line labor leaders were not equipped to
deal with Reuther's program.

Walter Reuther himself did not publicly develop the
social implications of his strike program. The briefs prepared in his behalf by the UAW Washington representative, Donald Montgomery, were detailed *economic* proofs
of the validity of the strike program, but they were sig-
nally silent on the social consequences of that program.
It is not hard to guess at the causes of this silence.
Reuther's strike program was a halfway stand: an implicit
rejection of the kind of unionism which acquiesces to the

capitalist status quo, while yet not ready to state that rejection openly. The program, in fact, excellently illustrated Reuther's own social views, with all their difficulties and internal contradictions. What, for example, asked Reuther's critics, would you say if the auto corporations really "could not afford" to pay a 30 percent wage increase? Reuther could only reply (from a labor point of view, inadequately and lamely) that he would then agree to scale down his demands. As soon as he said *that,* he was open to the serious charge that he was basing labor's demands not on the objective needs of the workers for improved living conditions but on the transient, war-stimulated profits of the corporations.*

For others, too, the GM strike program presented programmatic difficulties. The Communist Party never quite adopted a consistent line toward the strike or the UAW program for the strike. At the beginning it was highly enthusiastic about both, and George Morris, the *Daily Worker* labor expert, hailed the strike as "the battle that will decide" the future of all labor wage demands in 1946. "Today," he wrote, "labor is challenging the concept that an employer is the sole judge as to whether his business could or could not give the workers a living wage."[23] But by January, 1946, Nat Ganley, CP whip in the auto union, was saying that, "We do not think the one-at-a-time [strike] plan is working out." He proposed that the union "follow Murray's plan." Murray, he said, "isn't going to shut down one company at a time."[24]** By March 15th George Morris was writing in the *Daily Worker* that Wal-

* A few weeks after the strike, a flurry of comment was caused in the UAW by a statement attributed to Reuther in a Detroit paper: "The demand that GM open the books was just a maneuver to win public support and to get the company over the barrel."[22] Reuther denied having made the statement and claimed that he had been misquoted.
** Which was quite true—Murray wasn't going to shut down *any* plants.

ter Reuther "is working desperately to unload from himself the major blame for the mismanagement and consequent prolongation of the General Motors strike to 113 days."[25] And by April 23rd Morris was delighted at the fact that the anti-Reuther majority of the UAW executive board had "chucked out of the window" Reuther's " 'ability-to-pay' wage theory."[26] Finally, the party's major trade-union theoretician, Jack Stachel, wrote in its magazine:

> Another weakness in the General Motors strike resulting from Reuther's tactics was the manner in which he coupled the fight for wages with that against price increases. It is absolutely correct and essential for the entire labor movement and all the people to fight against price increases, for price control, and to emphasize the ability of the capitalists to grant the workers' full wage demands without price increases. . . . But it is another thing to do as Reuther did, so to couple wages and prices in one industry as to play into the hands of the employers and endanger the strike."[27]

Despite these fluctuations in line, the CP was consistent about two things: its bitter opposition to Reuther and its readiness to allow its followers in the UE to cut the ground from under the GM strike.

Within the labor movement, only two groups, the Catholic unionists and the socialists, tried to examine the Reuther program in terms of its ultimate, underlying meanings. In its paper, *The Wage Earner,* the Association of Catholic Trade Unionists supported the Reuther program because it rejected GM's theory that labor was merely a commodity to be bought in the market rather than a partner to be given a share of the profits.[28] In addition to this ethical ground for supporting the GM strike program, the ACTU people shrewdly analyzed the possible consequences of the strike:

If Reuther succeeds in forcing GM, one of the country's largest industrial empires, to redivide the fruits of its production, the day of gigantic profits in American business will be done.

Every union will then insist that the profit and price structure be examined in collective bargaining and wage increases be absorbed out of profits if possible. The result may not be the end of capitalism but it will certainly be the beginning of a new kind of capitalism.[29]

The socialist interpretation of the GM strike program emphasized its consequences in terms of "class relations." One socialist writer, Max Shachtman, said that the linking of prices, profits and wages implicitly signified "a demand for direct intervention by labor in the running of the economy as a whole . . . From this demand to the demand for a government which will control wages, prices and profits, in the interests of labor and of the consumer is only one step . . . You, the workers, say that the industry, while paying a fair profit to the corporations, can still pay a decent wage to the workers without charging a monopolistic price to the consumers . . . if you say that industry can do these things and the monopolists say that industry cannot, then it is perfectly logical for you to take over industry and prove in practice that your demands are realizable . . . Suppose the [corporation's] books show that the company is losing money. Does that mean that you would advocate . . . a wage cut? The best that Reuther could do in reply was to say that in that case he would scale his demands down to zero." Here, continued the writer, Reuther was unwilling to face the consequences of his position: namely, that if the corporations were unable to satisfy the socially-desirable demands made on them, they had proven themselves bankrupt and the union should call for their nationalization.[30]

Though this line of reasoning is politically unpalatable to most UAW leaders, it seems a valid deduction from the GM strike program. Thus, it would seem that the significance of the GM strike program was best understood by the extreme right and the extreme left, the reactionaries like Sloan and the socialists. But, it should be emphasized, these were the interpretations given to the program by outside commentators; in the union, no such rigorous extension of its meaning was developed. In practice, the major effect within the union of the GM strike program was to help dramatize Reuther's position as an aspiring national leader and to consolidate his reputation as the most imaginative and boldest UAW leader.

The Rise of
the Reuther Group

7

SINCE its disastrous experience with "dual unions" in the late twenties and early thirties, the American Communist Party had sought to gain a new base for activity in the labor movement. AFL craft unions were difficult to penetrate, more difficult to influence. When the CIO was formed it seemed an ideal place for the CP to work. During its early days the CIO did not look too closely into organizers' credentials; in fact, John L. Lewis allowed CP followers to gain influential posts and Harry Bridges to become West Coast CIO director. The formation of new unions gave articulate and experienced men, such as the CP had, chances for quick ascents to leadership. As thousands of unsorted workers flocked in to sign cards, even a wary leadership would have had difficulty in ferreting out CP people.

For the first time in its history, the American CP gained

a considerable grip over a number of important unions: maritime, transport, electrical, mine and smelter, parts of auto, and others. In the UAW, the actual CP "fraction"* has always been quite small, not more than 500 nationally at any time during the past fifteen years. But the size of such a fraction is inconsequential in comparison with its strategic location, mobile discipline, and ability to influence non-party union leaders. What did it matter, for instance, that George Addes was not a member of the CP, so long as he seemed always to agree with its union policies? More than that no commissar could ask.

The defeat of the R. J. Thomas–George Addes group in the UAW turned out to be the decisive event in the gradual destruction of Stalinist power in the CIO. Had the Thomas–Addes group licked Reuther, it seems most unlikely that Philip Murray would have been jolted out of his traditional position of "neutrality" with regard to internal affairs of CIO unions—and that was all the Communists wanted from Murray: neutrality. With control of the electrical and strong influence in the auto union, the Stalinists would almost have been in a position to make a serious bid for domination of the CIO; they could certainly have pressed Murray against the wall. But once they were beaten in the UAW, their influence declined in the other CIO unions.

It is worth noting, too, that had the Thomas–Addes group defeated Reuther in the UAW, the union might well have supported Henry Wallace in the 1948 elections and thereby given his semi-Stalinist campaign the mass labor

* As used in union circles, the terms faction and fraction have the following distinct meanings: a faction is a grouping of unionists which desires to advance a particular program for, or to gain leadership of, a union; a fraction is a grouping of union members who belong to a political party and work in the union as a disciplined unit.

base it lacked. Wallace understood this: hence his attack on Reuther as the "greatest single obstacle" to his party.[1]

What made the Reuther group's victory so significant was the way in which it was achieved. On the whole, the Reuther group conducted a principled fight against Stalinist totalitarianism and for democratic trade unionism. Reuther hammered away at the idea that he opposed the CP not because it was a political party, good, bad or indifferent, but because it was the docile agent of a totalitarian power. He stripped the CP of its most valued pretense: that it is a legitimate expression of native discontent. Of course, not all the spokesmen of the heterogeneous Reuther group were as clear about this as its leader, for some were simply "agin' the Reds."* But Reuther understood that the Stalinists' "subservience to the Kremlin and their shifts on trade-union issues as Moscow winds veer [could] become the Achilles' heel of the domestic

---

* Perhaps the best example of this difference of approach within the Reuther tendency was an incident that took place somewhat later in the UAW's history. In March, 1947, Michigan's Governor Sigler testified before the House Committee on Un-American Activities and accused Thomas, Addes and Leonard of being "Communist captives." Reuther then issued a press release stating in part: "the reactionaries of the country have launched a red-hunt whose ultimate victims are intended to be, not Communists, but all effective labor leaders and labor unions. . ." He said that Governor Sigler's testimony was "an attack upon the entire UAW and the American labor movement."[2]

Shortly afterward the *Wage Earner*, organ of the Association of Catholic Trade Unionists, attacked Reuther's statement: "It seems to us that he [Gov. Sigler] is performing a service to the people of Michigan in exposing a lot of Communist monkey-business. . . ."[3]

Two divergent approaches to the problem of the Communist Party in the unions could here be seen: the ACTU favored government intervention in the unions, while Reuther believed that the government should keep its hands off and that the unions should take care of the CP problem themselves. Of course, the implications of this difference are far larger than the issue itself.

Stalinists if honest progressives in the labor movement carry the fight to them."[4]

It should be noted that Reuther's formula, "Against Outside Interference," could be misleading. If it was meant to signify opposition to the CP fraction, it was legitimate, though obscurely worded. But it could too easily be seized on by those conservative unionists who object to any political discussion in the union or to the participation of any politically minded members of the union. The term "outside" is full of dangerous implications—for have not many of Reuther's *own* ideas come from "outside" the unions?

POLITICS AND "POLITICS"

The antagonism between the two main union factions had been festering for years. During the war it had come to a boil on issues of first importance to the ranks: the proposals of the CP and Addes that the UAW accept piecework and "incentive pay." As discussed in a previous chapter, Reuther opposed piecework and "incentive pay" on the grounds that they destroyed the fundamentals of unionism. By and large, the ranks supported him and his influence among them grew. The antagonism was still further sharpened during the 1945-46 GM strike when the question of socio-economic strategy for a modern trade union was raised by Reuther's "higher wages without higher prices" program.

In 1946 the bitterness between the two scuffling groups was heightened by events outside the union world. After the war the Russians had won significant political victories in Europe, and the morale of the Communist Parties rose everywhere. Concurrently, the period of uncritical adulation of the Russians came to an end, and relations between the Western powers and Russia began to deteriorate. In the union movement, the consequences of this power fissure soon made themselves felt. To the Stalinists, Reuther now seemed the most dangerous enemy, for, unlike the old-style business agents, he really understood what they were up to—and they knew he did. The Stalinists are always most ferocious in suppressing dissidence from the left, which they sense as most dangerous for them.

For years the *Daily Worker* had directed a barrage of fulmination against Reuther. As recently as June, 1948, the Communist Party frankly declared in a resolution on its failures in the UAW, that "Since 1939 our main line has been to weld a progressive coalition of communist and non-communist auto workers to isolate and defeat the Reuther policy and leadership . . ."[5] This CP policy had reached, by 1946, its climax. The CP had made a more or less "left turn," and was again an opposition party, which in the UAW meant: get Reuther. But it was not an easy matter for either side in the UAW faction fight of 1946 to win decisively. The ranks were weary of the petty maneuvering and endless bickering that choked union meetings. They were ready enough to defend democracy in the locals but they were weary of "politicians." Anyone, with almost any point of view, could get up in 1946 at a UAW meeting and win applause by denouncing "politics in the union." It became a ritual for all factions to print denunciations of factionalism in their factional programs.

But the ranks had a point. What they meant by "politics" was careerism, power-bickering, clique-maneuvering. That is, they resented the spectacle of a struggle for power in which there were no clear issues at stake. Yet the Reuther group could win only if it made dramatically clear the *political* as well as the union issues in the UAW fight. It had to use politics—generalized ideas about the union's role in socio-economic life—in order to defeat the opposition's "politics." The workers' suspicion of "politics" was to be used to raise their thinking to a higher level of political consciousness. It was not an easy thing to do.

Reuther organized a faction, not as well disciplined as the CP fraction in the union, but bound together by certain common ideas which were enough to keep it moving. In addition, of course, for many of his supporters among union officials and would-be officials, there was the magnet of jobs. But it would be crude vulgarity to reduce the UAW fight of the 1946-48 period to a mere job hunt, as did some reporters.

The Reuther faction worked on two levels. In the locals it hammered away on the simpler union aspects of the fight; at city-wide factional meetings it discussed these issues in more generalized and political terms. Thus, in Detroit the Reuther faction meetings would have as many as 700 unionists, leaders in the locals and shops, in attendance. There Reuther would patiently explain the nature of Stalinism, the way the CP worked in the unions, and why its rule always meant the end of democracy in a union. In some quarters, this division of emphasis was assailed as undemocratic; Reuther, it was said, was telling the ranks one thing and the secondary leaders another. Actually, he was merely recognizing the existence of varying levels of political consciousness in the union. It would have been as false to ignore the needs of the politically alert members at caucus meetings as it would have been disastrous to ignore the less articulate ones to whom the Reuther program appealed only on a simple trade-union level. Since they can so easily be abused, factions are sometimes dangerous to union democracy. But those that have a fairly clear program, some reason for existence other than ambition for jobs and power, can be a means of clarifying and organizing the discussions held by a union.

In a sense, then, the Reuther group was functioning as a political coalition in the union. But it was open and above-board, responsible only to itself and to its adherents. Its line could not be changed by a cable from the East.

LINEUP OF FORCES

Reuther had succeeded, over the years, in attracting to himself a small group of secondary UAW leaders who formed a kind of semi-personal, semi-political following. Some of these people had, like Reuther, once been in radical politics but had drifted out in the mid-thirties to work in the CIO organizing drives. A much larger stratum of his supporters arose in the union's secondary leadership: the local officials, shop committeemen, and stewards who formed the indispensable base of the Reuther group. During the war some of these secondary leaders had adhered to the short-lived third group which fought against the no-strike pledge, but now they supported Reuther because of his role as leader of the GM strike. Simultaneously, Reuther won the support of a number of political groupings in the union: on the right, some of the conservative leaders who wanted merely to defeat the CP, and the Association of Catholic Trade Unionists

(ACTU)* which saw Reuther merely as a leader in an anti-communist fight; on the left, the anti-Stalinist radicals and socialists of various sorts. This coalition was by no means homogeneous or indestructible, but for the time being it hung together.

In Reuther himself it had a leader increasingly respected by the ranks. He was not an old-line unionist; he was hardly "one of the boys." Yet the very fact that his attitude toward the ranks was somewhat like that of a mentor helped increase his prestige. In the postwar period there was strong dissatisfaction in the union. The GM strike program, discussed in a previous chapter, seemed to the workers a way out—*Reuther's* way out.

Against this array the opposition just did not have enough. It had a majority of the UAW top officers—president R. J. Thomas, vice-president Richard Leonard, sec-

* The Association of Catholic Trade Unionists was first organized in New York City in 1937 as a local group; it became a national organization in 1940. Its major purpose has been, it claims, to propound Catholic doctrine and morality among unionists; its specific role has been to support the more conservative union leaders and to combat both Stalinist and radical influences. In the UAW, it has supported Reuther but quietly opposed his more radical allies. One of ACTU's big triumphs has been in the Transport Workers Union where its specially-trained followers helped defeat a Stalinist machine that had run the union for fourteen years. At present, there are 100 Catholic labor schools, from which 7,500 students graduate each year into the union movement.

In the UAW, ACTU gained prominence through its paper, *The Wage Earner,* which printed "inside information" about the UAW faction fight from 1945 to 1947. ACTU's numerical strength in the UAW is quite small, but its influence stems from the fact that its people are active and articulate, as well as from the union leaders' fear of antagonizing the Catholic Church (or what they take to be its labor appendage). ACTU does not exert the sort of tight and monolithic organizational discipline over its members that the Stalinist movement does (there are seldom, if ever, ACTU caucus meetings), but its members and followers are intellectually disciplined by a rigorous dogma. In each ACTU chapter there is a priest who acts as its "advisor." (CONT'D.)

retary-treasurer George Addes. These leaders were largely committed to orthodox penny-ante unionism, and viewed Reuther's "schemes" with much distrust. (Malicious wags said one reason R. J. Thomas was against the GM strike program was that he couldn't understand it.) Some secondary UAW leaders supporting Addes believed they were following the policies of Philip Murray, for was not Murray's personal antipathy to Reuther the worst-kept secret in the labor movement? Doubtless, too, some of the UAW militants, though certainly only a minority of them, supported Addes.

But central in the anti-Reuther group was the Communist Party. Small though its fraction was, it alone had the political drive and homogeneity to give ideological direction to the group. Over the years, it had entrenched itself in some leading posts (it controlled Local 600 at Ford, the largest in the world) and it had a sizable bloc of votes to deliver to Addes. Not for free, of course. None of

---

Though official ACTU philosophy favors industry-labor "co-operation," individual ACTU members are sometimes militant unionists. Sometimes too, there is a conflict between ACTU members and the Church hierarchy —e.g., when the Church frowned on a teachers' strike in Buffalo in 1948 and ACTU supported the strike; when Cardinal Spellman openly proclaimed himself a strikebreaker during the 1949 New York cemetery-workers' strike and ACTU people in Detroit deplored his attitude.

What of ACTU's general role in the labor movement? ACTU itself says that its purpose is merely "to permeate the unions with that good spirit which should direct them in all their activities."[6] Its intra-union critics charge that ACTU is merely a makeshift for the fundamental policy of the Church: to create separate Catholic unions such as exist in Europe; that it is the agent of an institution which is fundamentally authoritarian in outlook and which came to agreements with fascist states in Europe; and that it sets the precedent of separating workers into religious groupings within the labor movement, thereby creating dangerous sectarian fissures. In any case, with the decline of Stalinist influence and the absence of any large radical influence in the American unions, it seems likely that ACTU strength in the unions will increase during the next few years.

the leaders of the Addes group was a Communist, none accepted the party's totalitarian outlook, but the CP could deliver a large bloc of votes, it could work out clever strategies, it could supply neatly formulated programs, and it even claimed to be pro-Murray, as, in contrast to some of Reuther's radical union proposals, it was.

The issues on which the two sides lined up were simple but basic. A chart readily illustrates the programmatic differences between them:

REUTHER	*ADDES*
Had opposed wartime "incentive pay" and piecework.	Had favored them.
Had supported the GM strike.	Had considered it unwise.
Championed the "GM Strike Program" of "higher wages with no price increases."	Bitterly fought it.
Was anti-CP and proposed to destroy "outside political interference."	Accused Reuther of "red-baiting" on this issue.

These were, so to speak, the "original" issues. As the fight developed, others, of course, arose as well.*

---

* The faction fight in the UAW also created a bitter dispute between the two Trotskyist groups, whose several score members in the UAW wield an influence, because of their militancy and coherent views, far outweighing their numerical strength. Originally, the two groups had split in 1939 over political attitudes toward Russia—the "orthodox" Trotskyists of the Socialist Workers Party favoring "critical defense of the Soviet Union" on the grounds that it was a "degenerated workers' state" and the dissidents of the Workers Party refusing to defend Russia on the grounds that it was a totalitarian state. In the UAW faction fight, the SWP supported the Addes-Stalinist bloc, while the WP (which changed its name in 1949 to Independent Socialist League) supported Reuther. Though small, both groups played a considerable role in several locals in rallying critical support for the two factions.

THE FIRST TEST

As the battle of invective, propaganda, charges and counter-charges flared before the UAW's March, 1946, convention, it soon became clear that the anti-Reuther elements had badly miscalculated. They had begun by expecting easy victory—didn't they have a majority of the union executive board? Wasn't the union apparatus in their control? Weren't Thomas and Addes the two major officials? But they had failed to understand at least three things:

1) The extent to which the Communist Party, their under-the-counter partner, was by now despised in the ranks.

2) The likelihood that the recent internal disturbance in the CP (Browder out, Foster in) would prevent it from giving the political guidance and organizational support that had previously sustained the anti-Reuther coalition.

3) The fact that Walter Reuther had developed into a leader of national consequence, with oratorical talents, organizational skills and popular rapport that far outshone any of his competitors.

Addes was a skilled intra-union politician, but not a figure with mass appeal. Thomas was the fruit of an historical accident and, like most such fruits, beginning to decay; he bumbled, clowned, boasted, wept, cajoled. Addes knew with whom he was traveling politically and understood in his shrewd way what the fight was all about. Thomas seemed to think it was a personal insult when he was told he was playing into the hands of the CP. The modern world was just a little too complex for him.

When they saw that sentiment in the ranks was beginning to turn against them, Addes and Thomas tried to

depreciate Reuther's role in the 1946 GM strike. To gain
support from conservative unionists, they denounced
Reuther for "sacrificing the GM workers in a long, unnecessary strike"; to win the votes of more militant unionists,
they scorned Reuther's "one-at-a-time" strategy, thus im-
plying they were in favor of more "radical" tactics. And
finally they sneered at his "fancy economics" as imprac-
tical, R. J. Thomas especially delighting in mocking at
their intricacies.

The answers the Reuther people gave to these criticisms
were blunt and generally effective. Insisting that the GM
strike had been necessary, they pointed to the 18½-cent
raises won by the Ford and Chrysler workers as proof
that the strike had forced the other corporations into line.
Reuther noted on the "one-at-a-time" matter that his
opponents, although in charge of organization for Ford
and Chrysler, had done nothing to make the isolated
GM strike industry-wide. He further defended the "one-at-
a-time strategy" on grounds of economy: the union simply
didn't have enough money to finance another strike. And
as for the "fancy economics," he challenged Thomas to
debate with him. Thomas had enough sense to refuse.
Finally, the Reuther group pointed out with some acerbity
that the CP-controlled electrical workers had signed a
contract with GM before the end of the strike, for wages
considerably below the UAW demands.

When the 1946 UAW convention opened in Atlantic
City, there began one of the most furious gatherings in
American labor history. Seldom had the union been put
to so severe—and satisfactory—a test. The convention
really took place on two levels: the formal sessions and
the evening caucus meetings. It was not an open-and-shut
convention where all delegates are pre-pledged and speakers go through useless performances. Large groups of

delegates floated between the two camps, some voting with one side on certain issues, some with the other side. At evening caucuses, the two groups tried to convince wavering delegates. These caucuses were not of the "smoke-filled-room" variety, but large meetings in which speakers tried to give motivating explanations for the debates that had taken place during the day.

Reuther seemed to have suffered a severe blow at the convention's opening when Philip Murray virtually endorsed R .J. Thomas for the UAW presidency by declaring: "I have a soft spot in my heart for the big fellow." That the tenderness of Murray's heart was hardly an issue did not matter; his voice swayed votes. Actually, there were reasons more substantial than his uncontainable sentiments which led Murray to support Thomas. Between Murray and Reuther there were serious differences of opinion, and temperamentally Murray found himself closer to "the big fellow" with his simple bluster than to anyone as uneasily "intellectual" as Reuther.

But Reuther soon recouped a good deal of lost ground by challenging R. J. Thomas to debate "at a night session of the convention with the press and public excluded so that no punches need be pulled." (That last phrase was just a bit of fun, since no one, as far as the naked eye could see, was pulling any punches.) Thomas was rescued from this unhappy possibility by the skillful chairman of the convention, George Addes, who quickly discovered a rule that such a proposal would have to carry the convention by a two-thirds majority. The motion fell short by just a few votes.

The convention reached its peaks of excitement at night. Very probably it was at the night caucus meetings that Reuther won his presidency, for there he showed his impressive superiority as a political leader. At the caucuses of the opposition, there was neither a personality as attractive as Reuther's, nor a programmatic slogan as compelling as his GM strike program. The opposition's sessions too quickly exhausted themselves in emotionality, demagogy, and irrelevant cries of "support the CIO!"

When Reuther spoke at his caucus meetings he assumed the role of a political educator, hammering away at the meaning of CP domination of the opposition. As Reuther spoke, one could observe a painful but encouraging intellectual cohesion among his listeners. True, there *was* hoopla and wild talk and demagogy at the Reuther caucus meetings. But in the main these sessions were remarkable for the frequency with which the issues managed to break through the emotion and agitation in which the convention was engulfed.

Reuther won the UAW presidency by a narrow margin of 104 votes.

Then something strange happened. The delegates who had been impressed by the "red-head's" ideas and talents turned around and gave a majority to his opponents on the union's executive board. Addes was re-elected secretary-treasurer and R. J. Thomas and Richard Leonard vice-presidents. Reuther would reign but not rule. Why this strange result? Some said the delegates did not trust any leader very much and wanted to provide a check against any "dictatorial ambitions" Reuther might have. Some felt that the mixed vote showed that the ranks still didn't quite understand the issues at stake in the convention fight. Probably both observations were true.

Only one other event of importance took place at this convention: the election of Emil Mazey as a member of the UAW executive board. Mazey, who had gained prominence as a "firebrand" leader in the UAW, became director of the union's East Side Detroit region. He was to become increasingly important in the UAW in the next few years.

INTERIM SLUGGING

The next year and a half was a nightmare for the UAW. The faction fight raged with a complete lack of restraint, and the bulk of the union's energy was directed to self-agitation. It would be useless and wearying to report in detail on this period, but let us note a few central events:

On April 20, 1946, the *Daily Worker* gleefully reported that a statement on union policy which had not even been shown to Reuther, had been introduced by Addes and Thomas at a meeting of the union's executive board. There was no longer even a pretense of co-operation; majorities were all that counted.

The Reuther forces were later to charge that this resolution was written by the Detroit CP leaders, a matter of interest but small consequence. For no matter who had written the resolution, he had obviously been well trained in the *Daily Worker* school of dialectical composition. At a time when Russia was beginning to swallow half of Europe, the resolution's authors turned their eyes the other way and piously demanded "independence of all colonies." Not so much by what it said, but by what it failed to say, the resolution clearly showed that the CP leaders in auto had reasserted themselves after Browder's expulsion, and were now ready to give some ideological backbone to the Thomas-Addes group.

One of the more clever sections of this resolution denounced "Catholic-baiting, Protestant-baiting, Jew-baiting, Negro-baiting and red-baiting." In other words, when Reuther attacked Nat Ganley, CP leader in the UAW, as an agent of a totalitarian power, he was behaving in the same way as those who indulged in anti-Semitic remarks or practised Jim Crow!

After the executive board meeting, the faction fight entered a period of sustained slugging. Everything that came up at a local meeting—from the election of a sergeant-at-arms to sending members to the UAW summer school—was a factional issue. Philip Murray said the faction fight had "sunk to a level of complete moral degeneracy." Union meetings lasted till all hours of the night, drawn out by endless speeches and wearying motions. In many unions the Stalinists had learned that an effective way to capture control was to prolong meetings till late at night when workers would go home and the hardened core of party followers would remain to "win" the vote.

Each UAW or CIO divisional convention in Michigan became a test of strength. One of the more important of these was the June, 1946, convention of the Michigan CIO. Curiously enough, the representatives from Philip Murray's steel workers, whose natural affinity would seem to be with Reuther, supported the Addes-CP bloc. Apparently, Murray still felt that the Stalinists at the rear of Thomas and Addes were less dangerous or less irksome than Reuther and his clever ideas.

This was the moment of widest divergence between Murray and Reuther. At a meeting of his supporters, Reuther implicitly attacked Murray by saying: "The torch we lit during the General Motors strike was not picked up by the steel workers."[7] For Reuther knew perfectly well that Murray, having thrown a monkey-wrench into the GM strike, would be just as ready to throw one at him. Though relations later improved, and they called each other "Phil" and "Walter," in this one speech Reuther let himself go as a politically-conscious leader and seemed to express something of his inner opinion of Murray's policies. Despite the injudicious intervention of the steel-union delegates, the Reuther supporters won at the Michigan CIO convention.

Reuther's strategy at that time was to approach Murray and dispel his suspicions. Since Murray was becoming worried about the power of the Stalinists in the CIO, he received Reuther's overtures with a new friendliness. Shrewdly, Reuther invited Murray to a meeting of the UAW executive board in October, 1946. Here Murray made his remark about "complete moral degeneracy" and it was clear that in the main he was referring to the anti-Reuther people. With Murray neutral, Reuther would now find his task easier. Furthermore, when at the November, 1946, CIO convention Murray sponsored a resolution which declared that the CIO delegates "resent and reject efforts of the Communist Party or other political parties and their adherents to interfere in the affairs of the CIO,"[8] it was clear that he would henceforth put no major obstacles in Reuther's way.

Early in 1947 the annual UAW local elections were held in the usual factional atmosphere. For the more active unionist, life became a constant round of local caucus meetings, district caucus meetings, city caucus meetings. Tons of literature were printed and passed out in the early hours at factory gates. Each side claimed victories, but the results were inconclusive; the ranks, wary and weary, were waiting. One straw in the wind was that Thomas' slate was defeated in his own local.

But soon attention was deflected from the local elections to a UAW fiasco: the Allis-Chalmers strike in Milwaukee. The strike, led by close followers of the CP, had been dragging on for weeks (it was to last 329 days). Started in April, 1946, it was badly organized and contaminated by damaging political activities. The CP was then bouncing back from Browder's "revisionism" to Foster's "radicalism," and the Allis-Chalmers leader, Harold Christoffel, behaved in an especially wild fashion. He prolonged the strike long after a clear-cut victory was impossible. When Reuther and John Brophy finally went to Milwaukee to patch up the sad situation, the Thomas-Addes group charged that Reuther and Brophy had made a secret deal with the company. (Actually, the company refused to negotiate with Thomas or the local officials, and, as Brophy was to write, "Thomas was thoroughly acquainted with the attitude on the part of the company and assented to our continuing to handle the matter."[9])

Reuther made the Allis-Chalmers affair a key issue in the factional struggle, pointing to it as dramatic evidence of how Stalinism harmed the union movement. He wrote:

> Our failure at Allis-Chalmers was the result of the open interference on the part of the Communist Party in the affairs of the local union involved. This Communist Party interference served to destroy the confidence and loyalty of the workers in the local strike leadership. It gave the vicious management of this company an all too effective weapon to exploit in breaking the strike. Such incidents as the circulation on the picket line of Communist Party petitions on behalf of the party's gubernatorial candidate afforded the company a perfect basis for its propaganda campaign against the union.[10]

In the spring of 1947 came the climax of the faction fight, when the Thomas-Addes group dreamed up a bright proposal. In the CIO there is a small union, of some 35,000 members, called the Farm Equipment Workers Union, whose jurisdiction sometimes touches that of the UAW. Why not, proposed Thomas-Addes, end jurisdictional difficulties by bringing this union into the UAW?

The majority of the UAW executive board immediately voted for unity between the two unions.

It was a clever scheme. The FE was to be an autonomous part of the UAW, its staff to be placed on the UAW payroll, and its members to have 500 votes at the coming UAW convention. That the FE was led by officers strongly under CP influence and ready to vote unto death with the Thomas-Addes group, did not lessen the attractiveness of the merger proposal to Reuther's opponents. And it seemed easy to sell to the membership, for on the face of it unity is always desirable.

A referendum of UAW members was to be held on the proposal. Here again the strategists of the Thomas-Addes group appeared to have schemed cleverly. The referendum would be held in the summer when local meetings are poorly attended and an organized clique can easily push through majority votes. And once the FE was in the UAW, its votes would ensure the defeat of Reuther. The two unions together, shouted the advocates of the merger, could work better against their common enemies, etc. etc. Is Reuther afraid of the FE workers, etc. etc.? All the surface union arguments were on the side of the proponents of merger.

But here the rudimentary political training Reuther had given his followers began to pay off. When he and his supporters emphasized that what counted was not some abstraction called "unity" but rather the specific meaning of this particular unity proposal, when they pointed out that the FE merger proposal was merely a trick to give the opposition a mechanical majority, the ranks, in large measure, understood. Reuther's task was made easier by the over-confidence of his opponents. When Grant Oakes, FE president, made a public slip and admitted that "The merger would set up a powerful unified and *autonomous*

FE division of the UAW . . ."[11] the Reuther spokesmen were able to attack the merger as one which would create a special-privilege group within the UAW, an industrial union. A series of open debates took place on the merger question, the first of which was held on July 11th in Detroit when Reuther debated Addes before 2,500 UAW activists. On a lower level the debate was repeated in all the locals. When the returns were in, the merger proposal had been defeated—two to one. It was clear now that the Reuther group was on the upgrade.

BREAKTHROUGH

As the victory of the Reuther group became more certain, the desperation of its opponents grew wilder. For the Stalinists knew who would suffer most if Reuther won. The publicity material of the opposition became increasingly irresponsible and foul. A few examples:

> Tipped off by some provocateur, Drew Pearson broadcast a rumor that Reuther would run for national office with Senator Taft. Immediately, the story was whisked through the shops. Taft, of course, was something less than popular among unionists, and *what do you think about that goddamned red-head selling out to Taft.* . . . That it was a false rumor, as a minute's check could have shown, did not deter those who hoped to profit from it.

> The opposition published a booklet calling Reuther "The Bosses' Boy."

> Local 45, UAW, of Cleveland, long under pro-Addes leadership, published a special edition of its paper, *Eye-Opener*, charging that Reuther favored the speedup and had spoken to a meeting of Studebaker workers urging them to accelerate production. That Reuther had never said such a thing, that he had never even spoken to a meeting of Studebaker workers in three years—did it matter?

The opposition published a sheet called "FDR" in which a letter purportedly written by Gerald L. K. Smith to his followers was printed.* Smith was supposed to have written:

"This is to warn all key workers in the Nationalist movement to avoid enthusiastic praise of Walter Reuther. He is doing such an excellent job from our viewpoint that any public statement complimentary to him by one of our known leaders might limit his sensational usefulness in curbing the leadership of such men as Thomas, Addes, Sugar and Hillman.

As much as I appreciate his value I am careful never to compliment Mr. Reuther in anything I write or speak. Inside informers tell me that Mr. Reuther is thoroughly alert to the Jewish issue.

Destroy this letter immediately upon reading its contents." [12]

Once this filth was cleared, Reuther won a tremendous victory. R. J. Thomas was defeated in his own local. Ford Local 600, long under Stalinist leadership, gave a majority to Reuther. Even in Detroit's Local 155, long under the domination of Nat Ganley, CP auto leader, the Reuther group won a majority.

The 1947 convention was completely different from the one the year before. Now there was little turbulence, and very little suspense. The night caucus meetings changed the votes of few delegates, for lines had been drawn hard and fast before the convention. Reuther was in, and nothing could stop him—not even, had he so desired, Philip Murray. At this convention the Reuther group reached its peak of self-consciousness, the height of its political cohesion.

Debate on the floor was desultory, routine. When the

* Reuther subsequently filed suit against the publisher of "FDR," Cy Aaron, and named "one Bert Cochran" as also responsible for this "false document" which was "known to be such by the defendant."[13]

Thomas-Addes group, in a desperate espousal of "militancy," proposed that the union not sign the anti-Communist affidavits required by the Taft-Hartley act, the sentiment of the majority of the delegates was neatly expressed by one delegate from Chicago, Willoughby Abner: "Look who's talking militant now. The piecework boys."

Reuther was reelected president with only token opposition. The overwhelming majority of the executive board was composed of his supporters. Emil Mazey, a leading radical in the Reuther group, was chosen as secretary-treasurer, defeating George Addes, who had held the post for eleven years. Two of Reuther's more conservative supporters, John Livingston and Richard Gosser, were elected vice-presidents.

The daily press hailed the elections as a victory of the "right wing" over the "left wing." But what did these words mean in the UAW? Who was the "left wing"—the Stalinists who had supported piecework and speedup during the war, or the Reuther people who had been against it? Actually, if the terms meant anything at all, it was within the Reuther group that there was a genuine left: trade unionists, who while opposed to Russian totalitarianism, are militant and inclined to radical politics.

In a speech at the end of the convention, Reuther said: "If the editorial writers . . . are inclined to write that the UAW and the leadership in this convention are drifting toward a more conservative policy, I say to those editorial writers they are wrong, because this convention and its leadership is committed to the kind of militant, fighting trade-union program that will mobilize not only our union but the people in America in support of an aggressive overall economic, social and political program. . . ."[14]

Emil Mazey was blunt enough about his views. He said

that he had certain differences with Reuther from the left and that he was "a dues-paying member of the Socialist Party."[15]

In any case, the first part of the Reuther group's history was at an end. It had gambled on the idea that the Communist Party could be defeated in a trade union not by repression but by exposure; not by turning to reaction but by more consistent and aggressive militancy; not by shouting "red" but by showing the totalitarian strings to which the CP danced; not by high-echelon maneuvering but by going to the rank and file to debate issues. And it had won. The question now arose before one's mind: what would be done with the victory?

8 --

W H A T the Reuther group will ultimately do with its victory, it is still too early to say. Very probably, no definitive answer to that question will be possible until the UAW is forced to face a domestic economic crisis, if one occurs, within the next few years. In the meantime, however, certain signs can be noted.

As a militant trade union, the UAW has retained its position of leadership in the American labor movement. In each of the major postwar wage disputes, the UAW set the dominant pattern for the CIO. In the spring of 1948, six months after the Reuther forces took control of the union, there arose the crucial problem of a "third round" of wage increases. For the labor movement as a whole, this was a period of gloom and retreat. Philip Murray had called President Truman a strikebreaker for his handling of the railroad strike. Relations between the CIO and the White House were, as the official phrase goes, strained. The Taft-Hartley leadership in Congress seemed power-

ful and self-confident. A sixty-seven-day strike of packinghouse workers ended in defeat, with pickets subjected
to violence of the kind that aroused memories of pre-CIO
days. John L. Lewis was ensnarled in injunction proceedings, which he could neither defy nor quash. The steel
workers' union, bound by a two-year contract which Murray had voluntarily negotiated, seemed helpless before Big
Steel's insistence that wages not be raised. And as of early
1948, there was no sign of any halt in the rise of the cost
of living. To the auto workers, this last, of course, was
most important of all.

These were the signs of what political analysts called a
"postwar swing to the right." The unions were stuck in a
deep sandtrap: though their antagonists in industry and
Washington were on the offensive, the men in the shops,
spurred by daily economic needs, grumbled for a third
wage round. For a militant union like the UAW, in which
the men expect yearly gains, this situation was particularly trying.

The tension and anxiety felt by the active strata of the
UAW members was deeply aggravated by the attempted
assassination of Walter Reuther on April 20, 1948. Reuther
was so badly wounded that he would obviously be in-
capacitated for some time. To the UAW people this
seemed a severe blow. Still, negotiations with Chrysler
had to be continued; negotiations with GM for a new
contract had begun in March. The general retreat of labor,
together with the attempted assassination of Reuther,
seemed then sufficient cause for the UAW to pull back,
at least temporarily.

Sensitive to every fluctuation of mood among their employees, the auto corporations felt that for once they had
the union on the run. Negotiations between the UAW and
GM and Chrysler were purely routine, since it was clear

that the corporations had no intention of granting any concessions. The company officials calculated that the men in the shops would be affected by the demoralization then sweeping the entire labor movement, and consequently believed that the union would not dare to call strikes. One Chrysler official referred to the workers in his plant as "dumb clucks" and later took no particular pains to deny having made the remark.

In the long see-saw battle between corporation and union, it has always been possible to sense the power relationship between the two sides simply by noting their manner, their aura of self-confidence or hesitation, before and during negotiations. And now it seemed that the corporations were on top and might stay there. But they quite underestimated the power of the UAW activists, as well as the eagerness of the new Reuther leadership to prove itself by gaining good contracts. In Reuther's absence, Emil Mazey became acting president and spokesman of the union.

Mazey is not a dramatic public figure; he lacks Reuther's flair for public statement and controversy; he is not so sophisticated in handling public relations; and he is not at all so effective a speaker as Reuther. Mazey has been a quite different kind of union leader: a radical who believed, above all, in militancy. His smooth and well-groomed appearance and his gentle manner are quite deceptive; they hide a toughness in strike struggle that the more intellectualized Reuther can seldom achieve. Mazey has been active in the labor movement since 1933 when, barely over twenty years of age, he led an Unemployed Citizens League campaign to help striking auto workers. In 1934 he was fired by the Gulf Refining Company, where he had begun a unionization drive, and in 1935 by the Rotary Electric Steel Company, for the same reason. Early in 1936, when he was working in Briggs, Mazey joined the UAW, and was soon fired; later in the year he became a union organizer. For five terms he served as president of the Briggs local, probably the most militant and hectic in the UAW. He remained in the Socialist Party long after Reuther quit it, since he is, by nature and training, a rebel against the social status quo— less the intellectual socialist than the aggressive, "class-conscious" unionist who has come to a general socialist view through years of labor activity. When the powerful flying squadrons from the Briggs local tangled with the Michigan police during the past thirteen years, Mazey was usually in the thick of the fighting. During the war he served as an army sergeant and later was a leader in the GI demobilization demonstrations in the Philippines.

Since becoming a top UAW leader, Mazey has followed a political course somewhat disappointing to some of his union associates who had hoped he would be the aggressive spokesman for a more militant and radical wing of the Reuther group. In early 1949, at least, Mazey was hardly such a spokesman. Whether his new reticence was the result of the "stabilization" in office which sometimes tempts radical unionists or due to a feeling that a fight for more militant views in the UAW would leave him isolated in the leadership and without sufficient support in the ranks, it is difficult to say. In the 1948 negotiations, however, his instinctive union militancy found a natural outlet.

Soon after becoming the acting UAW president, Mazey gave a number of talks to the secondary leaders. His approach was simple: "If we can't get a wage increase now, in a period of capitalist prosperity, when can we? The corporations can afford it, and we're going to get it. We're not going to be like some other unions; we know how to fight." These ideas began to catch on in the ranks, as they were spread there by the stewards and local leaders; soon a more vigorous spirit could be observed among the workers.

While preparing to come to grips with the Chrysler corporation, the UAW leaders, including the usually conservative Chrysler director, Norman Mathews, took a step that dramatized their intention of reversing the labor movement's drift of retreat. The Michigan state legislature had passed the Bonine-Tripp law, known as the "Little Taft-Hartley Act," which required a vote of all shop employees, union and non-union, under state mediation board auspices, on an employer's last offer to the union in negotiations. Then, if the men rejected that offer, another vote would be held on whether to strike. Arguing that it was an unconstitutional violation of workers' liberties and union rights, the UAW conspicuously ignored this law and took its own secret strike votes when it prepared to shut down Chrysler.

When the Chrysler corporation offered a wage increase of six cents an hour, it helped rally the UAW ranks for the forthcoming strike. For the men felt that the corporation's meager offer indicated that with struggle more might be had; at the same time, the offer was insufficiently attractive to induce a mood of compromise. On May 12th the men walked out. A few days later there was a skirmish with the police at Highland Park, which showed, if nothing else, that the UAW could still run pugnacious picket lines.

Meanwhile, negotiations with GM were completely stalled. To break this impasse, T. A. Johnstone, acting as director of the UAW's GM department in Reuther's absence, announced that "Our members will not trespass on GM property after May 28," the day the old contract was terminated. This Lewis-like flourish signified that the UAW—at a time when the rest of the labor movement was either in retreat or marking time—was challenging two of the auto industry's Big Three. The UAW leadership knew that the union's future, and certainly its own prestige, largely depended on its ability to wring concessions from the companies.

GM was the first to retreat—though, some unionists thought, in a very clever manner. Seeing that the Chrysler strike was successful and faced with the possibility of a major strike only two years after the 113-day walkout of 1946, GM reversed the national industry pattern by suddenly offering wage increases totalling 11 cents an hour. The contract the UAW signed with GM in 1948 has aroused so much discussion in the labor movement that it warrants a close analysis.

GM granted a six-cent basic wage increase immediately and another three-cent increase effective May, 1949, as a "standard of living annual improvement." In the eyes of the union, these nine cents represented labor's share, albeit an inadequate share, of the fruits of technological progress and the consequent increased productivity per worker.

A more controversial clause in the GM contract was the so-called escalator clause, according to which wages would be increased one cent per hour each time the Bureau of Labor Statistics cost of living index showed a 1.14 rise in the cost of living. In the event of a price decline, the decrease in wages was limited to five cents per hour below the wage level of May 29, 1948. This clause of the contract, proposed as a five-year provision by C. E. Wilson, GM president, caught the union leadership by surprise; after brief hesitation, it accepted the clause, though only for two years. In the UAW itself there had been considerable discussion about the escalator idea, Walter Reuther having recently opposed it in a debate with union oppositionists in Flint. Its proponents had based themselves on the experience of the CIO Oil Workers Union which had won substantial automatic wage increases in the postwar period as a result of such a clause.

In deciding which position to take with regard to the escalator clause, the UAW leadership had to make a quick estimate of the likely development of the postwar economy. Certainly, if Marshall Plan expenditures continued, if military spending mounted, if production remained near the war peak, the outlook was for a high price level, perhaps even for one continuing to rise in an inflationary trajectory. In that event, the escalator clause would serve to protect the workers' standard of living. As prices fluctuated, so would wages—and workers would not suffer from minor movements either way. If prices increased steadily, so would wages. If prices decreased, wages could drop only five cents below the May 29th level. Hence, if prices took a big drop, the workers would win a genuine gain in purchasing power. In any case, the GM escalator clause would be a good gamble for the union—if a gamble at all. From the corporation point of view, the clause was also valuable. The corporation apparently counted on a relative stabilization of prices and, desiring labor peace for the coming period, felt that slight wage increases occasioned by slight price increases would be preferable to strikes. For now that a buyers' market was in sight, no corporation looked forward to a strike in 1949—and it was really with regard to 1949 that the escalator clause had any meaning.

Once GM decided to make concessions to the union, Chrysler also had to. It raised its ante to a thirteen-cent-an-hour flat wage increase, which the UAW accepted; the strike ended on May 29th. Soon afterwards the Ford workers obtained a thirteen-cent-an-hour wage increase, although the company had previously proposed a cut to the union. Trailing behind but pleased to take advantage of the UAW's militancy, the steel workers' union found itself the recipient of a similar pay increase, which the steel corporations announced without even formally negotiating with Philip Murray.

In September, 1948, a three-cent hourly wage increase for 270,000 GM employees under the escalator provision was taken as a matter of course, but in February, 1949, when the cost of living index dropped sufficiently to result in a two-cent-an-hour wage cut, the GM contract again became nation-wide news. Throughout 1949 Reuther's factional opponents inside the union tried to make capital out of this wage cut, but they failed to win many converts. UAW members had not forgotten that these same oppositionists had, in 1948, either voted approval of the GM contract to which they now objected, or had been against any strike action at the time. It is still too early to offer a final assessment of the escalator clause, but there seems little reason to oppose it, the two-cent wage cut notwithstanding. If a recession sets in, the GM workers will lose five of the original eight cents obtained as a cost-of-living bonus, but their six-cent basic increase will still be retained; in the meantime, prices will fall. If inflation continues, the escalator clause will provide protection.

One voice in the union movement has recently been raised against the GM contract. David McDonald, secretary-treasurer of the steel workers' union, has said: "I am, with all the vigor, disdain, condemnation and disgust I am able to muster, opposed to the terms of the contract recently negotiated between the CIO and the General Motors Corporation." This contract "means that if a worker's take-home pay allows him enough money to buy one loaf of bread this year, this time next year his purchasing power will still be only one loaf of bread. He will be forced to remain, along with the peon on the Chile pampas and the rickshaw driver in China, a motionless entity on the economic ladder of life."[1] Leaving aside the silly comparison with the peons and rickshaw drivers, it is clear that McDonald's statement, quite typical of the thinking (or lack of it) of run-of-the-mill union leaders, is based on a misunderstanding of the GM contract. There is nothing in that contract or in the UAW position on wage increases which will prevent the union from fighting to raise the *base wage* from which rates go up or down in accordance with fluctuations in the cost of living. McDonald's statement comes with particularly poor grace from one whose leader, Murray, failed to support the UAW in its 1946 fight for higher wages without price increases, and also received a 1948 "gift" in wage increases largely due to the UAW's struggle. It is significant, however, as a sign of potential divergence in the CIO.

By mid-1949, the GM contract was almost forgotten in the UAW, as preparations were made for a fall campaign to win new security provisions for the auto workers. The union has come increasingly to realize that while wages remain one of its major points of interest, the wage-price vicious cycle forces it to reinforce its economic struggle with a number of other demands. (Nathan Weinberg, UAW economist, has estimated that for all factory workers to regain the purchasing power they had at the beginning of 1945 a 30 percent wage increase would be necessary in 1949. The fight against inflation had largely been lost once the GM strike program of 1946 failed to carry.)

For coming negotiations with the corporations, the UAW has prepared a demand of a $100-a-month pension for workers over sixty years of age. There are an estimated 75,000 such men in the industry. This time the major battle will be with Ford. In 1947 the Ford corporation had offered its employees a pension plan, which they rejected in favor of a flat wage increase largely because the Ford plan placed too heavy a share of the financing on the workers, the pinch of inflation made cash increases seem more attractive, and there was no provision for union participation in its operation. But, in the opinion of the UAW, the important thing is that Ford has already publicly recognized its responsibility for a pension plan. Again using its "one-at-a-time" strategy, the UAW hopes that Ford's reluctance to face a long strike at a time when competition among the auto companies is increasingly sharp, will result in the acceptance of the UAW pension plan.

Worried by the UAW's plan, the Ford corporation has announced that "a wage increase in 1949 might mean a loss of jobs" and that "no pension plan could be set up without a pay cut." After having laid off a large number of older maintenance workers, the Ford company sought to maneuver the Reuther leadership into an unfavorable position. "There is only one way to pay for a pension plan . . . for our customers to pay for it in higher prices . . ."[2] Here again the problems raised by the GM strike program reappear. The Ford company was obviously either fishing for a deal with the UAW whereby pensions will result in sanctioned price increases or is trying to justify in advance any price increases which it might impose to avoid financing the plan out of current profits.

Reuther has further added to his problems by announcing that GM will be asked this year for pensions and death and hospital insurance. Undoubtedly, demands will also be made on Chrysler. There is thus good reason to believe that in the second half of 1949 severe conflicts may break out in the auto industry. As many times before, the rest of the CIO doesn't mind letting the UAW assume the brunt of the struggle.

In the meantime, a series of wildcat strikes has been breaking out in the auto industry. During the first four months of 1949 nearly 200,000 auto workers were involved in wildcats—among other plants, at Briggs, Chrysler, Hudson, Ford, Dodge, Plymouth, Bendix, and Flint Fisher. These wildcats were due to speedups which, the union charged, had made working conditions intolerable. For the UAW, however, they represented a serious problem and threatened to upset its entire 1949 wage-and-pension strategy. While realizing that it had to back up the Ford workers who voted to strike against speedup, the UAW feared that if strikes broke out over this issue it would be extremely difficult to use the strike method again, if necessary, in the pension struggle later in the year. The UAW was thus in danger of being maneuvered into a defensive fight at precisely the time it was planning an offensive.* Simultaneously, the UAW was carrying on a guerrilla war with several other CIO unions. A number of

---

* In the Detroit Ford plants a three-week strike broke out in May, 1949. It was provoked by the Ford management which apparently hoped that a strike on the speedup issue would weaken the union in the later struggle over pensions. The UAW leadership feared that this strike might be strategically unwise, but had to accede to the demands of the workers that it be called. At the time of writing, the strike's outcome seems inconclusive and its possible effect on pension negotiations uncertain. A strike vote is being held in all Ford plants, in preparation for the big clash between Ford and the UAW that will probably take place in the fall of 1949.

locals of the CIO United Electrical Workers Union which opposed its communist leadership left it in disgust and affiliated themselves with the UAW. Because the UE leaders refused to sign the Taft-Hartley non-communist affidavits, UE locals had run into considerable difficulties. Anti-communist locals were also harassed by the UE leadership. There was therefore considerable truth to the UAW claim that it was not "raiding" the UE but was merely providing shelter to workers who could no longer tolerate its leadership

In the altercations between the UAW and the Farm Equipment Workers Union, CIO, the UAW had a rather less admirable record. At the 1948 CIO convention Philip Murray ordered the small, Stalinist-influenced Farm Equipment union to dissolve itself into the UAW. Pleading organizational autonomy, the FE refused. Thereupon the UAW, through its own farm equipment division led by vice-president John Livingston, began a campaign to take over the FE's shops. In Moline, Illinois, where there are both UAW and FE locals, a fierce battle broke out in February, 1949, in which 250 workers from FE shops attacked forty-five UAW organizers. The great bulk of FE members are certainly not Stalinists, and the fact that they have rejected the UAW would seem to indicate that the UAW campaign to absorb them has been poorly conducted. The UAW appeal to FE workers, molded by the conservative and unimaginative Livingston has been largely "red-baiting" and a call to "loyalty to the CIO." Neither of these appeals is likely to inflame workers with passion for joining the UAW. Unless the UAW develops a more democratic and attractive program for asking members of the FE to join the UAW, it will be open to the charge that it is merely raiding a weaker union.

HOUSES BY THE MILLION

In the spring of 1949 Walter Reuther announced another of his ambitious plans, this one for mass-produced, cheap housing. As usual with Reuther's plans, it was both an immediate economic proposal and a statement of his social philosophy. In this chapter, the plan will be considered largely as an economic proposal.

Testifying before the Senate Banking Committee on February 14th, Reuther urged that idle aircraft plants be utilized to produce 20,000,000 low-priced pre-fabricated houses. According to Reuther, the millions of feet of idle floor space in airplane plants could be used for assembly-line production of houses. The project would cost $120,000,000,000 over a sixty-year period.

As he usually does in his plans, Reuther suggested that private enterprise backed by government finances be given the first opportunity to carry out this program. But since private industry has thus far shown remarkable reluctance to invest in large-scale low-rent housing, the Reuther plan envisages the intervention of the government directly to produce the houses if and when sufficient private capital is shown to be unavailable.

Reuther subsequently estimated that if all possible mass-production economies were realized, a two-bedroom house with all functional equipment could be manufactured to sell for about $6,000. Twenty million of such houses would cost $120,000,000,000, but since there would also be matching expenditures in utility expansion, ground clearance, construction of streets and sewage facilities the total cost would come to $240,000,000,000. The plan, it is estimated, would result in 1,000,000 new jobs, few of them competitive with the work currently done by AFL craft building-trade unions. Reuther also said that assembly-line manufacturing would not necessarily result in complete standardization of houses, and that as much lee-way in their appearance might be possible as is now had in the manufacture of automobiles. The problem of stand-ardization of appearance (one imagines a country with everyone living in the same kind of box) has apparently not yet been adequately solved by the authors of the plan, for it is obviously necessary to have greater diversity of construction in housing than in automobiles.

While it would be impossible for anyone not an eco-nomic or production expert to pass judgment on the tech-nical aspects of Reuther's plan, it does have the merits of dramatizing a serious social problem. Reuther's housing program would be too large in scope, requiring too consid-erable a co-ordination of financial and productive facili-ties, to be undertaken by competitive industrial units. The plan helps to underline the irrationality of a situation in which there is a great need for mass, low-cost housing while productive capacities that might be used to satisfy that need remain idle.

At present there seems little likelihood that Reuther's plan will receive serious consideration in Washington, and therefore discussion of some of its implications must seem slightly academic. But what is involved is more than a mere plan; it is a way of looking at American life. It is therefore interesting to question Reuther's apparent as-sumption that the plan could be carried out by private industry, even if it were government financed. (Of course, it is quite possible that Reuther does not really believe private industry could do this, but has put that provision in his plan for reasons of public polity—we do not know, we merely raise the possibility.) For his plan would re-quire at least as great, and probably greater government regulation of industry than existed during the war—a situation American business would resist to the most bitter end. Because of the highly competitive nature of the building industry, and because of the large amount of overall top planning of material priorities, plant allocations, production directives and schedules that would be necessary, the plan might well result in economic wastefulness if undertaken by private industry. There is therefore some grounds for the conservative suspicion that it leads, willy-nilly, to government production of houses— the desirability of which depends, of course, on one's larger social views.

Another important aspect of the Reuther housing plan is that, in effect, it is an attempt to develop a scheme from the liberal point of view whereby the U.S. can have its cake and eat it too—that is, can spend immense amounts of money for both armaments and social services. (To justify a housing program even partly in terms of war preparations is a dubious procedure; housing is a social need regardless of its relation to armament production.) Reuther's scheme is based on the assumption that what the U.S. military program requires is not a large accumulation of armaments that may soon become obsolete, but rather a plant geared to rapid conversion to war production which, in the meantime, can serve civilian needs. If nothing else Reuther's scheme is extremely ingenious. It raises the general problem of the relation of such unions as the UAW to an economy increasingly based on armament production—a problem which it will be advantageous to discuss in greater detail in the last chapter of this book.

Walter Reuther, a Portrait

9

AS THE story of the UAW moves further along into the late forties, the name of Walter Reuther becomes increasingly intertwined with it, and increasingly important in American affairs as a whole. It therefore becomes necessary, at this point, to look into his career, his mind and his personality. What are his motivating ideas? What influences molded his mind and character? What is his relationship to American life?

The strongest individual influence on Walter Reuther's personality and thought has undoubtedly been his father, Valentine, a man who devoted most of his life to the rising American labor movement. From his father, a German emigree who had come to America to escape political persecution, Valentine Reuther inherited a strong strain of Lutheran feeling: a binding sense of duty and a belief that life had to be guided by strong moral pointers. (Valentine's father is said to have remarked once that churches try to do too much for God and not enough for men.) Valentine Reuther's political thought was shaped by a blend of influences: the German Social Democratic tradition and the American movements of rebellion in the early 1900's, populism and Debsian socialism. At the age of twenty-three he became president of the Ohio Valley Trades and Labor Assembly—a post which then entailed more risks than honors. When his second son, Walter, was born on Labor Day eve of 1907, Valentine Reuther was working in a Wheeling, West Virginia, brewery for $1.50 a day and running the local union.

Valentine Reuther was a socialist and a friend of Eugene V. Debs; he ran for Congress on the party ticket. He was a man capable of large and generous social feelings; he passionately believed in progress and educational "improvement"; his whole approach to life was direct and active. In recent years it has become fashionable to sneer at the era in which Valentine Reuther's ideas were formed, the era of Debs and Bryan. And in truth, if one had to define precisely the ideas of Valentine Reuther, it might be difficult to do so, for the people who admired Debs and Bryan were more adept at releasing enthusiasms and indignations than at formulating ideas. They were characterized by social rebelliousness, a deep feeling for the down-trodden and a ready faith in the possibilities of social amelioration—attitudes a later, more sophisticated generation cannot afford to pass by with a shrugged shoulder.

Valentine Reuther spent many hours supervising the education of his sons. On Sunday afternoons he would arrange impromptu debates and discussions on the issues agitating the 1920's, and train his sons to think of problems quite beyond the intellectual range of the usual American boy. As in so many other immigrant families, the younger generation was prodded to intellectual activity by the parents' passion for education and "improvement"—an experience a boy in a more established and secure American family might not have had. Even the

Reuther family's recreation was often tied in with the labor movement: union picnics on Wheeling Island and socials at the union hall. In its internal organization, the Reuther family was marked by typical German immigrant cleanliness and orderliness. It was in this kind of atmosphere—intensely serious, politically self-conscious, socially extroverted—that Walter Reuther grew up. With the passage of years, he has seen fit to discard or modify parts of the intellectual training he received, but even if he would wish to he could not so easily abandon its motivating passions.

Before he had completed his third year at Wheeling High, Walter Reuther had to quit school to take a job and help support the often struggling family. For three years he worked as an apprentice toolmaker at Wheeling Steel's corrugating plant, where his older brother Ted (the only one who never went into the labor movement) already had a job. Top wages at Wheeling for his kind of work were then forty cents an hour. Reuther, soon restless, gagged at the idea of working on Sundays. His political father had taught him it was a day for reading and discussion, his religious mother that it was a day for prayer. We need not imagine that Reuther's only motives were those absorbed from his parents; perhaps he just wanted to rest or have a good time on Sunday. In any case, he tried to organize the shop in protest against Sunday work, and was fired for his pains. Jobless, without any visible economic future in Wheeling, the young Reuther left for Detroit where, he had heard, there was work to be found in the factories. In 1930 his younger brother, Victor, joined him and later Roy, the third Reuther to become active in the UAW, came to Detroit.

In the late 1920's Detroit was an open-shop city, with

the insipid AFL craft unions a mere fringe along the life of the auto workers. Reuther worked for several of the big companies, breaking in as a tool-and-die maker. First, he worked a thirteen-hour night shift at Briggs for eighty-five cents an hour, and then he brazened his way into Ford where he received $1.10 an hour as a tool-and-die man. The impressionable young radical saw enough of the life of the auto workers to convince him that unionism was a burning necessity; it was his central conviction, and he has retained it throughout his life.

But, while deeply interested in and sympathetic with the workers, Reuther did not intend to remain a worker for the remainder of his life. Nudged by the intellectual curiosities and ambitions he had acquired at home, he resumed his education, first at high school and later at night sessions in Wayne University, known as Detroit's poor man's college. In those days of depression, when radicalism was popular in the colleges, Reuther organized a Social Problems Club at Wayne, which led a campaign against an attempt to install an ROTC unit on the campus and also joined in a number of Detroit's labor struggles.

In 1932 Reuther was attracted to the Socialist Party, which was then experiencing a considerable growth after its sharp decline in the twenties; it recruited hundreds of young workers and students who held radical views but were antagonized by the Stalinists. In the 1932 presidential campaign, when the socialists made their most considerable electoral effort since Debs' great campaigns, Reuther was an active soapboxer for Norman Thomas, whom he had met and come to admire.* Like other young

* It is an amusing comment on Reuther's career that a recent biographical sketch released by the UAW does not mention this well-known participation in the socialist movement . . . as if it were some youthful indiscretion that had best be passed over in silence.

socialists of the time, Reuther considered himself a left-wing socialist, which meant in part one who admired "the Russian experiment." Though no definitive date is available, Reuther is believed to have remained in the Socialist Party until 1938.

In 1933 Reuther was fired from the Ford plant for union activity, and found it difficult, at the peak of the depression, to get another job. Rather than consume the several hundred dollars he and Victor had saved, they decided to leave both Detroit and the depression behind them and take a hand-to-mouth world tour. Such a rather bold and imaginative step reveals a great deal about these two young men; still in their early twenties, aflame with radical ideas, eager for new experiences, they set off on their own version of the grand tour that so many Americans had taken before them. But with what a difference in purpose and method!

Of all the countries they were to visit in Europe, only England had a semblance of political order; there they saw the auto plants, the textile mills and the coal pits. On the Continent they took bicycle tours, spending nights in farmhouses and in cheap hotels. They came to Berlin twenty-four hours before the Reichstag fire and inspected its ruins; they lived with some anti-Nazi students, a few of whom they helped smuggle into Switzerland; and they visited their mother's home town where they saw a young worker horribly beaten by Nazis whom he had dared to challenge. Germany had nothing but terror and fear to offer them; they moved eastward.

For sixteen months the Reuther brothers worked in an auto plant near the city Gorki, built for the Russian government by the Ford Company. They mingled with workers of many nationalities, among them American construction workers who lived at *Amerikanski Pasholik*.

Walter Reuther became a leader of a brigade of sixteen workers, and won bonuses for his production ideas; he wrote articles in Moscow's English-language papers giving suggestions on how to improve production.

It can hardly be doubted that the Reuthers were then extremely sympathetic to the Russian regime, as were also a great many non-communist radicals and liberals. As it happened, they were living in Russia at a time when the terror of the Stalin dictatorship was at its height, but reports of this terror were then extremely sparse and the last place in the world they were likely to reach was the city of Gorki. The enthusiasm of the Reuthers in 1933 and 1934 for the Russian regime was based on the misconception that some sort of genuine socialism was being built or would shortly be built in Russia; once the truth became known, this enthusiasm was quickly dispelled.

For years later Reuther was to be plagued by a letter dated Jan. 21, 1934, and signed by Victor and himself, though probably written by Victor, in which they lavishly praised the Russian regime. Victor Reuther has since claimed that parts of the letter are forged, though he has not specified which parts. The letter has been read into the Congressional Record by a Congressman wishing to show how dangerous a radical Reuther is, has been used by inter-union factional opponents, and has been picked up by magazines eager to paint a gaudy picture of Reuther. But anyone who was familiar with the socialist movement of the thirties knows that the Reuther brothers were merely the victims of a then-prevalent uncritical enthusiasm for the Stalin regime.

After leaving Russia, the Reuthers went to India, there to watch its movement for national independence, and then spent two months in Japan, there to see the growth of militarism. No one could have asked for a more direct education in modern realities, and no one was to need it more than these young men soon to lead the largest union in America. They saw every social tendency of our time, and if in the future they might prove inadequate to their responsibilities, they could hardly plead ignorance. History had been thrust into their faces, its lessons scrawled in blood before their eyes.

YEARS OF STRUGGLE

When Walter Reuther returned to America, he again went to work in a Detroit shop. The men in the factories were restive; talk of union was in the air. Still very young, Walter Reuther already enjoyed more than the usual range of intellectual and political vision, certainly far more than that of the average union organizer. His experience near and in the socialist movement had taught him how to organize vague notions into precise propositions. (Whatever his later depreciation of that experience, it had been one of the major formative influences in his life.) His travels had shown him that America, for all its ease and wealth, could not forever escape the social crises that were tearing Europe. And as his thought crystalized and his ambitions expanded, his personality became more assertive: he learned that he could throw his weight around in the shops, he tested his growing power to persuade men. Walter Reuther discovered that he was blessed with one of the rarest of human gifts: he was a natural leader.

Reuther threw himself into the campaign to organize the auto workers. As a member of the Ternstedt local, he rapidly became known throughout Detroit as a union leader and was blacklisted in most of the auto plants. As a volunteer organizer in 1937, he set up a tiny office at Twenty-fourth and Michigan Avenues, and began the wearisome job of amalgamating the scattered and puny West Side UAW locals into one big local. Within a year the West Side Local's membership rose from seventy-eight to 30,000. Reuther played a leading role in the Detroit and Flint sitdown strikes. He was in the forefront of the 1937 drive to organize Ford, and gained national fame as one of the men who was severely beaten by Ford Servicemen in the "battle of the overpass." In 1938 his house was invaded by thugs who again severely beat him; Reuther claimed they were in the employ of the Ford Service Department.

The prevalent image of Reuther in recent years has been that of a brainy young fellow, quick-witted and quick-tongued, who wins his fights in debates and meetings. But it must be remembered that before having reached this relatively luxurious status, Reuther had to spend a good many years doing the dangerous dirty work that goes into building a union. The "red-head" was as ready as the next man, perhaps more so, to go out and risk his neck—and in the mid-thirties you did risk your neck in union work.

As he rose in the UAW, Reuther must for a time have felt—here we can only speculate—that his political opinions and his new role as leader did not conflict. But sometime between 1936 and 1938 there seems to have arisen in his mind an acute awareness that, since the socialist movement showed no signs of growth and his participation in it might inhibit the free and easy maneuvering he felt union leadership to require, he would soon have to choose between the two. Either the lonely rectitude of radical politics or full participation in the union world, with doctrine straggling as best it could behind power and prestige—that seems to have been his choice.*

But to put it so bluntly is to indicate that he never hesitated in making his choice. All the evidence shows that Reuther was by now so deeply immersed in the union world that he did not hesitate a moment to abandon his political ties. He felt that those socialists who wished to exert an immediate, substantial influence on American life would have to abandon their party and its doctrines and join the New Deal parade. He chose power, with the hope that power would then enable him to convey his vision to millions of people; but, asked his critics, what would be the value and meaning of that power if achieved by at least the partial sacrifice of vision? It was an old question and in one form or another it is still being debated today; it was a question that particularly disturbed many of Walter Reuther's generation.

In any case, Reuther became a national figure. He saw to it that there arose a public image of himself which is far different from that of the usual labor leader. He once remarked that if labor leadership merely meant winning six cents more an hour for his members, it would hardly interest him. In every public act, he shrewdly arranged to give the impression of a man whose imagination could

---

* Reuther's decision to leave the Socialist Party was partly based on a disagreement with it on Michigan electoral policy. In 1938 he felt it was necessary for unionists to support Governor Frank Murphy, a New Dealer, for re-election, while the party inclined to running its own candidate. Reuther offered to resign from the SP rather than place it and him in the embarrassing position of having two contrary policies followed by socialists in the UAW. Norman Thomas asked Reuther's associates to urge him not to resign, since a resignation could only be interpreted as a hostile act. Since, at the time, Reuther disagreed with but did not feel hostile to the Socialist Party, he postponed his resignation until the end of the Homer Martin faction fight. Apparently, there was not much bitterness on either side when the separation came.

not be contained by his limited status. "Pure and simple" trade unionism he dropped once and for all.

The talents he showed in these years were amazing. He learned how to build a powerful machine inside the union and to compete for public attention with such schemes as "the Reuther plan." He learned how to make himself the symbol of aggressive leadership to the union's members while at the same time delicately balancing between sections of his supporters. He learned how to sense the moods of his supporters—and to anticipate them. He became a first-rate speaker and leader, the only union official of his generation who succeeded in capturing the public imagination.

Once he had broken with the socialists, Reuther did not develop an explicit, tightly formulated political point of view. To his more radical supporters in the union, he would sometimes imply that at heart he remained a socialist, and that while his exposed public position prevented him from going as far as he might like, he still would place no impediments in their way. Nonetheless, as a public figure, Reuther aligned himself with what might be called the "left-wing New Dealers." This group, represented by such figures as Leon Henderson, Arthur Schlessinger, Jr., and Senator Hubert Humphreys, feels that the sharp opposition "capitalism-socialism" is unrealistic in America at the present time, and that what is necessary is a series of New Deals, each going a step further than its predecessor in the direction of social reform. The economy envisaged by this group would be of a "mixed" kind: partly privately owned, partly statefied—not too different, that is, from the sort being constructed in England by the Labor Party government. The strategy proposed by this group has been to work within the framework of the Democratic Party in order to "liberalize" it and eventually gain control of it.

Now whether Reuther completely agrees with such people as Henderson and Humphreys or merely feels it necessary to work along with them for a time, it would be difficult to say. The point at which Reuther diverges from the left New Dealers is where the force of his own personal tradition occasionally reasserts itself and where pressures from the union influence his behavior. He is certainly not a revolutionary; the remark of George Romney, auto-industry publicist, that "Walter Reuther is the most dangerous man in Detroit because no one is more skillful in bringing about the revolution without seeming to disturb the existing forms of society"[1] is nonsense that Romney can hardly take seriously himself. But though Reuther's formal ideas may seem very similar to the left New Dealers, he speaks with an urgency and power which stem directly from the fact that only ten years back he was being beaten by company guards. Reuther's role in American life cannot be understood merely by subjecting his political statements to formal scrutiny; it is always necessary to remember the dynamic potential, as well as the dynamic history, of the union he heads.

Still, it must be granted that there is a distinct quality of improvisation in his recent political thinking. One can see it in a curious, sometimes amusing, shift of tone from one of his speeches to another. When he appears in public view, he indulges in all the fluffy phrases and verbal vagaries of liberal rhetoric; the tone of his speeches becomes flat and impersonal. When he speaks at a meeting of his more sophisticated and radical followers in the UAW, he occasionally lets himself go a bit and returns to the characteristic inflections of socialist terminology. On such occasions, he seems to speak with more spontaneity and directness. How conscious he is of this difference in emphasis, it would be hard to say.

Perhaps the political difficulty in which Reuther finds himself can be clarified by a dialogue he held with GM representative Harry Coen during 1946 wage negotiations:

REUTHER: I think when monopolies like the aluminum industry, owned 85 percent nowadays, and magnesium, when the monopolies jeopardize the safety of the country, they can no longer be trusted in private hands to use them for a profit. That is my private philosophy. It hasn't got a damn thing to do with automobiles or industries operating on a non-monopolistic basis. And it has nothing to do with the question of wages in this case.
COEN: It all colors your thinking. . . . Do you believe we have to learn to live 50 percent better, or do you believe first we have to learn how to create that much more wealth? What has that got to do with dividing up the profits and reducing the salaries of the people in the corporation?
REUTHER: Because unless we get a more realistic distribution of America's wealth, we don't get enough to keep this machine going.
COEN: There it is again. You can't talk about this thing without exposing your socialistic desires.
REUTHER: If fighting for a more equal and equitable distribution of the wealth of this country is socialistic, I stand guilty of being a socialist.
COEN: I think you are convicted.
REUTHER: I plead guilty. . . .[2]

This plea of "guilty" is one Reuther might not be willing to repeat publicly at the present time. Involved here is not the problem of sincerity, for it is certain that Reuther is as sincere when he says he is merely an "independent voter" as when he pleads guilty to being a socialist. Involved rather is the difficulty he finds in reconciling

different strands of his tradition and thought—and even
the most pragmatic of pragmatists cannot avoid such
difficulties.

UNFINISHED PERSONALITY

In many ways Walter Reuther is an admirable person—
quite apart from his obvious public talents. For all his reserve, he is warm and friendly at least amidst people he
trusts; he is unostentatious and modest in his relations
with people; he is neither a mere bureaucrat condescend-
ing to the workers nor a demagogue pretending to be a
regular guy. That he is different from the bulk of the
workers in personality and attitudes both he and they take
for granted. He gains from them, not uncritical admiration, but strong respect; and in his seeming aloofness from
the ranks, his readiness to recognize the difference between a worker and a labor-political intellectual, there is
an implicit respect for the workers in the UAW. Nothing
is more painful and harmful in a union leader than the
false "democracy" of calculated condescension. Reuther
rarely succumbs to that fault.

In Detroit Reuther's moderate personal life has become,
at least among his admirers, a source of unmalicious hu-
mor. That he does not drink, that he is a model husband,
that he seldom uses foul language except on those occasions when union politics force him to—all this is accepted
as an interesting, if not too important, anomaly in Detroit.

Yet there is something here that is intriguing, and not
because of any reasons of prying curiosity. There is good
reason to believe that a man as receptive to stimuli as is
Reuther could have developed a more rounded intellec-
tual-cultural existence than he has. Reuther eats, sleeps,
and talks union; he is as close to being a political machine

as any man alive today. He has forgotten how to relax
and how to play; according to his own admission, he becomes bored when he tries to taper off by reading a mys-
tery novel. (It is possible, however, that some interesting
personality changes may result from his recent enforced
rest after the attempt to assassinate him. Since his long
and very painful convalescence Reuther seems to have
slowed down his pace a bit and to have opened himself
to a greater variety of experiences.)

But what has happened to Reuther in general is that,
to a considerable extent, he has slipped into the character
mold of the American managerial type: the personality
of neutral efficiency. Reuther's private personality has increasingly been absorbed by, or become a function of,
his social role. As he has consolidated his power in the
UAW, he has unwittingly, perhaps unavoidably, taken
on a number of characteristics and outlooks of the managerial caste which functions in large areas of American
industrial life. The way he dresses, the way he talks, the
large, almost frightening emphasis on *efficiency* in his
recent statements would all seem to support this hypothe-
sis. Reuther is not yet fully settled into this rut, of course—
and that is what makes him so interesting to watch. There
can be seen in his public personality, as it has recently
developed, a disturbing *distance*—a distance between himself and his followers; between the ultimate ideas tucked
away in the back of his head and his immediate actions;
between his own image of himself and his need to be a
popular leader; between his long-range passions and his
day-to-day compromises.

No doubt, Reuther does not believe these opposing elements of his personality to be in conflict, but he seems at
times to be aware of at least some discrepancy between
them. The sense of distance we have described is perhaps

unavoidable in any public leader, but it is especially pressing for one who has not fully reconciled his past with his present. This split between tempting power possibilities and the grip of social conscience is not unique to Reuther. It is characteristic of a generation of radicals that came to feel leftist politics a dead-end but could not throw off the moral compulsions that had led them to such politics.

As long as Reuther is disturbed, no matter how slightly, by this problem, his action proceeds from tension generated by a clash between the demands of power and the demands of vision. He remains, thereby, an *unfinished* personality and retains the possibility of dramatically drawing on the large potential of his talent. In the meantime this difficult condition prevents him from using his full powers, which is why, as one sees him in action, speaking at a union meeting or debating an opponent, one feels that, despite his evident talents, something is being held back, some resources remain unreleased and unavailable to him. It may help explain why he speaks so many different ideological languages to so many different men: vibrating tensely to the hot and slackly to the cold.

In crude terms that hardly do justice to the problem, Reuther faces the choice of playing it safe, becoming a not too heterodox union leader and thereby almost certainly rising to the head of the CIO, or letting loose a recently inhibited social imagination, giving free reign to great gifts for popular leadership and thereby perhaps suffering for a time at least, some degree of isolation and rejection. To become a "social engineer" manipulating men or a social leader in close rapport with them—that has been and still may be Reuther's choice. And it presses harder on him than he knows.

Without doubt, this description of Reuther's personality

in terms of his social development involves a kind of dramatic exaggeration. Reuther is convinced that he *has* succeeded in reconciling power and vision. (Of course, power tends to hedge vision in, and creates the illusion that a tight row of bushes is actually a vista of forest.) An unsympathetic observer, regarding Reuther's political history from a thoroughly formulated political position, might conclude that he has chosen in favor of power, has taken the road of the opportunist. In a certain sense, this is no doubt true. But in some men there lie buried strands of the past and ties to a possible future which can be brought to the foreground of consciousness by a shock of experience. The whole pragmatic, deliberately flexible outlook of Reuther is designed to prepare himself to receive shocks. Which means that while he probably will not try himself to initiate any sweeping political realignment in America, he will quickly lend his support to one if he sees it in the making.

Perhaps it will help clarify this analysis if we briefly compare Reuther with some other American labor leaders. That Reuther is different from the run-of-the-mill union organizer, especially of the AFL variety, should by now be obvious and need no longer be stressed. But how does he compare with such unorthodox labor leaders as Eugene Debs, the socialist, and Bill Haywood, the "Wobbly?"

The comparison is striking and in many ways disadvantageous to Reuther. Whatever one may think of the ideas of Debs and Haywood, few would deny that there was a certain uncompromising *wholeness* to their personalities, a wholeness that Reuther lacks. Even their political opponents were moved to admiration because of their commitment, their unwillingness to compromise ideas in order to gain power. By comparison with Debs' profound compassion, or Haywood's robust vitality, is there not something undeveloped and contrived in Reuther's personality?

There has always been a fatal split in American character between the "idealist" and the "realist," which only a few Americans have ever succeeded in transcending; and Walter Reuther, still tied by a lax string of recollection to Debs after having abandoned most of his ideas, is but the latest in a long line of public leaders to be trapped in that opposition of character types. Yet, in fairness, it must be remembered that Debs and Haywood lived in an era in which it was far easier, perhaps far more "natural" to dedicate oneself to an idealistic objective than it has been in the past decade. The forties have been conducive to compromise, not intransigeance. Reuther is the archetypical figure of a generation that has tried desperately to reconcile its image of the social good with its participation in day-to-day politics.

Reuther's unique importance, we would suggest, stems from the fact that in his career, as in few others, it is possible to find so many representative strands of recent American experience. Here is our new version of the labor leader: a product of the depression and New Deal eras; a man of unusually broad social interests and intellectual capacities; a former socialist trying to blend recollections of traditional radicalism with a power-conscious appreciation of business and engineering techniques; and a bright young man of the 1930's who, rather than capping the usual socialist flirtation with the usual New Deal job, chose to work his way up in the CIO. In Walter Reuther's career one can thus see a reflection of the experience of a generation of American radicals and liberals whose work and thought betray an irksome split between a commanding urge to power and a weakened but still restive commitment to a social vision. In all his talent and attractiveness, Walter Reuther is important not only in his own right, but also as a symbol of twentieth-century American experience.

Part III

PROBLEMS

Negro Workers:
The Road to Equality

10

The American Negro, his mind still torn by the welts of slavery, was first forced to enter this country's major industries as a strikebreaker. He had no genuine choice and could hardly have foreseen the tragic consequences. In the early 1880's Negroes were imported from the South to help break steel strikes in Pittsburgh; they were later employed as strikebreakers in the Kansas and Illinois coal mines. In 1894 they came to the Chicago meatpacking plants as strikebreakers and were frequently utilized as such until the early 1920's.[1]

It is a depressing bit of irony that Negroes could not get into the auto plants largely because white auto workers were unable to call sustained strikes. For where strikebreakers were not needed, Negroes were seldom wanted. Many auto companies excluded them as a matter of course. Only at the River Rouge plant were Negroes hired in large numbers, a policy, by the way, the Ford organization extended to none of its other plants. Henry Ford's willingness to employ thousands of Negroes at the Rouge has often been a matter for perplexed dispute; a reasonable assumption would be that it was the result of his characteristic blend of paternalism and ruthlessness, his desire to help Negroes and his shrewd readiness to utilize them against unions. But even after including the 10,000 Negroes at the Rouge, the Negro labor force in the industry before 1935 never amounted to more than 4 percent.

The great bulk of the Negroes was confined either to janitorial chores or to those unpleasant and back-breaking jobs, such as foundry work, which white men did not want. Except in the Rouge plant, Negroes were everywhere barred from skilled work. Even after the industry's unionization, this discriminatory policy remained prevalent, and it has not yet been eradicated.

For the companies racial discrimination proved advantageous in several ways. It assured them of a large pool of cheap and docile labor, which could be used to beat down demands made by white workers; it meant, too, that the sharp color line drawn in the plants would help prevent the organization of workers into one united group. Employer defense—or rationalization—of discriminatory hiring policies was either that Negro workers were incapable of performing skilled tasks or that white workers refused to work beside them. In the latter claim there was, of course, considerable truth, for racial prejudice cuts deep into all classes in American society. But the essential point was that the companies, while they had not themselves originated racial prejudices, were often ready to take advantage of and deepen the antagonisms already present.

By being confined to the dangerous foundry jobs, Negroes suffered accident and death rates higher than those for white workers. As late as 1940, the severity rate for accidents in foundry work was nearly three times as high as the average for the entire industry.[2] Respiratory ailments especially plague foundry workers, among whom "pneumonia is . . . more than twice as frequent as among all occupied males."[3] One investigator summed up the situation in an interview with a white worker.

> I asked if Negroes were not employed anywhere in the plant. He said, "Yes, some jobs white folks will not do; so they have to take niggers in, particularly in duco work, spraying paint on car bodies. This soon kills a white man." I inquired if it never killed Negroes. "Oh, yes," he replied, "It shortens their lives, it cuts them down but they're just niggers."[4]

By 1948 Negro employment in the industry had risen to 9 percent, and Negro auto workers were protected by the same contract provisions as white workers—which is not to say that they have yet reached economic equality. They have, however, been organized into one of the most democratic and dynamic unions in America, whose action against Jim Crow has won the approval even of skeptical students of race relations.[5]

MISGIVINGS AND HESITATIONS

When the big sitdown strikes broke out in 1936 and 1937, few Negroes participated. During the Studebaker sitdown at South Bend in November, 1936, the Oldsmobile sitdown at Lansing in January, 1937, and the one at Flint General Motors in February, 1937, most Negroes simply stayed home until the strikes were settled. They neither co-operated with the strikers nor served as scabs; they were passive and watchful.

It is not hard to understand why they took this attitude. Past relations with white workers in the plants had usually been bad. At Flint Chevrolet, for example, there had been sharp clashes for some months before the sitdown. The AFL, then still the dominant labor group, had often been viciously discriminatory, and Negro workers had little reason—as yet—for supposing the UAW would be better. On the few occasions that Negroes had co-operated with white workers, the results had not been very happy. In Toledo, a few years before the sitdowns, a strike at the American Can plant had broken out in a department employing many Negroes. When the strike collapsed, disgruntled white workers had blamed the Negroes; and management, seeing a chance to divide its workers, had fired all the Negroes.[6] Such memories rankled. And it must be remembered that to the Negro workers the union did not yet represent something *new;* it was merely a regrouping of white workers, whom they had good reason to suspect.

But perhaps the strongest reason for the Negro workers' skepticism about the sitdowns was that they had become habituated to following the leadership of the Negro middle class, a precarious social group which, particularly in Michigan, depended on the patronage of white industrialists. The Ford Company had a powerful hold on Negro politicians and ministers, who repeatedly advanced the persuasive argument that, while AFL unions discriminated against black workers, Ford hired and befriended them.

Of course, both the UAW and the CIO as a whole, fearing that Negroes might again be used as strikebreakers, formally pledged themselves to non-discriminatory policies. The very nature of industrial unionism made impossible the racial divisions prevalent in the AFL. Where AFL craft groups appealed to limited sections of a labor force, often pitting skilled against unskilled, white against black, and thereby aggravating racial tensions, the new industrial unions could not have consolidated their power without winning some support from Negro workers.

During the period of its early organization, the UAW took special pains to win Negro workers. Special organizers were appointed; the UAW press and publicity hammered away at the theme of racial equality; if a stray organizer showed prejudice he was quickly removed; and white workers were slowly, painfully taught that if they failed to co-operate with Negroes they would never win their demands. When a Negro worker showed leadership capacities he was quickly encouraged; in the March, 1937, Chrysler sitdown a Negro, Sam Fanroy, was elected to the strike committee. As a rule, wherever the Negroes were a substantial fraction of a plant's labor force, they co-operated much more readily than where they were a small isolated group. In the former instance they felt strong enough not merely to fight with the white workers against management but also, if necessary, by themselves against the white workers. In the Detroit Midland Steel plant, where about half the workers were Negroes, relations were excellent; at the Dodge plant, where fewer Negroes were employed, clashes broke out.

An interesting account of how the color problem was temporarily solved in one small shop on Detroit's East Side has been given by Frank Winn, a UAW official. Twenty-five percent of this shop's workers were Negroes, the remainder whites of whom many were Southerners bitterly anti-Negro. The union agent pleaded with the white workers to co-operate with the Negroes, but they bluntly refused; no mere speech could overcome prejudices so deeply ingrained. However, after the company refused to recognize the union, it became necessary to strike, and the white workers had then to consider what to do about the Negroes they had banned from the local.

Not without hesitation, the shop committee invited the Negroes to state their case. Winn continues the story:

> By special invitation a committee of Negro workers attended the next meeting to discuss ways and means of getting the Negroes to join the union. Their spokesman presented their case with dignity and intelligence.
>
> "We represent," he said, "most or all of the Negro workers in the plant. If we recommend that they join the union and participate in the strike, they will do so. We think we should be in the union and support the strike if one is necessary. We cannot recommend that unless we are guaranteed full membership privileges and equal consideration under the contract."
>
> The chairman of the meeting summed up the feeling of all those present: "Anything you want, brothers. Just get in here and help us win this strike!"
>
> And so the Negro workers came into the union and a few weeks later they struck, one of the first of Detroit's famous sitdown strikes. Negro and white workers sat down together in the plant, marched the picket lines outside the plant, shared the food from the strike kitchen, and when the strike was won they had a victory dance. If any white member had reservations about the Negroes' attending the dance, he did not say them out loud . . .[7]

Not everywhere did things go so smoothly. In many instances, co-operation existed only on a formal level, with the races within the union still separated or suspicious of each other. In other instances, once the cameraderie of the sitdowns had tarnished, white workers fell back into their old prejudice. And no one could have blamed the Negro workers for being wary; had not so much of their experience with whites ended in betrayal?

In the strike at Chrysler in November, 1939, about sixty Negroes tried to break through the picket lines at

the Dodge plant. A fight broke out. Negro unionists and
a few Negro community leaders urged the men not to
buck the strikers, but three days later 187 Negro men
marched into the shop under police protection. The picket
line of several thousand white workers could probably
have blocked them, but the union had the good sense to
realize that these Negroes, not being ordinary scabs, had
to be treated with special consideration. Consequently, a
race riot was averted and the way prepared for winning
the Negroes to the union.

In the South, where the UAW organized a few plants,
the problem was far more difficult, for the union came
head-on against a fervently defended pattern of prejudice.
At the Atlanta GM plant, union organizers could not persuade white workers to admit Negroes into the local, and
it was only with some difficulty that the whites were dis-
suaded from pressing for the discharge of the Negroes.
As late as 1941 Negro workers in the Atlanta GM plant
were still kept out of the union, and only subsequently
were they reluctantly admitted.

Yet the problem of organizing Southern workers on an
equal basis is not insoluble. The United Mine Workers,
which has large locals in the South, does not tolerate
Jim Crow arrangements, though it must be remembered
that its excellent policy is possible only because of the
deep tradition of unionism in the mines. In the auto
plants there was no such tradition, and consequently the
workers' prejudices were often insurmountable. Sometimes, however, sheer economic necessity forced a crack
in the hard surface of race hatred. Frank Winn tells the
story of his experiences in a Texas aircraft plant:

> About ten percent of the employees were Negroes. Many of
> them had already joined the UAW-CIO. They attended
> meetings and there was no Jim Crow seating arrangement.

A few days before the National Labor Relations Board election a local union officer, a native Texan, approached me and said he wanted to talk about the Negro situation.

"You know," he said, "we got a lot of niggers in that plant."

"Yes, I know," I replied with some nervousness.

"They're all going our way."

"Yes, I believe they are."

"I think we ought to be mighty damn careful we don't do anything to turn 'em against us. That's a big block of votes and we're li'ble to need them, by God, to win this election!"

And he was right. It was a close election. The Negro vote swung it in favor of the UAW-CIO. I hope, and believe, that he, his fellow officers, and the members realize it.[8]

In order to gain recognition, the UAW was sometimes forced to accept not quite satisfactory contracts, as a result of which old plant conditions were perpetuated. That meant that Negroes were still frozen in low-status jobs, and consequently that their original doubts about the union were reinforced. At other times, the UAW risked stirring dormant prejudices by demanding the improvement of Negro workers' conditions. When UAW pressures forced companies to upgrade and to grant seniority and promotion rights to Negro workers, some whites felt that their ethnic "superiority" was being threatened and their economic status endangered. No quick solution to such problems was possible, if only because the antagonism between skilled whites and unskilled Negroes was aggravated by general antagonism between skilled and unskilled workers. But the mere fact that industrial unions like the UAW soften competition between craft groups by bargaining for everyone in an industry, helped a lot. After some experience, white workers could be made to see that improvement of Negro conditions also meant the improvement of their own conditions.

Many of the racial tensions in the industry between 1935 and 1942 are directly attributable to the fact that working conditions of Negroes *were* being bettered. This seeming paradox is explained by an observation often made by sociologists: when an oppressed racial group is helpless and quiescent there is less *observable* tension between it and the dominant group than when it begins to claim equal rights. Which is why the propaganda of those Jim Crow defenders who contrast race riots in Detroit with race "peace" in Mississippi is so sophistical; by extension, one could argue that Stalin's Russia or Hitler's Germany solved the labor problem because there were no strikes in those countries!

Gradually, in their daily life experiences, at least a minority of Negro workers became convinced that the UAW could be trusted to defend them. Big rhetoric meant little, but little actions meant much. When Negro delegates to the 1940 UAW convention at St. Louis suffered from discrimination, the union voted to hold future gatherings only in those cities where Negroes would be treated exactly as white delegates. Precisely such small concrete actions impressed Negroes rightly skeptical of mere resolutions in favor of good will.

THE MAN WHO BOUGHT CHURCHES

Of all the auto companies, Ford had worked out by far the cleverest policy with regard to Negro employment. By hiring 10 percent of his workers from among Negroes, Ford gained the clinging loyalty of the entire colored community. White workers would remain at their jobs at the Rouge because they had no alternative; Negro workers because they considered it a lucky break made possible by Mr. Ford's friendliness.

Offhand, it often seemed that Negroes were hired on a highly capricious basis. In his excellent study of Negro auto workers, Lloyd Bailer writes that, "It became extremely difficult for applicants unknown to Ford personnel officials, or without the recommendation of some individual or organization known to those officials, to secure employment." He quotes a Negro worker as saying:

> One thing about Ford's—if you know a big shot you can always get a job there. They are always taking on somebody recommended by a big shot even though they aren't supposed to be doing any hiring. They'll hire 500 men and fire 500 more the same day.[9]

But such policies were no mere whims. By sprinkling donations through the Negro community and by employing thousands of Negroes, Ford had become a power in the Negro world. He had donated the Parish House of the St. Matthews Episcopal Church (colored) and befriended its Father Daniels; his Negro satrap, Donald Marshall, taught Sunday School classes at St. Matthews; and once a year Ford honored the church with a visit. He had also given substantial aid to the Second Baptist Church (colored), the minister of which, Rev. Bradby, was one of his personal favorites. When either Rev. Bradby or Father Daniels recommended a Negro for a job, it was as good as had. Negro politicians, though seldom as successfully, also served as labor agents for Ford.

Ford went out of his way to win the support of the Negro community He helped finance the all-Negro village of Inkster and provided jobs at $1 a day to its unemployed residents. The Fords entertained committees from Negro women's clubs, invited George Washington Carver to their home, and paid Marian Anderson and Dorothy Maynor to sing on the "Ford Sunday Hour."

These things made a deep impression on the Detroit Negro world, for no other wealthy white man was quite so bountiful.

Ford also helped finance and organize the Republican Party in the Negro districts, and in the 1932 election had placards favoring Hoover placed in the River Rouge plant. On one occasion when the Negro community switched its support to the Democratic Party, Donald Marshall was frank enough to say at a church meeting: "My employer, he was disappointed when he saw the returns from Negro districts—twenty to one Democratic!"[10] And his employer's word counted.

Because so many Negroes were employed by Ford, fear of incurring his ill-will affected virtually the entire Negro community. Several Negro churches and other institutions barred pro-union speakers for this reason. When A. Philip Randolph, head of the sleeping car porters' union, was invited in 1938 to speak at a church meeting, church members employed at Ford were threatened with layoffs. After Randolph spoke, some were dismissed and frankly told that Randolph's speech was the reason.[11] When Mordecai Johnson, president of Howard University, made a pro-union speech at a Negro church, a second appearance was denied him three months later. For in the meantime, said the minister of the church, "Don Marshall heard about the speech and was very angry . . . He said he would never hire another member of the Bethel Church if the church allowed any more speakers to come here and criticize the company."[12]

In the crisis, this policy paid off for Ford. In April, 1941, when he was negotiating with a puny AFL local in order to crowd out the UAW, a group of Negro clergymen calling itself the Detroit Ministers Conference urged Negro workers to support the AFL against the UAW. Pressure had been applied by the Ford Company for public support of the AFL, and though the ministers privately expressed their distaste for the AFL's dubious record on race relations, the Conference did Ford's bidding. It declared:

> We believe that the American Federation of Labor is a truly American organization, that it has acted in the best interests of the Negro ... We endorse this patriotic organization with all the powers at our command.

A Baptist minister who participated in the conference has been quoted as saying that "All but one of the Churches included in the Conference was mortgaged ... the average Negro minister is behind in his payments, and consequently fears that pro-union activity would invite foreclosures."[13]

For the Negro community in general, and for the Negro middle class in particular, the situation was very difficult. Negro storekeepers and professionals, ministers and politicians depended on Ford patronage, in the direct form of subsidies and in the indirect form of jobs. As Lloyd Bailer has put it: "Negro ministers have sought amicable relations with plant officials who can provide church members with jobs and perhaps supply the church furnace with a little coal in the winter. As long as the church membership is employed, the minister is able to keep his head above water. His ability to place job applicants swells church attendance and enables him to keep his flock."[14]

A minority of Negro leaders was sufficiently independent, however, to risk helping the union. Walter White, leader of the National Association for the Advancement of Colored People, came to Detroit to speak for the UAW, and the Rev. Horace White, one of the very few Detroit

Negro ministers who consistently supported the union (in 1937 he had debated Don Marshall on unionism before a highly aroused Negro audience), also helped. The UAW won the hesitant neutrality of the Ford Negro workers, which was enough to ensure the success of the strike. Later, the Negro workers would be convinced that their place was in the union. Of greatest ultimate importance was the fact that the unionization of Ford led to a basic change in the social structure of the Detroit Negro community—but of that, more later.

THE WAR YEARS

With the outbreak of the war in 1941, a new crisis in race relations arose in the auto plants. A few of the major causes may be briefly noted:

1) The influx of new Southern white workers brought into the union thousands of men who had not gone through strike experiences at the side of the Negroes and who knew nothing of the tradition of tolerance that had been slowly developed in the union.

2) The Detroit housing crisis aggravated tensions between Negro and white.

3) The exclusion of Negroes from auto plants at a time when government officials were bemoaning a manpower shortage aroused immense resentment among Negroes.

4) President Roosevelt's Executive Order 8802, establishing a committee for fair-employment practices and prohibiting discrimination in war industries, was hailed by Negroes. But when it was largely ignored by industry and loosely enforced by the government, Negro resentment against wartime Jim Crow was aggravated still further.

When conversion to war production in the auto plants

resulted in the upgrading of many Negro workers, large sections of the white workers rebelled. A series of stoppages against upgrading or working with Negroes broke out—and the union was usually helpless to prevent them. Two stoppages took place at Packard, one in November, 1941, and the other in June, 1943; four at Chrysler in February and June, 1942; two at Timken Detroit Axle in July, 1942; and one at the Hudson Naval Ordnance in June, 1942. These stoppages were part of the anti-Negro hysteria that was climaxed by the Sojourner Truth riot in 1942 and the Detroit race riot of June, 1943.

The one at Packard was typical. In November, 1941, white workers sat down on the job after two Negro metal polishers had been transferred to war work. The company readily withdrew the Negroes, and the officials of the Packard local did not defend them. In UAW circles there was talk at the time that the Ku Klux Klan was influential in the local and had threatened its officials with retaliation if they defended the Negroes. For months afterward the international union tried to persuade the white workers to allow the two Negro polishers to work on war production, and both the government and management came out in favor of the transfer; but only by April, 1942, could the two Negroes be transferred. One white Packard worker told an interviewer:

About forty percent of the workers here are Polish. There are also a lot of Southern whites. Both of them are very prejudiced. The rumor got out not long ago that Negroes were going to start working in the trim department—where I work. Most of the men there are Southern whites. They said, "I'll be goddamned if I'm going to work with a goddamn black nigger."[15]

To counter the hysteria sweeping the city, the UAW and the NAACP called a rally on April 11, 1943, in Cadillac Square which was attended by 10,000 Negroes and whites. The NAACP speaker, Dr. James McClendon, asked the blunt question: "Bullets, machine guns and submarines draw no color line. Why should our government?" Walter Reuther, in an excellent speech, pledged that "the UAW-CIO would tell any worker that refused to work with a colored worker that he could leave the plant because he did not belong there."[16]

But in some plants racial enmity flared again; it was especially bad at Packard. When in June, 1943, Negroes in the Packard foundry briefly protested because they were not being upgraded according to seniority provisions, 25,000 white workers walked out four days later. Walter White, NAACP leader, has written that "subsequent investigation indicated that only a relatively small percentage of Packard workers actually wanted to go on strike," but the sad truth would seem to be that he was wrong. Actually, thousands of Packard workers milled around the plant and listened to anti-Negro harangues. When R. J. Thomas, then president of the UAW, urged the men to return to work and charged that the KKK was behind the strike, the workers ignored him. Walter White later claimed that, "Certain officials of the Packard Company were clearly responsible in part for the strike. C. E. Weiss, Personnel Manager, George Schwartz, General Foreman, and Robert Watts, of the personnel division, urged strikers to hold out on their demand that Negroes not be hired or upgraded."[17]

But if the situation at Packard was appalling, Negroes were upgraded in such plants as Kelsey Hayes, Consolidated Brass and Briggs without any serious trouble. It is significant that in those plants, such as Briggs, where the UAW had its strongest and most alert locals there was least trouble.

In the picture of the war years the terrible anti-Negro riots and walkouts stand out most sharply, but it must be remembered that all the while the union leadership was trying desperately to educate new members and to remind old ones of its tradition of equality. During the 1943 race riot, there was no violence in the plants, though in the streets blood flowed freely. Attorney General Biddle attributed the peace in the plants to "efficient union discipline."[18] In his testimony before a Senate subcommittee, Walter Reuther summarized the situation well:

> At the bench and on the assembly line where white and colored men have undergone the everyday experience of discovering each other's common humanity, there was no violence. The UAW-CIO, through the practise of democracy ... had created an oasis of sanity in a city gone mad with frustration, bitterness, bigotry, and brutality.[19]

To educate its members in the fundamental attitudes of racial tolerance and democracy, the UAW established, in October, 1944, a "fair practices" committee, which was made into a regular department in March, 1946. The UAW leaders and responsible militants realized that the prejudice problem would remain for a long time to come. The friendliness that might develop during a strike would soon evaporate and in its place there would again arise the deep-seated fears and hatreds that are part of the heritage of so many Americans. The momentary enthusiasm of colored workers for the union could quickly give way to their more basic suspicion that all "white organizations" are their enemies. In the war years, the union had learned that once a riot started it could do little to stop it from spreading over an entire city; the patient work of education slowly and laboriously carried on over the years could be undone in an hour.

Race hatred ran deep. As long as men feared for their jobs, as long as they were economically and psychologically insecure, the UAW could make only slow progress in destroying it.

SPECIAL PRIVILEGES—JIM CROW STYLE

While the union was suffering from outbursts of anti-Negro hysteria, a highly significant debate with regard to Negroes was taking place at its conventions. Since 1940 demands had been raised in the UAW that a special post be created on its executive board for a Negro. Thinking that it was a way to protect its position in the union, a good portion of the UAW's Negro membership seemed to favor this proposal.

Here was a situation made to order for a group ready to exploit demagogically the Negro workers' grievances—at which point, naturally enough, the Communist Party bobbed up, ready and eager for the job. In 1942 it championed a separate UAW board post for a Negro at the same time that it urged Negroes, in the name of the war effort, not to struggle aggressively against Jim Crow. (The CP had violently denounced as sabotage of the war effort a proposed Negro "March on Washington" that was to have been led by A. Philip Randolph, head of the sleeping car porters' union.[20]) As with regard to so many other legitimate grievances, the Stalinists' position on Negro rights depended exclusively on their current political "line."

At the 1943 UAW convention in Buffalo, 150 out of 2,000

delegates were Negroes. A caucus of Negro delegates was held, to which all UAW leaders were invited to explain their views. In a principled and courageous speech, Walter Reuther told the Negroes that he considered any *special* position designated for a minority group an inverse form of Jim Crow which he could not support. But what with the demagogy of the CP leaders and the political inexperience of most of the Negro delegates, 90 percent of the Negroes voted to support the Addes-CP bloc because of its stand for a special Negro post. As a direct result, Addes defeated the Reuther candidate for secretary-treasurer of the union.

The debate on the convention floor was bitter and impassioned. Nat Ganley, a member of the national committee of the CP, first proposed that the special board post be restricted to a Negro; then he retreated by saying that "although the minority report does not make it mandatory that a Negro be a director of the Minority Department, I feel confident that [the UAW] would want to demonstrate to the entire nation our policy of racial solidarity by electing a Negro member to this post."

Victor Reuther spoke against the proposal: "We must not establish the practice of giving special privileges to special groups, because that is a Jim Crow privilege, and will . . . kick in the teeth the very people it is trying to help. If there is a special post for Negroes, then in all justice there should be a post at large for the Catholics, the women, the Jews, the Poles and the rest. That is not in keeping with true democracy . . ."[21]

Though the proposal was defeated, most of the Negro delegates voted for it. By sponsoring it, the Stalinist bloc had discovered a clever way of winning the support of Negro delegates, even though the result was that the

Negro issue became, for several years, a factional football.

The issue itself is of great interest. On the surface, the proposal seems eminently reasonable: there *is* a special Negro problem and there *is* need for special attention to it. Consequently, why not elect a special member of the executive board to handle it? And who could do that so well as a Negro—a special kind of Negro? But as the more alert Negro workers were soon to realize, the proposal meant that a Negro was to be "upgraded" in the union not because of his ability but because of the color of his skin—and was this not merely a special kind of inversion of the practice to which they so bitterly and rightly objected in the shops? Suppose, further, that the proposal were extended a bit: since Negro workers had special problems, why not help them by putting them in special locals? The conclusion was clear: whether through malice or opportunism, Addes and the CP had taken a roundabout, special path to Jim Crow.

CP supporters again made a similar proposal at the 1947 Michigan CIO convention. But there William Humphries, a Negro member of the Michigan CIO board, said that any self-respecting Negro would want to be elected to office not because he was a Negro but because he was competent. When Humphries ran for office, the CP bloc did not vote for him—the Stalinists would vote for a Negro only if he was in their tow and was plainly stamped "Negro." By then their motives were understood and the majority of delegates, white and colored, repudiated them. A crucial lesson in union democracy had been learned. True, the Reuther group's opposition to the "special post" demand had been politically disadvantageous in 1943, but by 1948 it had resulted in healthier relations between white and colored unionists.

THE RECENT YEARS

As soon as the war was over, the old patterns of racial discrimination in hiring were again clearly to be seen in Michigan; thousands of Negro women lost their jobs and, even if sometimes mistakenly, could not help feeling that this was due to discriminatory practices. "The Negro," Walter Reuther said, "has experienced the quick erosion of his wartime gains and today again, as in the days before the promulgation of the Four Freedoms, he represents the unwanted tenth . . ." The government's failure to enact stringent fair-employment legislation further embittered Negroes who had enjoyed higher wages during the war. Reuther told a Senate subcommittee that, "No single institution such as the CIO . . . can do more than fight a holding action until the community moves through law to guarantee basic freedoms."[22]

But in the UAW the problem has been one of molding deep-seated emotional attitudes rather than of taking formal actions. On the latter plane, the union has acquitted itself admirably. The FEPC department, co-directed by Walter Reuther and William Oliver, has called regular regional conferences to push union work against Jim Crow; its educational film "Brotherhood of Man" is an excellent piece of work; its printed material is attractive and persuasive. But the problem goes deeper.

In some circles there has been a stereotyped view that in the unions the militant and aggressive rank and file is held back only by the leaders' timidity. Often the product of wishful thinking, this view is especially false with regard to the Negro problem. The truth is that in the UAW it is the international leadership which has the best understanding of this problem and the best record in dealing with it. Time after time, many top leaders of the union have risked the displeasure of the ranks by advocating equal rights for Negroes. This is especially true of Walter Reuther and Emil Mazey, but it has also been true of some of their opponents, such as R. J. Thomas.

The records of the secondary officials, those who run the locals, vary widely. Some, such as the leaders of Briggs Local 212, have consistently fought for the rights of their Negro members. In other locals, the story is rather unpleasant: leaders who go through the motions of supporting the union policy but do not really exert themselves to defend Negro members. (Sometimes one almost wishes that someone in the union would get up and speak out against Negro equality, so that a fundamental educational discussion could be held; but none of those who dislike the union's policy has the courage to do so.)

Certainly, the experience of Ford Local 600 stands out as an example of what can be done to establish a sense of fraternity and harmony between white and colored workers. While no one in that local could seriously argue that discrimination has been completely abolished, it is clear to all Detroit observers that it has a qualitatively superior record on race relations. Since its formation, Negroes have actively participated in the local's affairs, holding major positions and exerting powerful influence in its politics. There is no visible discrimination at social affairs or any other local function. One reason, of course, for the exceptional record of this local is that the Negroes are so large a part of it that any official who ventured to make overt Jim Crow remarks would be committing suicide. Another reason is that the Ford employment policies have made it possible for whites and Negroes to work together in the shops and learn to know each other. But these are the passive factors; they have been made into active incentives to racial tolerance only because the local's leaderships—of whatever faction—have worked toward that end.

The blunt truth is that the bulk of the prejudice in the UAW is to be found in the ranks, especially among workers of Southern and Polish extraction. Among them it takes the form not of explicit opposition to the union's policy but rather of grim, tight-lipped refusal to grant Negroes more than is unavoidable. The union policy, for example, ensures Negroes equal promotion rights, but a recent upgrading of four Negroes to assembly-line work in the Chrysler Kercheval plant resulted in four months of turmoil, with the union leadership pitted against a large section of its own followers but still insisting that the Negroes be accorded their rights. The Negroes were promoted, but a good many white workers bitterly denounced the union for defending them.

Such prejudice has been absorbed with mother's milk, and it is not going to be dissolved very easily. Between prejudice and the education received in the union, there wages a constant subterranean war in the minds and hearts of the white workers. Two recent incidents in one plant illustrate how painfully inconsistent many white workers can be. In November, 1948, a Negro woman worker at Hudson was disciplined for what other employees considered an unjust reason; first her department and then the entire plant, all the white workers included, shut down in protest until her penalty was removed.* That would seem a heartening display of solidarity between

* How complex and irrational emotions about racial conflict can become is seen in the fact that while white workers at Hudson were striking in defense of a Negro woman, a rumor spread through the adjacent Chrysler plant that the strike was caused by a riot between Negro and white workers in which a Negro had stabbed a white man to death. For one seething day, the rumor was received with credence in the Chrysler plant.

white and Negro workers, would it not? Yet only a few days before the shut-down, this same local held a Hallowe'en party for which tickets were sold to all members but at which three Negro couples were barred by policemen who had been called by an unnamed local official to "keep the niggers out." After much maneuvering and two membership meetings, the local instructed its committees to refrain from discrimination in the future. But no one seriously believes that a mere resolution is going to solve the problem. Actually, more and more UAW locals are avoiding dances because their officers fear to face the problem of "mixed dancing."

Next to promotion and seniority, social affairs remain the largest source of racial friction in the union. White workers who have acquiesced or learned to work and strike with a Negro still are unwilling to go to the same dance with him. The Briggs local was compelled, as far back as 1937, to cancel its first dance when white members protested against the presence of Negroes. Several subsequent affairs were cancelled for similar reasons. But the local's leadership has since taken a vigorous stand against discrimination and in recent years has held completely unsegregated social affairs. There are other locals, however, where the leadership has not been nearly so vigorous and where, to this day, Negroes are seldom invited to social affairs. In such matters, the vision and courage of local leaders would seem to be decisive.

A similar difficulty has arisen with regard to sport activities. UAW locals have active baseball leagues in which white and Negro members play on the same team. No problem arises there. Yet some of the very same men who play baseball with Negroes vehemently object to the union's attempt to organize an interracial bowling league. When the UAW failed in 1948 to force the American Bowl-

ing League to remove Jim Crow provisions from its constitution, it started a new bowling league. The blunt truth
is that this new league has not exactly been a brilliant
success; it is doubtful if Reuther has ever taken a step
more unpopular with large sections of the ranks.

How explain the paradox that white workers will gladly
march with a Negro on a picket line but not want to go
to the same dance with him, that white workers will play
baseball with him but refuse to bowl with him? One possible explanation is that white workers feel that there is
greater impersonality in baseball than in bowling. When
the baseball game is over, white and colored usually dress
and go their separate ways; but the bowling game is itself
a social event in which wives participate, and which is
followed by beer drinking. Such contradictory attitudes
seem to be the result of strong feelings of prejudice being
jostled by new equalitarian ideas picked up in the union.
But the prejudice is at the center, and the new ideas at the
periphery of many workers' minds. One conclusion that
can be drawn is that the minds of white workers remain
compartmentalized: their frequent readiness to consort
on equal terms with Negroes in the shops and on picket
lines seldom extends to life outside the shop. For example,
in the May, 1948, Chrysler strike, Negroes participated
to an unprecedented extent in picketing, soup-kitchen
work and similar activities. The attitude of white workers
was warm and cordial. Yet when the local's FEPC committee proposed a campaign to destroy discrimination in
restaurants near the plants, many white workers were, at
best, lukewarm, and others were downright hostile. Three
locals—Ford 400, Briggs 212, Chrysler 7—have started
campaigns to end restaurant discrimination, but none of
them has been successful or popular.

These are serious drawbacks and weaknesses; we have

tried to describe them honestly and without equivoca-
tion. Yet it would be a grievous error to underestimate
the extent to which the union has improved the status of
Negro workers and educated white workers on the color
problem. The very fact that it is now possible to discuss
such matters as are raised in these last few pages, shows
how far the union has moved in the last few years.

BALANCE SHEET AND PROSPECTS

What does the UAW's experience with the Negro problem add up to? Can conclusions of general significance
be drawn? And what are the prospects for the future?
We would briefly answer these questions in the following summary points:

1) The problem of race prejudice in a union must be
solved by empirical means: most white and Negro workers can overcome their fears and prejudices only by working and living together in the plants and, afterwards, by
social contacts outside of the plants. But, in turn, this
empirical program can be instituted *only* by a leadership
which is motivated by a compelling, overall program of
social and economic democracy, an idealistic vision which
gives it the perseverance and patience to work at the day-
to-day tasks in combatting prejudice.

2) The role of white leadership is decisive. By the
nature of things, most unions begin with white leaders
who have it in their power gradually to win the confidence
of Negro workers and thereby to develop Negro leaders.
This they can do by a firm policy of equal treatment, without condescension or favoritism. We should say that few
of the Reuther leadership's actions has so helped it to win
the *eventual* confidence of the Negro militants in the
UAW as its refusal to support the demagogic proposal

for a "separate post" on the union's executive board. Since then several outstanding Negro leaders have developed in the UAW who have won and will win prominent status on the basis of their ability—and their ability alone.

3) For the Negro workers, the UAW has provided an unrivaled arena for expression and means of achieving personal dignity. Negro participation in union affairs, though still hampered and inhibited, is constantly on the increase; in recent local elections, higher proportions of Negro workers participated than did white workers. In the UAW, many Negro workers have learned to speak freely and boldly; they have learned that the whole white world is not a conspiracy against them but that there are unionists ready to risk their careers to help them; they have begun, shyly and slowly, to live, work, eat and play with white workers at the UAW summer camps. The spirit of Negro workers today is as different from what it was fifteen years ago as the spirit of Ford workers today is different from what it was in the era of Harry Bennett.

4) One of the most important consequences of the UAW's attitude toward Negroes has been a shift in class relationships within the Negro community in Detroit. After the plants were unionized, the Negro workers and middle class no longer felt so dependent on Henry Ford as they once had; even the Negro politicians and ministers began to show signs of independence. More important, sharp cleavages developed inside the Negro community. The Negro middle class no longer commands the undisputed intellectual and political leadership of the Negro community that it once did. Rev. Horace White admits that, "The CIO has usurped moral leadership in the [Negro] community." For, "Sadly, I must admit, the Protestant Church gives no moral leadership in Detroit."[23] While

in the past the Negro minister was the leader of the Negro community, his role is increasingly being taken over by Negro trade unionists—and the implications of this social shift are certain to be large.

5) The big crisis in race relations will come once jobs begin to fall off. The Negro is dedicated to fight for the right to work. The danger ahead is that his fight to work and that of his white prototype may occur in a society with not enough jobs to go around. Then the irrational pressures produced by fears of unemployment will drive many a white worker to feel that his job would be safer if the Negro were again relegated to the foundry and the janitor's broom. This is one of the most difficult problems the union will have to face in the next few years.

6) The biggest immediate job of the union is to try to percolate its anti-prejudice education down to the ranks, where it is most needed. Rational appeals, formal statements, impressive resolutions have only a limited value. It is necessary to make over, so to speak, the thought and feeling of the average union member, the one who comes only to an occasional meeting and who is not active except in emergencies. This is not an easy job; perhaps it is ultimately an impossible job if attempted by the union alone; and there is no dramatic way of doing it. But it is the fundamental job.

7) The whole atmosphere of modern society makes for prejudice and hatred, suspicion and fear; by the time the union reaches the ears of many white workers their minds have already been clogged. Only the removal of the fundamental causes of racial prejudice can ultimately eliminate it from American life—and that means the removal, first of all, of economic insecurity. Race prejudice may continue long after its economic causes have ceased to exist,

but the removal of these causes is the first and most important step to eliminating the disease itself.

In no other field has the UAW made such an admirable contribution to bettering the life of American workers; in no other field does so much yet remain to be done.

The Life of a Union:
Democracy and Bureaucracy

11 ....

T H O U G H few people have ever heard of Walter Paine, he is one of the more important men in the UAW. His union post seems minor; he is a chief steward at the Jefferson Avenue Chrysler plant in Detroit. But unless one knows something about him and others like him, one cannot understand modern industrial unionism.

When the seven-o'clock whistle blows each morning and the production lines begin to vibrate, Walter Paine does not work on a job. Under the agreement between the corporation and the union, he is allowed to spend some time each day on union business. Actually, he devotes almost his entire day to his duties as steward. Each week the corporation will send the union its usual letter complaining that stewards are taking too much "lost time" (time devoted to union work on company pay); each week the letter will be filed. Since the corporation knows that

235

the stewards adjust grievances that might otherwise lead to chaos in the plants, it does not try to press its complaint.

The chief steward has often been compared to an army sergeant, but the comparison is invalid for at least three reasons: the steward is a freely elected official, he can be recalled by his "constituents," and he cannot exert unquestioned authority over them. The 500 men and women on the motor line consider him their direct representative who, more than anyone else in the union, can be trusted to defend them. From a distance their grievances might seem inconsequential, but in practice they often involve the difference between distasteful working conditions and relatively tolerable ones. Consequently, to many of the workers on the motor line Walter Paine *is* the union. Speedup, favoritism, layoffs, disciplinary actions, poor conditions, reclassifications—all these matters come to him.

Perhaps a man feels he is being worked too fast. If the chief steward were incompetent, indifferent or timid, the man's complaint might go unanswered and a mood of irritation develop among the workers near him. Or suppose a layoff occurs. It is then of considerable importance that that the steward make sure that strict seniority rules are observed. Nor do such matters ever become merely "routine."

Because he is the hour-to-hour leader of the union, the steward gains a prestige that carries over to all aspects of the union's life. One of his jobs is to collect dues of $1.50 a month from his "constituents." Here he must serve both as the union's defender in relation to the workers and the workers' spokesman in relation to the union. When he collects the dues, he can tell how the men feel about the union—which is why his opinion is so closely heeded by the union's officers, at least those who intend to remain in power. Similarly, Walter Paine has to be able to explain

place without his consent. Since the rickety machinery for settlement of grievances was often ignored by the corporation and sometimes by the workers, the steward would be left to handle plant disputes on his own. Precisely the instability of plant relations allowed him considerable initiative and latitude in adjusting grievances. And because he had such large powers and responsibilities in the shop, he was particularly important as a link between the workers around him and the union's international office. Usually he even had to assume some of the functions of the office, the organizational laxity of which was then in direct proportion to the involvement of the leaders in factional struggles. As a result of uncertain conditions in the plants and chaos in the union, the steward was often the only adequately functioning representative of the workers.

By 1949, however, the steward, while still important in the shop, seemed to be less powerful in the union than he had been in the thirties. On some matters he was now merely a referral agent relaying problems to union committees; on other matters his initiative now counted for less because precedents had been set for handling them. The UAW's departmentalization meant that the steward's powers would necessarily be decreased, since such matters as housing, health service, legal counseling, veterans' aid, education, food co-ops and unemployment insurance are handled by special departments. The steward was still important as a representative of the workers in adjusting immediate grievances; but his role as a union leader had diminished.

Almost always, the expansion and inevitable departmentalization of the union results both in a decrease of the steward's *executive* power and a shrinkage of the area of initiative accessible to him. But the union's growth is only a secondary reason for his decreased power, the primary one being the changed relationship between the union and the corporations.

By the very nature of mass production, brief and unforeseen interruptions of work are extremely wasteful and costly. It is distinctly to the corporations' advantage to prevent grievances from erupting into quickie strikes—though sometimes non-economic factors, such as a corporation's desire to inflict a punitive defeat on the union, can over-rule immediate economic calculations. Usually, however, both sides want plant peace, for not even the most militant unionist can subsist on a perpetual diet of nerve-racking plant disputes. One method used to establish a semblance of plant peace has been the impartial umpire system, in effect in the GM plants since 1940. Since then some 30,000 written grievances have been filed in almost 100 plants. Of these only about 1,200 reached the umpire for decision, the remainder being settled at the shop level or between UAW and GM representatives on a national level. The result, says Walter Reuther, has been that, "The principles of interpretation established by umpire decisions have become a sort of common law of labor relations at General Motors. Thousands of grievances are settled every year because the parties realize that the umpire has already ruled upon the question in dispute."[1] It is obvious that this system tends to regularize shop relations, and hence to cut down sharply the steward's initiative.

A further important restriction on the steward's powers came in 1946 when Richard Leonard and Norman Mathews signed "company security" agreements with Ford and Chrysler, which gave the corporations the right to discipline and/or discharge union shop officials who participate in unauthorized work stoppages. In the view of many UAW people, this provision amounts to a surren-

der to the corporations of a basic union right—the right of
a union to discipline its own members. Since the presup-
position of any agreement is that both parties are able to
keep their word, the "company security" clause under-
mines the UAW's claim to authority and sovereignty. In
this instance, the UAW seems to have taken an easy way
out of a vexing problem: that of setting up a grievance
machinery efficient enough to enjoy the confidence of the
workers and thus eliminate the basic cause of wildcats.
For the corporations, of course, the "company security"
clause is a strategic weapon to hold over the stewards'
heads.

In practice, however, the very fact that the steward's
powers have been thus curbed does not lead to the elimination of wildcats. The major effect of the "company security" clause is to give the wildcat strikes that do take
place an occasional *anti-union* as well as an anti-company
flavor.

When the steward could threaten, as a last resort, to
close his department if a grievance were not satisfactorily
settled, he had a genuine reserve weapon at his disposal.
Now, however, he cannot make such a threat without en-
dangering his job. As a consequence, the workers, know-
ing that the steward is often unable to "get tough," may
take things into their own hands by starting brief work
stoppages without his formal consent. In such instances,
the local union leadership often privately supports a wildcat while publicly deploring it. The truth seems to be that
no repressive restrictions can be a substitute for genuine
collective bargaining. Strip the steward of some of his
powers through "company security" clauses, and the men
will merely be forced to assume those powers themselves.
That neither management nor the union enforces the
"company security" clause with literal stringency is evi-

dence that both are forced to recognize this fact in daily life.

How the union shop and the dues check-off* affect the steward's role is a matter on which there has been much discussion in the UAW. It has been argued that the union shop and the check-off decrease the steward's power, but this seems quite doubtful. We would suggest that they change the nature of his job somewhat, but do not at all lessen his possible powers. At the Ford plants, where there is both a union shop and the check-off, the steward (called a district committeeman) is able to devote his time to union leadership exclusively, while at Chrysler the steward has to spend much time at the tedious chore of collecting dues. With the union shop and the check-off, the steward *can* become a genuine plant leader; without them, he may too easily slip into the rut of mere dues collecting. (Some unionists argue, however, that when there is no check-off the workers can threaten to "withhold dues" as a means of stimulating union leaders and stewards into keeping on their toes.)

Fifteen years ago it meant risking one's job and sometimes one's neck to become a shop steward in an auto plant. Now the post not only brings honored status but also the advantage of not having to work a full day on the line or at a machine. "Lost-time unionism" has become a powerful factor in the auto plants, having partly sup-

---

* A union shop is one in which union membership is a requisite of permanent employment, a new worker usually being given thirty days in which to join the union. The union shop is suited to mass-production industries since it furnishes union security but does not impose a tight regulation of labor supply. By contrast, a closed shop is one in which a man cannot be hired until he has a union card. For craft unions in skilled industries, the closed shop is a highly desired goal.

The check-off is an arrangement by which a union receives the dues, fines and assessments of its members directly from the employer, who withholds them from wages.

planted idealistic or militant unionism—or more precisely, having blended with them. The more active UAW members, having created in the union a world of their own, naturally reach out for the privileges and status that can be gained in that world. Sometimes "lost-time unionism" is allowed to mushroom to an unwarranted extent—as, for example, the practice in the Detroit Dodge local of paying stewards to attend union meetings after working hours.

We have stressed this problem of the changing role of the steward because it leads directly to such central questions as: how has the recent growth and consolidation of the UAW affected its internal life? Can an organization as large as the UAW remain democratic? Are there bureaucratic tendencies in its inner life? But before discussing these questions directly, we shall have to make a brief excursion into the general theory of trade unionism in America.

BETWEEN REVOLT AND STABILITY

Neither among labor leaders nor students of the labor movement is there any general agreement on the purpose of trade unions. Opinions on that question always depend on the explicit or implicit social perspective from which they are launched. But it seems indisputable that most American trade unions fulfill two major functions: 1) they are agencies performing various services for their members, the most important of which is to represent them in contractual negotiations with employers; 2) they are, to one extent or another, movements for the general social betterment of the working people. This latter function may be conceived by a union leadership either in terms of social reform, class struggle or a blend of the two.

Unions may enter politics or confine themselves to "pure and simple" bargaining; they may provide their members with a rich institutional life or may offer them nothing but dollar incentives; they may train their members to democratic initiative or may rule them with an iron hand—but almost all of their activities can be placed under one or the other of the above two headings.

Actually, no union is or can be purely either a service agency or a movement for social change. The two functions always interweave, and the resulting mixture is the source of many of the intra-union tensions and conflicts. The UAW is a conspicuous example of a union blending continuous activity for social reform with occasional eruptions into "class-struggle" militancy.

Though by no means an invariable one, a correlation can be observed between a union's commitment to large social goals and its observance of internal democratic procedures. Correspondingly, the service or business kind of union *tends* frequently to succumb to bureaucracy. The AFL carpenters and building-trades unions are efficient at performing for their members certain contractual services, but the members have little voice in determining the course of these unions. A craft union protecting the favored position of a skilled labor stratum will often become bureaucratic because its members feel no pressing need to intervene in its administration so long as it "delivers the goods." The members feel no strong urge to self-rule because they often regard the union not as *their* organization but rather as an external body mediating between them and the employers. So long as the union wins economic gains for these skilled workers, they will often be willing to let the leaders "get theirs too." (This "business psychology" of the craft unionists, possible only in an atmosphere of economic well-being, is a major factor making for racketeering in the AFL.) There are, of course, unions of skilled workers which are democratic. The typographical workers' union is highly democratic, perhaps because of the superior intellectual level of many of its members. But by and large the usual AFL craft union tends to become bureaucratic because its members can afford the luxury of supporting a parasitic leadership.

In the mass-production industries, the situation is usually different. Here unskilled and semi-skilled labor predominate, and no "aristocracy-of-labor" outlook can take deep roots. Because they cannot establish the peculiarly advantageous and "monopolistic" arrangements of the skilled craft unions, the industrial unions are more militant and often seek amelioration of social problems through politics. Consequently, they must involve their members in campaigns that often result in greater union alertness and social consciousness. At the same time, it should be emphasized that there is no invariable connection between internal democracy and militancy or social consciousness. John L. Lewis' UMW is the classic example of a union that is both extremely militant and extremely undemocratic. But as a rule, the union with members actively participating in aggressive struggles against employers or in social-political campaigns will be more democratic than the union which merely exchanges contractual services for regular dues.

In practice, even the most conservative AFL union finds it necessary to make formal and practical concessions to the social-change notion of unionism. Though a union may really be interested only in limited economic demands for its members, it seeks, for strategic reasons, to identify itself with the general social and economic welfare. In the name of that latter phrase, it can undertake any number of actions—sometimes even actions in which the membership may be convinced that it is preferable not to press for a wage rise or, on rare occasions, to submit to a wage cut. If only because the seemingly isolated act of bargaining impinges on and is in turn affected by a great many other social and political events, few unions in the modern world can exist merely as bargaining agencies. But not only the pressures of a complex society force a union to take a certain minimum interest in the social events around it; the very needs of bargaining itself produce the same interest. The most conservative and accommodating union must be ready, at some time, to threaten a strike— which means that in addition to economic grievances it must have at its disposal certain ideological appeals (the welfare of our people, the justice of labor's cause, etc., etc.) with which to rally its members. Life in a competitive society is so organized that the most limited action requires a generalized ideological motivation or pseudo-motivation.

Now these two purposes, contractual service and social change, do not merely exist side by side; they conflict with each other, though neither can totally devour the other. In the early days of most unions, "the idealistic, democratic, emancipatory aspect is dominant . . . But with the growth and entrenchment of unionism, the businesslike service aspect inevitably comes to the fore." Yet "the old ideology, the old conceptions and phraseology, still persist as underlying tradition . . ."[2] In some instances, this conflict is not strongly felt, for a union can be built from above, with a minimum of initiative coming from the workers themselves and most of the organizers and finances being provided by another, established union. But even when a union is created through mass struggle and under radical leadership, it must, if it is to survive in a capitalist economy, place increasing stress on the "businesslike service aspect." Otherwise, it will become merely a political organization without immediate economic appeal to the workers in the industry.

As a union settles down (the official term is "matures"), its internal life increasingly resembles the temper and structure of the status quo against which it had once risen in rebellion. "The old primitive democratic structure," writes a skeptical student of the labor movement, "is never formally abolished and usually not even modified officially. It remains in a vestigial or fossilized form without greatly hampering the actual bureaucratic concentration of power."[3] This process has not nearly been completed in the UAW, though it has undoubtedly been begun. One would have to be intellectually blind or bureaucratically bland to deny that there are signs, inclinations, *itchings* in that direction. But the process of bureaucratization, at least in its more blatant forms, is *not at all* inevitable; the tendency toward that bureaucratization may be unavoidable, but its consummation is not. An alert membership and militant leadership can check and control it. The UAW is at present in a particularly interesting position: it has obviously outgrown its lusty primitive democracy, but has not yet suffered a thorough "bureaucratic concentration of power." In it democracy and bureaucracy square off, the still potent democratic tradition suffering certain flank attacks from a bureaucracy that has arisen during the union's stabilization in recent years.

THE DANGER OF BUREAUCRACY

The general sociological problem of bureaucracy has only begun to be discussed in recent years; there is as yet no encompassing study of bureaucratic formations in modern society. In fact, there even seems some disagreement on what the term "bureaucratic" means. Some writers use the term more or less to describe the elaborate administration of a state or an organization—this administration being characterized by a finely worked-out division of labor, with full-time leaders who enjoy specialized skills and considerable executive authority. If the term "bureaucracy" be used in this sense, it is not only unavoidable but actually desirable in a large union, for no organization of hundreds of thousands of members can exist without such an administration. But, obviously enough, if only this were involved, no one would become very excited about the problem of bureaucracy. In discussing bureaucracy, we mean something else; we mean certain habits and outlooks that can arise among leaders and increasingly dominate the life of an organization. The leader begins to identify the union with himself or with his group of co-leaders; he may suspect (sometimes rightly so) that he knows better than the members; and he may consequently become impatient with the "cumbersome" business of going to the ranks for approval and support. He then begins to arrogate to himself the decisive powers that formally and presumably rest in the ranks.

Usually, the problem of bureaucratic leaders in the unions arises not merely or even primarily from evil intentions or greed; it stems from the fact that men who run union offices can never, with the best will in the world, think and feel quite like the men who work in shops. Now this discrepancy of thought and feeling is not yet in itself a sufficient cause for the rise of bureaucratic leadership; it is, however, a factor making such leadership possible. The superiority of living conditions enjoyed by the union leader over the union member is, so to speak, the "material base" on which the bureaucratic outlook begins to form.

Trade unions soon find themselves pressured by powerful forces to conform to the social status quo. Once the
employers see that it is possible, as the phrase goes, to "do
business" with the union, the two work out a co-operative
arrangement. The union leader finds that the union is becoming stabilized, relations with the employers are being
"normalized," dues are flowing in regularly. So long as the
national economy is not in crisis, the leader can win moderate wage gains for his followers at occasional intervals
and thereby keep them more or less contented. In most
unions, especially those in the AFL, that is enough to ensure his continued tenure in office. The leader thus acquires a special reason for maintaining the union as a "responsible" organization and his post as a "responsible"
leader.

The union does not exist in a vacuum. It functions in a
social milieu in which bureaucratic fungi form on all institutions. Not only government, but the corporations are
shot through with the bureaucratic psychology (for all
the cant of their heads about "those bureaucrats in Washington".) In an age in which economic and political
institutions are increasingly centralized without mass participation and democratic control from below, most
people begin to take the bureaucratic outlook for granted.
It is absorbed in the very air they breathe; they expect
their leaders to behave bureaucratically.

The union leader discovers that in a period where the
government plays an increasingly dominant role in economic life, many decisions are made, not in the union halls
or even on the picket lines, but in government offices. He
is increasingly involved in mediation and arbitration proceedings and decreasingly in the old-fashioned kinds of
militant union action. Since he finds that, in order to function as an effective union leader he must range beyond

the union hall and into the centers of government, he may feel that his powers rest less on his members than on his relations with officials in the right places. He becomes a "labor statesman"—that is, all too often, a labor bureaucrat. The bureaucratization of the secondary leaders is a simpler process, based largely on their desire to maintain comparatively comfortable jobs that keep them off the assembly line.

Now this tendency toward bureaucracy is less powerful in the UAW than in most other American unions—but it *is* there. One reason why it can be found in the UAW is quite simple: its size. In so large an organization it becomes increasingly difficult to maintain the more direct kinds of democratic procedure in which masses of members can actively participate.

Of course, a union can be small and yet quite bureaucratic. One of the dangers peculiar to democracy in a small union is that the personality of its leader can exert an inordinate and unhealthy influence. In the National Maritime Union, members are often very intimate with Joe Curran in a way few UAW people would think of being with Walter Reuther. Yet Curran sometimes resorts to using his personal popularity as a demagogic means of influencing the membership. Cameraderie can exist between bureaucratic leaders and their followers, for democracy is not necessarily or merely a matter of friendliness. And while the problem of bureaucracy is inescapable in a large union, there is no rule that it will not arise in a small one.

Nonetheless, sheer size, and more particularly the consequences of size, does engender special bureaucratic dangers. A union as large as the UAW must necessarily become an attractive institution in which to work; it creates an entire hierarchy of status within itself; it has a

morally caressing ideological sanction which makes for a
sense of purpose among some of its employees; it acquires
a stake in the status quo (money, buildings, relations with
corporations, political power) which exerts subtle pressures on its leaders. Let us cite a few examples of how the
institutionalization of the UAW gives rise to certain bureaucratic dangers.

In recent years the UAW has hired a very considerable
number of specialists—economists, lawyers, newspaper-
men, lobbyists—whose work is valuable and indispensable.
There are good reasons to welcome this development. It
brings into the union men with a broader social vision
than that enjoyed by most union leaders; it makes possible
some contact between intellectuals and workers, with
benefits to both. Yet the presence of these specialists has
certain dangers. An unsatisfactory relationship can very
easily be established between the union official and the
intellectual employee of the union. A union leader needs
a speech for a certain occasion; he has to work out a certain problem. Why bother doing it himself? Call up and
get one of the "smart boys" to do it. That means that one
man has the power and the other man does the thinking
for him. At the same time, the intellectual employee of
the union, even though he is supposed to articulate its
ideas and defend it in public controversy, may find himself in a subsidiary position. Since he does not "rest on"
the ranks, he lacks the power of the local union leaders.
He finds that if, for any reason, he does not toe the line
set by the union leadership, he may be dismissed and have
no possibility of appealing his dismissal to the ranks. Too
often he is wanted more for the use to which his skills
may be put than for the ideas his mind may produce. This
separation of the leaders with power from the specialists
with skill is a sign of developing bureaucracy.

In the UAW, fortunately, the separation is not so extreme as in the above abstract description. Between the more intelligent UAW leaders, such as Walter Reuther, and the intellectuals employed by the union there is a certain, though not a sufficient, exchange of ideas. But there is no doubt that a number of routine UAW leaders, the more conservative supporters of Reuther, would be only too glad to get rid of the intellectuals who do a lot of the UAW's specialized work, or at least further to curtail their rights. Many of the more routine unionists feel uncomfortable with, perhaps secretly a little inferior to, the intellectuals working for the union. At best, they find them a necessary nuisance.

There is still another way in which the union's growth tends to curtail its democratic life. Negotiations between the UAW and the corporations have in recent years become so complex that not many shop workers are able to follow them closely. In 1948, for example, both Chrysler and Ford found themselves confronted by a very talented UAW economist, Nathan Weinberg. The unionists who observed Weinberg were highly enthusiastic about his skill. But the truth is that with the increasing complexity of negotiations the rank and file's role in them tends to become subordinate.

In the UAW, the membership remains the ultimate source of decision; when the Ford workers disliked a pension agreement worked out between the UAW and the Ford corporation in 1947 they defeated it, even though they hadn't read every line of its fine print. But, as men like Weinberg must undoubtedly know and be perturbed by, the fact remains that in wage negotiations the ranks are becoming increasingly dependent on the leaders and the specialists. "The wage policy of a union, like the foreign policy of a nation, is a matter poorly suited to the methods of primitive democracy."[4] There seems no way at present of avoiding this loss of rank-and-file initiative. All that can be done is for unionists to make sure that the membership retains the democratic right of approving or rejecting the agreements which specialists work out.

Another major danger to democracy, unavoidable in a large organization, is that too many decisions may be made in "the office" rather than among the workers. A large office structure in any organization is always a source of bureaucratic malformation. Since appointed employees depend for their jobs exclusively on the union's leadership, they cannot help being pliant to its will. On many secondary matters, however, the office begins to assume a life of its own, with its own interests and momentum, and to enjoy a certain range of power so long as it does not cross the top leaders. While presumably a mere subsidiary agent of the organization, the office may begin to think of itself as if it *were* the organization. Even worse, it may fail to recognize the possibility that in practice there can be a conflict of habits or needs between itself and the organization's tributary branches.

The leadership, seeking to perpetuate itself, tends to form a hardened group or clique, each member of which defends the other from attack or criticism. In most organizations, the leaders tend to bunch together in their relations to the members, for no matter how much leaders and members may respect and admire each other, their perspectives can never be quite the same. In early 1949, for example, the Reuther leadership prepared for an oncoming UAW convention by implicitly agreeing to retain in power all of its supporters on the union executive board. When a group of pro-Reuther unionists in Los Angeles tried to have the local regional director replaced by another pro-Reuther leader, it was vehemently opposed by vice-president John Livingston who insisted that the status quo be retained. Here the leadership was acting as a kind of mutual protective association.

These, then, are the first signs of bureaucracy: a leadership becomes so secure in office that it gets "careless" in its relations with the ranks; it begins to think of itself as a sacred entity to be protected from all criticism, even of a friendly kind. Of course, this is not yet the rule in the UAW, which remains one of the most democratic unions in the United States. But there are danger signs.

PORTRAIT OF THE PORKCHOPPER

In the pithy language of the rank and file, every full time leader of the UAW is a porkchopper.* Behind this half-friendly, half-aggressive designation, there is a shrewd appraisal of the inclination of the full-time official to remove himself from the ranks and become part of a group of functionaries with work habits, mode of existence and attitudes toward society different from those of the workers.** At the same time, this designation also sug-

---

* In his authoritative *The American Language, Supplement 2,* H. L. Mencken defines a porkchopper as a union leader who wishes to use his post for personal advantage. That is no doubt the original meaning of the term, though at present it is used in the UAW to refer to all full-time officials. Mencken gives a reference to the magazine *American Notes and Queries* where the term is discussed but its origin not explained. It seems likely that it goes back to IWW days.

** An interesting sidelight on the union leader's social status was revealed in a report by Professor Paul Hatt of Princeton University to the Eastern Sociological Society in April, 1949. In a poll of 3,000 people undertaken by the National Opinion Research Center, a series of questions was asked to discover the status they attributed to occupations. When Professor Hatt tabulated the answers, he found that they would have to be broken down into several overall categories if any meaning was to be assigned to them. After doing so, he discovered that the job of labor organizer was held, by those replying to his questionnaire, to be closest in status qualities, not to industrial workers, but to white-collar workers and small businessmen.

gests the rank and file's ambition, for many of the more active UAW members naturally want to become pork-choppers too.

What are the makings of a good porkchopper? As a rule, employment as a full-time union representative does not come easily and must be preceded by a long apprenticeship. In the union's early days, a union organizer had to be ready for rough give and take on the picket lines, and had to expect in some instances to face attack by thugs hired by anti-union employers. Most porkchoppers didn't have much time for eating pork chops, and didn't earn enough to buy many of them.

As internal schisms appeared in the union, the pork-chopper had to be endowed with another talent. Those organizers merely competent at mass leadership in and before strike struggles, but innocent of the fine—and not so fine—points of faction fighting often found themselves unemployed. The porkchopper had to be able to deliver the votes for his faction; otherwise, why keep him on the payroll? The staffs of competing top officers were like private armies maneuvering for position and power in the union. At the same time, each leader had to solve the delicate problem of finding subordinates able to deliver votes, yet themselves not so capable that one of them might supplant him. But delivering the votes is itself not a simple matter. The skilled porkchopper had to be competent not merely as factional agent but also as a union representative, for if he were inadequate as a union leader he would discredit his faction.

As the union grew, still another winnowing process took place. New kinds of porkchoppers became necessary: organizers who were skilled at negotiations as well as at maintaining picket lines, organizers who had enough political knowledge to carry out the union's political policies. The Reuther group is especially shrewd at balancing off one kind of porkchopper against another. Thus, for instance, everyone in the UAW knows that while X may be a regional director and an ally of Reuther, it is really Y who, while only an assistant director, is Walter Reuther's representative in that region. For while X is a hurly-burly old-line unionist with a certain routine competence, Y has had some experience in a radical group, is sophisticated in the ways of modern politics, knows something about economics and is therefore able to provide behind-the-scenes leadership of a kind simply beyond the capacity of X.

Now that there seems no serious possibility of the Reuther leadership being supplanted for some time to come, the secondary officials are beginning to feel secure in their jobs. So long as a porkchopper is reasonably efficient and does not make important personal or political mistakes, he can expect to keep his job. Personal mistakes? Don't get involved in scandals, don't be arrogant to the ranks, don't flaunt your superior economic status (a porkchopper earns from one and a half to two times as much as most auto workers). Recently, one UAW organizer made such a personal mistake when he bought a luxurious Lincoln car and drove it down to union headquarters. He was severely reprimanded by Walter Reuther, who told the organizers that they should not have luxury cars until union members could afford to buy them. Political mistakes? Don't flaunt your disagreement, if you have one, with the union's policy at election time; be careful in your relations with the union's top leadership. The safest formula for a secondary union official is to wait until the top decides policy and then to support it.

One of the distinguishing characteristics of the union official is usually his facility as a speaker. That does not mean that he is a polished orator; quite the contrary. It means that he has learned to speak the language of the ranks, that he can hold the attention of the members attending a local meeting. Most workers have difficulty in expressing themselves and are usually unduly impressed by people who speak well. Let a man get up on the floor and make a speech that is irrelevant or demagogic—he will yet get a hearing and win some support if only he is fluent and colorful. This excessive regard for verbalism is one reason why so many flashes in the pan, so many opportunists manage to acquire leadership in American unions. Walter Reuther's always cogent and serious manner of speaking is an exception to the style of oratory prevalent in the unions and is another of the differences between him and the old-line leaders.

Most union activists hope that some day they too will become porkchoppers. It is not hard to see why. The status of the union official can be very high; he is a leader of an organization which claims not merely to be improving the lot of a limited number of people but also to be working for the welfare of the entire population; he is usually highly respected by the workers for his presumed superior knowledge and greater articulateness; he earns a larger and more steady income than they do; he does not have to submit to factory discipline and can keep comparatively flexible hours; and he enjoys what is for Americans a very great privilege and mark of social superiority: he can wear "white-collar" clothes rather than work clothes.

All of these factors explain why porkchoppers defeated in union elections seldom manage to summon enough courage and stamina to return to the shops. To them it seems far easier and more convenient to get a full-time job in another, less turbulent union or to retire to private business. (The auto corporations delight in hiring ex-union leaders as labor-relations men.) Homer Martin became a businessman, as did Richard Frankensteen. John Anderson,* for years head of the powerful Local 155 and often associated with the Stalinist point of view, quit the union to become personnel director for some tool-and-die shops. Of the major anti-Reuther leaders of recent years none has had the gumption to return to the shop and gain mass support for his point of view. R. J. Thomas took a secondary post with the CIO. George Addes retired to run a cabaret. Richard Leonard tried to work in a shop for a few months, but soon took a minor post with the CIO. In effect, all of these people surrendered any possibility of regaining their power in the UAW and declared that they preferred the comfort of an innocuous CIO post or the privileges of working for the corporations to fighting for their views and for leadership in the UAW.

To the leader, the union soon becomes an institution with a life of its own, which is the major focus of his loyalty. It is his source of income, his center of existence and his area of status. Even the secondary leader who does not have any very idealistic notions about the ultimate significance of unionism and more or less keeps to the hewn path of simple economic unionism, is still willing to trade punches on picket lines and in clashes with rival unions. A major motivating factor in the life of the officials is rivalry with other unions, the struggle over who will gain more dues, greater power and prestige. The

* This John Anderson is not to be confused with the John Anderson mentioned in Chapter 5 as head of the 1946 Detroit GM strike committee. This John Anderson has been consistently pro-Communist Party; the other is an anti-Stalinist. This John Anderson is known in UAW circles as "Big John" and the other as "Little John." This one has left the UAW; the other remains an active member. About all they have in common is their name.

union, as an institution with loyalty drives and status attributes of its own, plays a highly important part in the life of the porkchopper, often more so than in the life of the rank and filer.

In the UAW there are none of the disgraceful special privileges that are to be found in other unions: no lifetime presidents, little sickening adulation of leaders, no $30,000 salaries. If the members remain alert, there will not be such special privileges in the future.

THE RESOURCES OF DEMOCRACY

It would present a one-sided picture of the UAW's internal life if the problem of bureaucracy and democracy were discussed merely in terms of its leadership. So long as there is a conflict between bureaucratic and democratic trends, one must consider the role of the union membership.

For a variety of reasons the UAW has never felt itself to be as secure as other unions. Relations between it and the large auto corporations have seldom been harmonious; to this day there are frequent, usually unreported clashes in the plants between union committeemen and company representatives. The continued, if sometimes subterranean, antagonism between corporations and union prevents the latter from sinking into bureaucratic sloth. Merely to survive, the union must remain vital, democratic and militant. The garment workers' unions, in New York, to cite a contrasting example, deal with small employers whom they can often crush at will; consequently they do not feel themselves so persistently threatened as do the auto workers. Rightly or wrongly, many UAW people believe that the last battle in the industry has not yet been fought and that the corporations still hope to destroy the union.

One result of this situation is that there exists in the UAW a layer of active and experienced members who are habitually alert in defense of its interests. This layer, often designated as the militants, provides the union's shock troops; the men who can be called upon for active work, for flying squadrons to help strikers. They are habitually jealous of their rights in the union; they have burned their fingers often enough with leaders and factions to remain somewhat skeptical of all of them; they have a rough but workable concept of internal democracy; and they have learned a good deal about how unions should and should not be run. Perhaps they would not formulate their attitude so abstractly, but they do seem to function on the implicit assumption that a democratic union is the best safeguard against possible inordinate ambitions or dictatorial inclinations of any leaders. Ultimately this layer of UAW members is the decisive power in the union, and any faction seeking to gain office must win its support.

The presence of such a stratum of members is possible only because of the peculiar history of the UAW. Unlike the steel workers' union, which never had a genuine convention or constitution during its formative years (1936–1941), the UAW was built from the bottom up. In it, no Philip Murray could have been ensconced as president by a John L. Lewis. For the UAW is largely the handiwork of the militants, and though their power in the union has recently declined (both because of their aging and the changing character of the union), they still remain a potent group.

Central to an understanding of the UAW's tradition of democracy is the fact that it has been a union that faced

repeated crises, both through external attack and internal
dissension. Each time it was only the rank and file, roused
to desperate action, that saved the union. This is true of
the Martin fiasco, the sitdown strikes, the Ford strike, the
wartime crisis. A union forced to repeated displays of
militancy is more likely to retain its democratic spirit than
one dozing peacefully in concert with the employers.
While it would be an exaggeration to claim that the majority of the UAW's members are actively involved in its
affairs (there is probably no organization of comparable
size of which that could be said), it does have a higher
degree of membership participation than most other
unions. And even the section of the membership that is
usually dormant has been called into frequent if intermittent participation by the union's militant actions and
internal crises.

A further stimulant to internal democracy in the UAW
is the presence of small groups of dissident radicals as well
as many people who have at one time or another been in
the socialist movements. These people are particularly
alert to any attempts by either the Communist Party or a
conservative clique to capture control of the union, for
they realize that, as dissidents, they would be the first
victims of such a development. Though few in number,
they often serve as the defenders of democratic rights in
the union.

But it should not be imagined that all the rank and
filers are proponents of democracy and all the leaders advocates of bureaucracy. Union members often lack the
patience to put up with democratic procedures; they
sometimes find it easier to hiss an opponent than to listen
to him. Some of them have been improperly trained by
modern society to favor instinctively the undemocratic ap-

proach which is so much "easier" than the democratic one. On the other hand, there are some secondary UAW leaders who, because they possess an intellectual awareness of the problems of the union, are particularly careful to defend democratic values. The problem of democracy is never cut and dried, never reducible to abstract propositions, never fought over between angels and devils. Rules can and should be made, but they are never enough. Russia has "the most democratic constitution in the world" and the most totalitarian society. For democracy to be preserved there must always be an active minority anxious to guard it.

There is one decisive proof of democracy in a union (or any other institution): oppositionists have the right to organize freely into "parties," to set up factional machines, to circulate publicity and to propagandize among the members. The UAW's history is particularly admirable in this respect. Each time a group has sought office, it has had to submit itself to the membership's decision. Full, heated and prolonged debates have always preceded elections. No leader has been above attack—in the 1947 faction fight, R. J. Thomas was subjected to sustained and stinging criticism in his own Local 7. Thus far, at least, there has been no attempt in the UAW either to abolish the right of factions to exist and function freely or the equally important right of the membership to express its attitude toward them; nor is there much evidence that such an attempt will be made in the near future.

Before conventions the union has assumed the appearance of an electoral arena with slates, caucuses, campaign literature, and public debates. In early 1949, for example, it was taken for granted that various caucuses would start working in preparation for the spring convention. The

Reuther group held meetings of its active supporters. The old Addes group had disintegrated and been replaced by the "Progressive" caucus, friendly to the line of the Communist Party, and the "Committee for Militant and Democratic Unionism," inspired by the "orthodox" Trotskyists. Neither opposition group is likely to muster much support, but the important thing is that they have been able to work quite freely in the locals.

What is most disturbing about the current situation in the UAW and what constitutes the greatest possible source of bureaucratic malformation is that, for the first time in the union's history, there is no significant opposition to the leadership. The presence of an opposition, particularly if it be an even partly intelligent one, is the best way of insuring that a union's democratic structure will be preserved. But the oppositions now existing in the UAW, both dominated by discredited political groups, can only help to entrench and calcify the present leadership. There is nothing most trade-union leaders like better than a ridiculous or discredited opposition, for by kicking it around they can forestall significant and intelligent criticism.

To defend the right of factions to exist is not at all to applaud this or the other faction. But that is the overhead (well worth paying!) of democracy: groups one considers detrimental to the union's interest will be formed. The alternative is dictatorship. As a rule, factions exist only in the more democratic and advanced unions. One of the reasons why "factional struggles often afflict most terribly the very unions generally regarded as the most progressive is that these unions have tried, in some degree, though inadequately, to educate their members both with regard to the facts in modern industry and society and with regard to the history, functions, and problems of the labor movement. The membership in such unions . . . makes more demands on the union, and at the same time is somewhat more clearly aware of the dilemmas the union confronts. They cannot therefore take things as they come, as is often the case among less sophisticated workers."[5] This description largely holds for the UAW and helps explain the complex interaction between its democratic life and its recurrent factional crises.

There is no denying that on many matters, especially in periods between conventions and contract negotiations, the union leaders are very much on their own, consulting the ranks only when pressure is brought from below or when passive resistance to a policy is encountered. But this is probably unavoidable in an organization like the UAW, in which considerable initiative on the part of the leaders is mandatory. Actually, what *has* been disturbing recently is the fact that most of that initiative has been centered in the hands of one person: Walter Reuther. His authority in the union is now at an all-time high, and not without good reason; yet it would be a very serious development if the present habit of many second-line leaders of "waiting for Walter" and of elevating him to semi-legendary status were to go unchecked. Bureaucracies can also be built by idealistic people with the best of intentions.

The democracy of the UAW of 1935-36 is not likely to reappear in the UAW of the coming few years. That kind of raw, primitive union life had more than a few attractive features. There is a story (probably apocryphal, but illustrative of the UAW's early spirit) about the reactions of David Dubinsky, head of the ILGWU, to a UAW convention. Dubinsky is supposed to have listened with amazement as the delegates jumped to their feet and violently denounced one leader after another. He turned to Victor Reuther and asked him what kind of madness this was. Victor Reuther replied that this was the UAW and such things had to be expected in a democratic organization. "Yes," Dubinsky is supposed to have replied, "I know. In my union there is democracy too—but they know who is boss!"

To use a hackneyed but still illuminating comparison, the early democracy of the UAW had something of the flavor of the New England town hall meeting: it was direct, spontaneous, intimate. It is hardly possible for an organization of one million members to preserve that kind of democracy, but it should be possible for it to preserve a less direct and intimate but still substantial democratic life.

Today the future of democracy in the UAW depends largely on the extent to which the rank and file can again be passionately involved in its affairs. Now that the union is established and not likely to face any immediate threats to its existence, what motives can lead the members, even the more active ones, to participate in its affairs? In the early days, the need for struggle, the call to sacrifice and to heroism played a powerful role. But now mere militancy is often insufficient, sometimes even unnecessary. The union, we think, can involve large layers of the membership in its work only if it offers them a new source of interest: a compelling program of political activity sustained by a large social motivation. On this rests the future of the UAW. If it becomes "just another union," a mere service agency, it will undoubtedly suffer from a hardening of the porkchoppers' intellectual arteries; if it becomes, as it can, the leader of the American labor movement, advancing a bold program for social change, it will remain one of the few genuinely democratic mass organizations in America.

SOME PROBLEMS IN DEMOCRACY

Since the Reuther group assumed leadership, serious and interesting internal problems have arisen with regard to the presence of Stalinists inside the labor movement. There is considerable discussion in the UAW on these issues, the significance of which goes far beyond their specific context.

In the winter of 1948-49 the Reuther leadership found itself extremely annoyed at the persistent eruption of Stalinist propaganda in the newspaper of Plymouth Local 51. The UAW executive board ordered a hearing at which the local's officers were to show cause why an administrator should not be placed over the local. The Reuther leadership refrained from placing an administrator over the local, for it realized that such an action, dubious in terms of union democracy, would create sympathy in the union for Local 51. When this explanation was offered by one of Reuther's lieutenants, Norman Mathews, at a Reuther caucus meeting in January, 1949, a rank and filer took the floor to dissent. In blunt fashion, he said to Mathews: "Either you got the goods on them and you move in, or else you shut up." The rank and filer was correct: either the top leadership had specific evidence that the CP-oriented Plymouth leaders were *acting* against the union's interests, in which case disciplinary action was required, or it was merely trying to silence dissenters, in which case it was behaving undemocratically.

The democratic method works best. Instead of imposing a receivership over the Plymouth local, the Reuther people organized a caucus inside the Plymouth local and took over its leadership by winning its recent election. There is a moral here for those who want to learn it.

A more important issue with regard to the Communist Party arose after the November, 1948, convention of the CIO. At this convention, the UAW advocated a policy of expelling "those who put loyalty to the Communist Party ahead of their loyalty to the CIO and loyalty to the Soviet Union ahead of loyalty to their own country." Walter Reuther explained this position in the UAW paper:

> We believe that those who assume positions of leadership have a responsibility that goes with that leadership. That responsibility is to adhere to CIO policy . . .
>
> Officers of CIO affiliated international unions who take advantage of the privileges and protections of CIO affiliation, must also assume the responsibilities that go with CIO affiliation. Those who have failed to assume those responsibilities in the past should make up their minds once and for all either to get all the way in or all the way out of the CIO.
>
> Members of the Communist Party and those who follow the Communist Party line do not accept this democratic principle because they are not trade unionists. They are colonial agents using the trade-union movement as a base of operations for serving the foreign-policy needs of the Soviet Union.[6]

While Reuther's description of the CP is undoubtedly accurate, the wisdom of his present proposal for dealing with it may be questioned on the grounds of democratic principle and union hygiene. In effect Reuther is proposing that the CIO adopt the kind of discipline exerted only by a tightly centralized political party. But the CIO itself was born in a rebellion against an attempt to impose that sort of discipline. The 1935 AFL convention voted by a majority against allowing the organization of mass industries on an industrial-union basis; yet John L. Lewis and the other CIO leaders violated that decision. Would Reuther now argue that Lewis was wrong in doing so, or that his expulsion from the AFL was justified since he did violate its false discipline? Or would it not be more reasonable to say that a labor federation has no right to impose that kind of tight discipline on its affiliates?

Reuther's proposal that all officials of CIO unions must publicly support CIO political policy would violate the autonomy of international unions and was, in fact, rejected by Philip Murray on those grounds. There is something particularly surprising in Reuther urging anyone to "get all the way in the CIO or all the way out," when it is remembered that as recently as 1945-46 he advocated a program in the GM strike which, at the very least, was not traditional CIO policy and which, as everyone then knew, Murray did not accept.

Most fundamental, however, is the fact that Reuther wants unions to exert *political* discipline over their functionaries. Now a political party has the right to say to one of its members: either you support our candidate or get out. A union has the right to exert union discipline: that is, when a strike is called it can insist that all its members stop working. But does it have the right to insist on political uniformity among its officials and leaders? This is a dangerous notion.

The same might be said for its proposal to expel CP members from the CIO. During the 1947 UAW faction fight Reuther himself showed best how to defeat the CP in the unions: win the union members away from the CP by exposing it politically, in the arena of intellectual debate. To expel workers who belong to the CP is to run the risk of fighting Stalinism with Stalinist methods and, further, to set dangerous precedents. No union member should be expelled, and deprived thereby of his livelihood, unless *specific and grave* charges such as scabbing can be proved against him. For the totalitarians will either be defeated by democratic methods or they will not be defeated at all.

Thus far, the Reuther leadership has not tried to expel members of the UAW on the grounds that they are also members of the CP. One of the UAW locals, Briggs 212, has taken a good position on this problem. In March, 1948, there was a work stoppage at the Vernor plant (a Briggs subsidiary) when workers refused to work with three men charged with being communists. Ken Morris, president of the local, issued a statement saying that, "If on one hand we are opposed to Communism because of their undemocratic principles, we cannot hope to defeat them successfully by taking undemocratic actions ourselves. . . . We vigorously disagree with the policies of the Communist Party, and refuse to deny a communist the right to his job."[7] This seems both a more democratic and effective means of fighting the Stalinists than the view advocated by Walter Reuther.

The reader may have noticed that in this chapter a see-saw rhythm of references to UAW democracy and bureaucracy has established itself. This is a matter of necessity, for the two are interlaced in union life. No union, not even the UAW, can be realistically described as merely democratic—that is the language of publicity releases or of uncritical supporters of a leadership. Nor can a union such as the UAW be honestly described as merely bureaucratic—that is the language of anti-labor propaganda or of blinded factional opponents of a leadership. In the UAW, the two forces, democracy and bureaucracy, are in constant interaction and frequent conflict; thus far, no union, or organization of comparative size, has succeeded in maintaining a healthier balance.

But its future as a democratic organization will probably not depend on internal procedures, measures or maneuvers. If the UAW succeeds in coping with, or even seriously tries to cope with, the complex problems facing it in the coming years; if it succeeds in transforming union energies into drives toward political action and social change which alone can fulfill the larger purposes of an alert union—then it will arouse sufficient enthusiasm and interest among its members to preserve its admirable democratic tradition.

Political Action:
The Future of the UAW

12

No LARGE or important trade union can today avoid the deepest involvements in politics; it cannot raise the simplest economic demand, engage in the most seemingly isolated bargaining conflict without soon touching on the central social problems of our time. The question facing the unions in the United States is not whether to be in or out of politics, but whether to enter aggressively or be dragged in limply, to act as an independent force or as an adjunct of an existing party. For the major CIO unions, Samuel Gompers' idea of "pure and simple" unionism has long been dead; the unions are in politics, some knee, some neck deep; the real problem they face is what *kind* of politics to engage in.

There has never been an articulate group in the UAW which opposed its involvement in politics, though there have undoubtedly been plenty of leaders and members who felt that the union should largely confine itself to economic issues. Since its formation, the UAW has had several divergent, sometimes conflicting, strands of opinion about political action: one favoring mere occasional endorsements of candidates; a second urging the unions to plunge completely into a major party, usually the Democratic Party; a third believing the UAW should build an independent political apparatus (the PAC) while supporting liberal candidates of the major parties; and a fourth propagandizing for an independent labor party.

In 1936, at the first UAW convention, a resolution in favor of a farmer-labor party was passed while, under the pressure of John L. Lewis, President Roosevelt's bid for re-election was endorsed. This kind of duality—general belief in the need for a new party and specific support for one of the old ones—has since characterized the political thinking of many UAW leaders and members. Very probably, sentiment in the UAW for a new party was at its peak in 1936 and has since declined somewhat. Almost all of the then influential radical groups favored a new party of some sort, and the militant temper of the UAW activists inclined them at least to regard the idea with friendliness. But as the union grew, became stabilized, and managed to throw some weight around in the Democratic Party, its leaders became increasingly skeptical of immediate action for a new party.

During the war years, the UAW generally supported the Roosevelt administration but found itself in sharp conflict with it on many specific matters (see Chapter 5). At its October, 1943, convention the UAW voted only "conditional support of the President", as the *United Automobile Worker* said in its headline, in spite of fervent pleas by Stalinist unionists for unconditional support of

Roosevelt. At this convention Emil Mazey spoke against Roosevelt and was booed so loudly by the CP delegate bloc that he had difficulty in finishing. The overwhelming majority of delegates agreed with the views of Victor Reuther, who spoke for "conditional support" of the President.

By early 1944, however, sentiment for a new kind of political action was so strong in the UAW that a number of its secondary leaders started a new party in Michigan, the Michigan Commonwealth Federation, obviously modeled after the Canadian Commonweath Federation. For a time it seemed as if the MCF might become a powerful factor in Michigan political life, but it ultimately dissolved, or was pressured back into, the safe ranks of the CIO's Political Action Committee. However, the MCF experience was of some importance, for it was the first time that UAW leaders not directly affiliated with a radical group tried their hand at independent political action. They were hardly helped by a UAW Executive Board statement attacking the new party. Nevertheless, the new party did find considerable support in important sections of the UAW—the Ford locals, Chrysler Highland Park and the Flint Chevrolet locals.

All the political trends of 1944 were unfavorable to the MCF. The CIO leadership worked out an alliance with the Michigan Democratic Party, itself quite weak and able seriously to contest elections only when it had labor support. In return for CIO support, the Michigan Democrats endorsed the New Deal program and gave the PAC several minor posts in the party apparatus. Both the CIO leadership and the conservative press tried in different ways to create the impression that the Michigan Democratic Party had been taken over by the CIO, but actually the old-line politicians retained essential control over the party machine. To most CIO people, however, the close working alliance between the CIO and the Michigan Democrats seemed sufficient reason for not supporting the MCF. So strong were the pressures applied on the MCF by Sidney Hillman and other CIO leaders that it soon became clear that it would not long remain independent—and if it wasn't independent, what reason did it have for an existence separate from the PAC? Though the MCF ran a large slate of candidates in the 1944 local elections, its leaders individually supported Roosevelt for re-election and refrained from nominating candidates against PAC-endorsed Democratic Party candidates. Unable to decide between supporting the PAC and striking out alone, caught between the conflicting pressures of a CIO leadership which wanted it to follow the PAC line and those of its members who wanted it to break sharply from the two old parties, the Michigan Commonwealth Federation soon faded away. A political party cannot be built on indecision.

The next major political incident involving the UAW soon became a rather dubious intrigue. In May, 1945, the erratic Richard Frankensteen, then a UAW vice-president, announced his candidacy for Mayor. A few days previous, a political committee representing Michigan CIO units had denied that Frankensteen would run as its candidate. This mixup can be understood only against the background of the faction fight then being waged in the UAW. The faction of which Frankensteen was a leader hoped that his campaign and possible election would greatly magnify its intra-union strength; the Reuther wing correspondingly frowned on the Frankensteen candidacy. (Not only, by the way, because of factional reasons; there was considerable speculation in UAW circles about what Frankensteen might do if elected.) One former UAW official, Charles Edgecomb, said in a radio speech that Frankensteen was "a self-starter who put the officers of our union in such a tight spot that they can pursue no other course than to hand him a reluctant endorsement."[1] In the UAW, Edgecomb's remark was considered tactless— but it was true, nonetheless.

In Detroit's primary run-offs, Frankensteen polled the largest vote, but before the actual election a coalition of conservative and reactionary political forces was formed to support Mayor Jeffries. The official opposition to Frankensteen was wild enough, but its anonymous quasi-fascist supporters were often viciously anti-Negro. Thousands of handbills appeared in the streets of Detroit charging that if Frankensteen were elected Mayor "you couldn't keep the niggers out of City Hall".[2] Frankensteen, in turn, did not distinguish himself either by dignified behavior or a serious discussion of political issues.

Rallying the entire conservative vote, Jeffries defeated Frankensteen, who could not win a united labor vote. Two years later, oddly enough, both wings of the UAW supported Jeffries for Mayor. Neither Frankensteen's off-key performance nor the political gyrations of the CIO leadership in Michigan did much to develop a high political consciousness among Detroit unionists.

Before the 1948 presidential elections, it again seemed as if the UAW were preparing for some sort of independent political movement. The Reuthers had occasionally expressed themselves in favor of a new party, Victor Reuther having written in late 1945 that, "The time is now ripe for labor to divorce itself from the two old parties and resolve to build the base for an independent, indigenous, new national political party."[3] In early 1948, when Truman's popularity in the labor movement could have been tucked away in a thimble's worth of space, and when it seemed that the Republican Party could win with almost any candidate capable of smiling into a camera, Walter Reuther began to hint that the UAW might strike out on its own politically. He denounced in writing both the Democrats and Republicans for "playing fast and loose with the welfare of the American people."[4] He also described Truman as "hopelessly inadequate."

At the same time, the Wallace movement seemed to be gathering considerable support in the shops. During the war years the CP fractions in the UAW had been the most vociferous opponents of either the MCF or any possible third party, but now they worked like demons for the Wallace candidacy. Had Wallace not so thoroughly discredited himself because of his close relations with the Stalinists, he might have rolled up a very impressive vote in the auto cities. In early 1948 he had not yet been debunked as an appeaser of Russia, and the UAW leadership was worried about the amount of support he might win in the ranks.

Meeting in March, 1948, the UAW International Executive Board adopted a political resolution which denounced the Wallace candidacy as "a premature and ill-advised adventure" and "a Communist Party maneuver," and adopted as its official political objective the formation of "a genuine progressive party" after the 1948 elections.[5] Though this resolution did not contain an endorsement of President Truman, it left the door wide open for one. After the 80th Congress aroused the most bitter feelings among both the union leadership and the workers, Walter Reuther issued a special statement, in the August, 1948, *United Automobile Worker*, in which he pledged to devote "my full support and my full energy for a new political alignment." However, when the CIO endorsed President Truman, the UAW adopted the same position, though two members of its executive board, Emil Mazey and Martin Gerber, voted against the endorsement. Subsequently, while officially supporting the CIO and UAW positions, Mazey let it be known that, as in previous elections, he would vote for Norman Thomas.

After Truman was elected, the UAW, for all practical purposes, junked the idea of immediate action for a new party. It had scheduled an educational conference devoted primarily to political problems for January 19, 1949, the day when Thomas Dewey was supposedly to be inaugurated; at this conference the first steps would presumably be taken to form a new party. But with the election of Truman and a number of liberal Congressmen, Reuther quickly swung back to the view that labor should function within, while not identifying itself with, the Democratic Party. Mazey, however, continued to believe that "we can only hope to solve the problem of jobs by building a powerful organization of labor and farmers that will have the courage . . . to democratically plan and use the facilities that our nation has . . ."[6] As usual, a mixture of the two ideas became the actual UAW program. Although there is little immediate possibility that the UAW will openly diverge from official CIO policy by boldly building a new political alignment, there are many signs of impatience in both the leadership and ranks with the union's cautious policy since Truman's election. In Michigan the inability of the UAW to convince old-line Democrats to concern themselves with very much besides patronage has resulted in a marked chilliness of relations between the "UAW Democrats" and the "regular Democrats." Nationally, the honeymoon between the Truman administration and the labor movement has not proved quite idyllic, as Reuther reminded the President at a White House conference. In this atmosphere, the problem

of political action by the labor movement will persist, and,
it may be expected, more voices will be raised for a new
party.

WHAT SHOULD LABOR DO?

The likelihood is that the union will veer and tack
politically, pursuing a highly flexible (or, if one prefers,
opportunist) policy, which will frequently provoke discussion in the union ranks. One such discussion (incidentally,
an excellent testimonial to the continuing democratic tradition in the UAW) took place at the January, 1949, educational conference the union held in Milwaukee.

Some 2,500 delegates listened to two main political
speeches. Congressman Andrew Biemiller, an ex-socialist
from Wisconsin and now a member of the liberal wing of
the Democratic Party, expressed one point of view. "The
election of 1948," he said, "proved that a genuine liberal
non-Communist labor party is not necessary nor a united-
front party wanted." Professor Robert Lynd, Columbia
University sociologist and author of *Middletown*, urged
the UAW to take the lead in forming a new party. "If
labor is to seize the initiative," he said, "it has to go
political; I mean form a labor party. There is no use in
you trying to take over the Democratic Party . . . A labor
party would have to make up its mind about capitalism
and about democratic national planning."[7]

The floor discussion largely reflected this split in opinion.
Most of the delegates from Michigan spoke in favor of
working inside the Democratic Party, with the possible
aim of capturing it in some localities. Delegates from Chicago told how they had helped the Democrats win the
election and had later been shunted aside by the regular
party leaders; they felt that even if the UAW were to work

within the Democratic Party it should retain an independent political machine of its own.

And that will probably be the dominant formula for UAW political action for the coming period: to work within the Democratic Party but to build "an independent machine." At the Milwaukee conference Walter Reuther said as much: "We in the CIO are committed . . . to build independent political forces outside of existing political parties and to use that power in the manner we deem most effective for our needs."[8] The UAW leaders now fear that any great reliance on a Democratic Party whose commitment to their program is lukewarm may create serious political difficulties for them. Emil Mazey has argued this point in UAW circles: "We'd be fools to bank on a party which can't solve either the basic economic problems of the working class or the question of war."[9] The UAW is preparing to support one of its former officials and a political ally, George Edwards, for Mayor of Detroit in 1949. This will be a major UAW venture into independent local political action. Though Edwards may try to give his campaign a "non-partisan" tinge, the conservative press will force the issue of the UAW's political role to the forefront of the campaign. It is therefore likely that the campaign will take on some of the characteristics it might have if there were an independent labor party functioning in Detroit.

Yet the problem of the labor movement's political course cannot or should not be settled merely on the basis of momentary twists of political leaders or momentary shifts in power relationships. Involved here is a matter of principle: what is or should be the political aim of the more advanced American trade unions?

The argument of those who favor continued co-operation with the liberal wings of the major parties usually proceeds along the following lines: "Neither of the two major parties is as tightly set up, either organizationally or ideologically, as the conservative or reactionary parties of Europe. No doubt, the dominant forces in both the Democratic and Republican Parties favor the continuation of capitalism, but then the American trade unions have not become revolutionary organs to destroy capitalism, nor are they likely to. All the unions want or need is a series of concrete demands which can be won through a liberal administration and Congress; in fact, some already have been. So, while the Democratic and Republican Parties may be abstractly 'capitalist,' in practice they contain a wide variety of political views, some of which the unions oppose and some of which they can support. Furthermore, the structure of American politics is such that a third party would have little chance of success. Many states make it difficult for new parties to get on the ballot. Actually, it is easier for the labor movement, using its own political apparatus, to fight out its battles in the old-party primaries than to set up a new party of its own. And finally, if a new party were created, it would tend to divide the liberal vote and ensure the victory of the reactionary right. Mind you, we are not opposed to a new party for all time and under all conditions; a reshuffling of the old ones may result in some sort of liberal-labor party; but the labor movement would stand to lose a great deal if it immediately cut itself off from its allies in the Democratic and Republican Parties and set up a party of its own."

In contrast, the argument for a labor party would run something like this: "There are at least two kinds of possible reasoning in behalf of a labor party. One of these is the socialist view. Socialists in the trade unions believe that just as the unions have established themselves as independent economic organs of the workers, so should there be created an independent political organ of the workers. Such a party might very well not have a socialist program, particularly at the outset, and could probably not solve all the problems of modern society. But it would at least represent a political coming-of-age for the American workers, a declaration of political independence from the old parties which, however 'loosely' organized, still defend the capitalist status quo. Then there are non-socialists in the unions, those who are simply labor militants and are not concerned with the general idea of a labor party as a step toward 'class independence.' They favor a labor party because they believe such a party would be the best way to win what the unions want, particularly if such a party could gain the support of farmers and sections of the urban middle class. (From here on, the socialist and non-socialist arguments for a labor party converge.) Time and again, labor's experience has been that the 'liberals' elected with its support did not come through as they had promised; they used the labor movement rather than served it. The liberals as a whole are too undependable; once a liberal gains power he too often becomes a conservative. If we have our own party, we will be able to control our representatives more adequately, and the best and most courageous of the liberals will come with us anyway. It is true that there are practical difficulties facing a new party, such as getting on the ballot, etc. But we'll just have to face them. However, we don't think a labor party would give a helping hand to the reactionaries. The kind of 'deal' labor gets will depend far more on its own organized strength than on the number of dubious liberals in Congress; a new party capturing the imagination of the American people, even if it did not win immediate electoral victories, would change the whole political temper of the nation, raise to a higher level the national political discussion, and provide a tremendous pressure force which the labor movement does not at present have. Finally, there is one more reason to favor a new party. If a depression comes in the reasonable future, a political swing to the left among many Americans is probable. To prevent them from falling into the CP trap, it is necessary to have a genuine, idealistic and aggressive alternative of the non-communist left; only a labor party could be that alternative."

This debate could, of course, be prolonged indefinitely with rebuttals and counter-rebuttals, but these two statements provide, we hope, a fair version of the general motivations of those holding both views. The authors of this book themselves favor a labor party for America, but must acknowledge—at least as of mid-1949—that their view will probably remain a minority one in the UAW during the immediate future. Yet such matters are not settled through an exchange of abstract statements; the experiences of life, we think, will lead the most idealistic and militant unionists to work for a new party based on labor and its allies.

THE WAR ECONOMY: GUNS OR BUTTER?

It is a mark of the intellectual backwardness and laziness of the American trade-union leadership that, with a few exceptions, it has failed to consider the general question of the role of the unions in American postwar life. The UAW leadership has made a few tentative, hardly sufficient moves toward thinking about the place of trade unions in an economy increasingly geared to war production. Yet this problem may well turn out to be the major one for the labor movement in the coming years.

Is the drift of American economy toward a kind of liberal "garrison economy" compatible with labor's desire for greater federal support of social services? Can the unions continue, at least in present form, their traditional bargaining functions in a society where the government increasingly orders and dominates production? Can even American society, the wealthiest in the world, indefinitely provide both guns and butter?

These are difficult, complex questions, an answer to which would require another entire book written by a skilled economist. But while not pretending to exhaust these problems, we wish here to mention a few of them, particularly with regard to the probable role of trade unions in the next few years.

The major direction of modern capitalist society is toward statism; laissez-faire, as fact or idea, is an anachronistic joke. By statism we mean the tendency of government to set rules for private enterprise, to become one of its main buyers and thereby indirect controllers, to subsidize industries facing financial difficulties, to abet the drives of industry itself toward various forms of monopolization, and in extreme situations to nationalize defunct or bankrupt industries. So powerful is this economic drive that it is to be found in both democratic and dictatorial nations, though of course in considerably different forms. In pre-Hitler Germany, there was the intense cartelization of business; in Hitler Germany, the consolidation of gigantic trusts, controlled jointly by the old capitalists and the new Nazi state bureaucrats; in fascist Italy, the corporate state in which employers and employees were aligned in parallel economic regiments; in postwar England, the labor government's supervision of private industry and the nationalization of certain industries, such as coal. The state thus tends to become the force that: 1) protects the central profit-and-private-ownership aspects of capitalism while depriving many individual capitalists of secondary privileges; 2) acquiesces in the tendency to increasing monopolization; 3) regularizes the conditions of economic life to prevent, if possible, extreme dislocations; 4) acts to help equalize profits and losses, as if it were a holding company of overall "capital" in behalf of the many scattered and competitive industrial units.

In the United States, this development has also taken place, though in somewhat milder form. The New Deal, writes the sociologist C. Wright Mills, "was an attempt to subsidize the defaults of the capitalist system. Part of this attempt consisted in the effort to rationalize business and labor as systems of power in order to permit a continued flow of profits, investments, and employment." The NIRA gave labor the right to bargain, but equally important, it was an attempt by government to regulate on a national scale business and labor cartels. Businessmen were given wide powers for the inner regulation of their industries—and the inclination of New Deal thought was to regard each industry as a compact unit. As a formal setup, the NIRA failed, largely because the government did not yet have enough power to enforce it. But in practice the tendency toward industry-wide regulation was strengthened during the war—and before the war by the Wagner Act, which helped unions become dominant bargaining agents in each industry. The U. S. Government assumed powers during the war that would have made the hair of Adam Smith or Thomas Jefferson stand on end. It had to; that was the only way to run a capitalist economy for war purposes.

Where then does all this lead to? It leads, says Mills, to "a stage where the state, in the interests of domestic stability and international security, increasingly appropriates the aims of the employer and expropriates or abolishes the functions of the unions . . . Increasingly, this state becomes the regulator of the national labor force, a task previously performed by individual employers and their unions, with only the courts intervening . . . Confronted with state encroachment upon labor business relations, the economic power of the unions declines. *Every economic tactic is as dependent for its success upon the political authorities as it is upon the economic strength to withdraw the worker from the process of production."*[10] (Our emphasis—I. H. and B. J. W.)

Yet the drive toward statism in America has only begun; its first major signs are the behavior of the government during and after the war. The powerful overall intervention of the government during the war is too well known to require description, but the degree to which it has helped stabilize private industry in the postwar period has been insufficiently studied by unionists—even by those who study anything at all. By 1949 the postwar consumers demand had largely declined to a normal level, and the market was changing from a sellers' to a buyers.' Unemployment was growing. Now, if the government had not been pumping billions of dollars into Marshall Plan aid and armament production, a good part of which returns to American industry, might there not soon have been an economic depression of catastrophic proportions? The government thus becomes a major force confronting and sometimes opposing the unions in economic life; as the private economy and the state interpenetrate, the unions cannot act with regard to one without affecting their relations to the other.

And there the union movement finds itself in difficulty —as it will undoubtedly find itself in increasing difficulties

in the years to come. The unions are primarily oriented
to limited economic activities within an industry; yet the
major decisions affecting their futures and the lives of
their members are increasingly the work of the government. This is the central fact which will either drive the
unions to full-scale independent political action or leave
them withered and anachronistic. But it must further
be emphasized that the trend toward greater government
intervention in and control of business does not occur in
a social vacuum; at present it is intimately related to, in
fact is inextricable from, a fierce armament race. The
American economy is undertaking, not only to equip the
U. S. Army, but the armies of half of Europe as well. The
unions must therefore ask themselves: how long is it possible for any government, even one based on so rich a
country as the U. S., to continue armament preparations
and yet maintain social services—to do both and yet
prevent inflation?

To some extent, Walter Reuther has at least recognized
the existence of this problem (which is more than can be
said for most labor leaders) by proposing his housing
plan, described in Chapter 9. In this plan, he seems
to think, he has found a scheme for providing the country
with both guns and butter. Yet, even if his scheme is
feasible and houses can be built in factories that could
quickly be converted to war production, that does not
solve the basic problem which he has touched. For there
is no getting around it: a gun is not a pound of butter and
a pound of butter is not a gun. Sooner or later, a government faced with the two alternatives must choose—which
is one reason why the Truman "Fair Deal" is not likely
to set any sensational records in passing liberal social
legislation. Its international policies and commitments are

such that, if forced to choose, it will have to prefer guns to butter. What answer do the unions have?

Perhaps the union leaders, particularly those with a greater political sense, will be forced to say that, in the interest of preventing Russian domination of the world, they are ready to acquiesce in a lowered American standard of living. If any do say this, they will be open to attack from two sides: first, from the workers in their unions who are more interested in immediate conditions than in overall world policies; second and more cogently, from those unionists who feel that if the labor movement offered the people of Europe an attractive radical and democratic alternative to either Russian domination or their present misery, Stalinism in Europe would be more decisively defeated than if confronted with ten boatloads of atom bombs.

What is most important with regard to these matters is that even the more alert and intelligent unionists pay so little attention to them. The pragmatic tradition of the American labor movement, its unwillingness to anticipate "theoretical" problems, may in this instance cost it dearly. But such unions as the UAW must, if they are to flourish, consider their relationship to an increasingly statified economy; they must find political means of influencing or controlling or changing the political organism that absorbs individual economic units into itself; they must face the problem of war economy and/or social services; they must find political means of helping the European people get on their feet so that they can live independently, dominated neither by East nor West. Why union leaders should dislike facing such problems is only too easy to understand; perhaps for some the reason is that they know they would then have to come to funda-

mental and radical conclusions by which they would prefer not to be troubled.

TOWARDS A NEW UNIONISM

America needs a new kind of union, one that will maintain the virtues of the older unions but will take the lead
in reacting to the problems that have arisen in the postwar
world. This new union would be as organizationally canny
and negotiations-wise as the AFL craft units; as militant
and ready for struggle as the CIO unions in the days of
their birth; and as rebellious and libertarian in spirit as
the old IWW. Here are some of the things it might do
to solve the problems that will soon be plaguing the
American labor movement:

It could orient itself toward an independent role in politics, serving as the focus for a realignment to include the
more militant unionists, the homeless anti-Stalinist left
and the thousands of people who would like to see a genuinely indigenous labor-radical coalition movement in the
U. S. This political realignment would neither be tainted
with the Moscow touch nor crippled by the usual timidity
and double-talk of what passes for liberalism in America.

Such a union could enrich its inner life, raising the
political, intellectual and cultural levels of its membership, rooting out all traces of racial prejudice and fiercely
guarding its democratic tradition.

Such a union could react sharply to the dangers of a
possible "liberal" version of the corporate state by fighting
every inch to maintain its independence; it could offer an
attractive radical and democratic alternative to the two
major political trends in the world today, that which looks
to Moscow for the new salvation and that which hopes to
regain the old salvation with the aid of the atom bomb;

and thereby it could prevent the American economy from preferring armaments to social services. If the unions continue to muddle through as they have been recently, that does not mean they will be able to exist in the style they have become accustomed to. Conservative unionism may well prove incapable of conserving the unions—as it proved incapable in pre-Hitler Germany. Conservative unionism would be adequate only if, while it stood still, everything else in modern society stood still too. But that is obviously impossible. The developments of modern society, which we have so briefly noted here, imperil the continued existence of the free trade-union movement.

The UAW is both the closest thing to the kind of union we have described as desirable and yet still far away from it; but in few other unions are there so many people who, in one way or another, would like to make it this kind of union.

In the Reuther group there are conflicting pulls. Some of Reuther's associates, such as the UAW vice-presidents, John Livingston and Richard Gosser, are routine conservative unionists, who want the UAW to become a powerful, affluent, respectable and "stabilized" union closely meshing with the status quo. The ACTU people have a similar perspective; they supported Reuther against the Stalinists because they would like to root all radicals, genuine or false, from power; now they apply pressure on Reuther from the right.

Since the triumph of the Reuther group in November, 1947, the more conservative of his allies and followers have been dominant. They have controlled many of the union's positions of power; the general social atmosphere of recent American life has favored them; and the more radical wing of Reutherites has not been particularly coherent or self-confident. Yet it is more than likely that the heterogeneous assortment of socialists, semi-socialists and militant unionists whom we designate as the radical wing of the Reuther group, will yet have an opportunity to win the union to its ideas and programs. Between these two conflicting pressures, Reuther skillfully balances, pragmatically testing which side can summon the most support in the union and among the people as a whole.

But in the long run it is not Reuther or any other individual who counts most. "To have an American labor movement capable of carrying out the program of the left, [and] making allies among the middle class . . . there must be a rank and file of vigorous workers, a brace of labor intellectuals, and a set of politically alert labor leaders. There must be the power and there must be the intellect."[11] In the UAW, more than in any other American union, there are potentially both. The militants have now spent over a decade in building their union, protecting it from attack from within and without; they are tough; they are self-confident; they know how to build organizations and now even have some rudimentary political experience. But they need political education and assistance. There are also in the UAW people with ideas who can give them that assistance. Will the power be welded to the intellect?

The achievements of the UAW are great; no other union has helped so many Americans improve and elevate the quality of their lives; no other union has brought so large a measure of decency and dignity to people who before knew only the regimen of factory rule. For that achievement, its members have every reason for pride. But now they face a greater challenge: Will the UAW settle into the usual union rut and become just "another union," or will it use its vast resource of energy and power to become a new social force in American life?

Walter Reuther has said of the UAW: "We are the vanguard in America . . . We are the achitects of the future."[12] Where will this vanguard lead, and what will these architects build? On the answer depends much of the future of this country.

Notes

1

The statistical and some of the analytical material in this chapter is based on the following sources: Current Population Reports: Population Characteristics of Detroit and Metropolitan Area, *1947. U.S. Census Bureau;* The Economic Base, *Master Plan Reports, City Plan Commission, Detroit, 1944;* The People of Detroit, *Master Plan Reports, Detroit City Commission, Detroit, 1944;* Tenth Annual Report, *Detroit Housing Commission, 1944;* Eleventh Annual Report, *Detroit Housing Commission, 1945–1946;* Social and Economic Rating of Detroit, *Detroit Bureau of Governmental Research, 1945;* Movement of Negro Population Within the City of Detroit by Census Tracts, *Detroit Bureau of Governmental Research, 1941;* Community Survey, *Citizens Survey Commission of Metropolitan Detroit, 1948;* Ammunition, *1948;* Automobile Facts and Figures, *Automobile Manufacturers Association, 1948;* Fifty Years of Men and Autos, *UAW pamphlet, undated;* Rise of the Auto Workers, *Edward Levinson, UAW pamphlet, 1947;* The Auto Workers Union,, *Frank Marquard, UAW pamphlet, undated.*

1. *Life,* Aug. 17, 1942.
2. *My Life and Work,* Henry Ford, in collaboration with Samuel Crowther, Doubleday and Co., 1922.
3. *ibid.*
4. *Detroit News,* Jan. 12, 1914.
5. "The Hill-Billies Come to Detroit," Louis Adamic, *The Nation,* Feb. 13, 1935.
6. *Detroit News,* Rex G. White. Aug. 12, 1947.
7. *The Detroit Murders,* edited by Alvin Hamer, Duell, Sloan & Pearce, 1948.

8. "The Life Story of Joe Louis," *New York Times,* Nov. 5–12, 1948.
9. "The Truth About the Detroit Riot," Earl Brown, *Harper's Magazine,* Nov. 1943.
10. *Michigan,* Oxford University Press, rev. ed., 1946.
11. *ibid.*
12. *Ammunition,* Aug. 1948.
13. *Business Week,* April 21, 1948.
14. Estimate obtained from Ed Hill, financial secretary, Local 7, UAW.
15. *Community Survey,* Citizens Survey Committee of Metropolitan Detroit, 1948.
16. *Tenth Annual Report,* Detroit Housing Commission, 1944.
17. *Eleventh Annual Report,* Detroit Housing Commission, 1945–46.
18. George Edwards, chairman of Detroit City Council, in testimony before the House Banking Committee, May 17, 1948.
19. *Today and Tomorrow,* Henry Ford in collaboration with Samuel Crowther, Doubleday and Co., 1926.
20. W. J. Cameron, Ford Sunday Hour Talks, Nov. 7, 1937, Dec. 18, 1938; quoted in *The Legend of Henry Ford,* Keith Sward, Rinehart and Co., 1948.
21. From a survey by Prof. C. Wright Mills, Columbia University, as summarized in *Ammunition,* Aug. 1948.
22. "Ford Puts on the Union Label," Victor Waybright, *Survey Graphic,* Nov. 1941.
23. From personal interviews with B. J. Widick.
24. Henderson Report for the National Recovery Administration, Jan. 23, 1935.
25. *Race Riots Aren't Necessary,* Alfred McClung Lee, Public Affairs Pamphlet, 1945.
26. Article by Martin S. Hayden, *Detroit News,* April, 1942.
27. *Detroit News,* Feb. 3, 1948.
28. *Race Riot,* Alfred McClung Lee and Norman Humphrey, Dryden Press, 1943.
29. "Race Riots Coming," Walter Davenport, *Collier's,* Sept. 18, 1943.
30. *An American Dilemma,* Gunnar Myrdal, Harper and Bros., 1944.
31. Davenport, *op. cit.*
32. *The American Jitters,* Edmund Wilson, Chas. Scribner's Sons, 1932.
33. *Journey to the End of the Night,* Louis-Ferdinand Céline, New Directions, 1947.
34. "On Popular Music," T. Adorno, *Studies in Philosophy & Social Science,* Vol. IX, 1941.

2

The most authoritative analytical account of early union struggles in the auto industry is by A. J. Muste, cited below. Also very valuable is Edward Levinson's book, cited below. Much of the literature about this period has been written by writers under the influence of the Stalinists and is therefore of doubtful reliability, one such account being a book by a former UAW official, Henry Krause.

1. *Labor Relations in the Automobile Industry*, William H. McPherson, The Brookings Institute, 1940.
2. *The Automobile Industry and Organized Labor*, A. J. Muste, A Christian Social Justice Fund pamphlet, 1936.
3. *Report*, Wyndham Mortimer to second annual convention, UAW, Milwaukee, Wisconsin, 1937.
4. *Detroit News*, May 3, 1936.
5. *ibid.*
6. *CIO*, J. Raymond Walsh, W. W. Norton, 1937.
7. *Labor on the March*, Edward Levinson, Harper and Bros., 1838.
8. *The Flint Auto Worker*, Jan. 12, 1937.
9. *The New York Times*, Jan. 22, 1937.
10. Levinson, *op. cit.*
11. *ibid.*
12. Told by Lewis in speech to UAW convention, St. Louis, 1940.
13. *Local 7 Citadel*, March, 1947.
14. *Business Week*, April 10, 1937.
15. UAW convention resolution, Milwaukee, 1937.

3

There is no single authoritative account of the material covered in this chapter, though a great mass of unreliable documents exists. Daniel Rosenblatt's GM-UAW Labor Relations, *an unpublished master's thesis, University of Michigan, 1946, contains a chapter giving a detailed, quite objective version of the Martin episode. Benjamin Stolberg's* The Story of the CIO, (*Viking, 1938*) *has a chapter completely pro-Martin and re-*

markable for its erroneous predictions. A more sober though insufficiently critical section of Edward Levinson's Labor on the March, op. cit., is anti-Martin.

The radical press is indispensable for this period of UAW history, though it is also one-sided. Anti-Martin material can be found in the files of The Daily Worker and The Socialist Call, from quite different points of view, of course. Pro-Martin material appeared in The Workers' Age, Lovestone's paper. Critical though inconsistent coverage was offered by The Socialist Appeal, the then Trotskyist paper.

The UAW press itself merely reflected the views of whichever group controlled it, but if consulted for documents rather than veracity it is indispensable.

We are grateful to Dick Artalo, Ford Local 600, for allowing us to examine his extensive file of materials on the Martin period.

1. *New York Times*, June 18, 1937.
2. *Detroit News*, Nov. 11, 1948.
3. *West Side Conveyor*, Nov. 1937.
4. Stolberg, *op. cit.*
5. *Daily Worker*, Feb. 6, 1949.
6. *New York Times*, July 23, 1938.
7. Letter of the Four Suspended Officers, Aug. 3, 1938. (From Artalo files, *op. cit.*)
8. *New York Times*, Aug. 29, 1938.
9. *Detroit News*, Oct. 12, 1938.
10. *Detroit News*, Jan. 25 and Jan. 27, 1939.
11. *Detroit News*, Jan. 30, 1939.
12. Rosenblatt, *op. cit.*
13. Statement, Committee for American Democratic Unionism, Aug. 1941.

4

It is impossible to write on the subject of this chapter without being indebted to Keith Sward's The Legend of Henry Ford (*Rinehart, 1948*). A first-rate contribution to American *history, his book has been scandalously neglected. Part of the material in this chapter is based on Sward's book, particularly the opening description of the Ford institution, though our portrait of Ford diverges at several points from that of Sward and our analysis of the 1941 Ford strike is based on different materials and is different in view from his. Nonetheless, the debt remains, and is gladly acknowledged.*

Other general sources consulted for this chapter were: "Automobile Unionism" by R. J. Thomas, a UAW report including a section on Ford organization; Upton Sinclair's The Flivver King (Haldeman, Julius, 1937); and the personal files of Ford union materials which Dick Artalo of Local 600 and David Averill, editor of Ford Facts, Local 600 paper, have kindly made available to us.

1. Sward, *op. cit.*
2. "Model T . . . the Peacemaker," Niven Busch, *The New Yorker,* March 10, 1928.
3. *The World's Foremost Problem, The Dearborn Independent,* 1920.
4. "A Talk with Henry Ford," James Bone, *Manchester Guardian,* April 8, 1947.
5. Sward, *op. cit.*
6. "Model T Tycoon," *Time,* March 17, 1941.
7. "Model T . . . Tintype," Niven Busch, *The New Yorker,* March 3, 1928.
8. "Model T . . . Turkey in the Straw," Niven Busch, *The New Yorker,* March 17, 1928.
9. See footnote 7.
10. Culled from Henry Ford's autobiographical works and his statements to the press.
11. "The Little Man in Henry Ford's Basement," John McCarten, *American Mercury,* May, 1940.
12. Quoted by McCarten, see note 11.
13. Sward, *op. cit.*
14. "Mr. Ford Doesn't Care," *Fortune,* Dec., 1933.
15. Sward, *op. cit.*
16. *Detroit News,* Jan. 28, 1933.
17. *Detroit News,* April 2, 1941.
18. *Detroit News,* April 4, 1941.
19. *Detroit Free Press,* May 23, 1941.
20. Interview with Emil Mazey by B. J. Widick.

5

1. *Proceedings,* UAW convention, July–Aug. 1940.
2. "The Strange Story of the Reuther Plan," George R. Clark, *Harper's Magazine,* May, 1942.
3. *ibid.*
4. *ibid.*
5. Cf. *War Lords of Washington,* Bruce Catton, Harcourt, Brace & Co., 1948.
6. *The United Automobile Worker,* Dec. 15, 1941.
7. *Proceedings,* UAW emergency conference, April, 1942.
8. *Proceedings,* UAW convention, Aug. 1942.
9. Harold Lavine, in *PM,* July 20, 1942.
10. *Modern Economic Society,* Sumner H. Slichter, Henry Holt & Co., 1931.
11. *Business Week,* April 3, 1943.
12. *Wage Policy in War Production,* Pamphlet by Earl Browder, 1943.
13. *Daily Worker,* Feb. 25, 1943.
14. Advertisement in *Detroit News,* May 14, 1943.
15. *Detroit News,* May 9, 1943.
16. *Daily Worker,* Oct. 10, 1943.
17. *Proceedings,* UAW convention, Oct. 1943.
18. *How to Win for the Union,* UAW Shop Steward Handbook, 7th ed. Edited by Jack Zeller.
19. Victor Riesel, *New York Post,* Feb. 1, 1944.
20. Catton, *op. cit.*

6

We are grateful to Daniel Rosenblatt for allowing us to use his master's thesis on GM-UAW relations, cited in the notes to Chapter 3. Some of the material and references in this chapter are drawn from his study. Other sources that present interesting reports on the GM strike and the ideological issues related to it are: Time *Magazine;* The Wage Earner, *organ of the Catholic unionists; and* Labor Action, *a socialist weekly.*

1. *The Wage Earner,* July 20, 1945.
2. *The Automobile Worker,* Sept. 1, 1945.
3. *Detroit News,* July 10, 1945.
4. *How to Raise Wages Without Increasing Prices,* Walter P. Reuther, UAW pamphlet, 1946.

5. Transcript, UAW-GM negotiations, 1945–46.
6. *Detroit News,* Nov. 24, 1945.
7. *New York Times,* Jan. 11, 1946.
8. *Here Is the Issue.* Pamphlet published by General Motors, 1946.
9. *New York Times,* Dec. 30, 1945.
10. *Detroit News,* Dec. 3, 1945.
11. *Detroit News,* Dec. 11, 1945.
12. *New York Times,* Dec. 5, 1945.
13. *New York Times,* Dec. 29, 1945.
14. *Detroit News,* Feb. 12, 1946.
15. *The Wage Earner,* Dec. 21, 1945.
16. *The New Leader,* Feb. 23, 1946.
17. *The General Motors Strike. The Facts and Their Implications.* Alfred P. Sloan, General Motors pamphlet, 1946.
18. *Detroit News,* Dec. 30, 1945.
19. *New York Times,* Oct. 18, 1945.
20. *Detroit News,* March 26, 1946.
21. Transcript, UAW-GM negotiations, 1945–46.
22. *Detroit News,* March 26, 1946.
23. *Daily Worker,* Nov. 27, 1945.
24. *Detroit News,* Jan. 7, 1946.
25. *Daily Worker,* March 15, 1946.
26. *Daily Worker,* April 23, 1946.
27. *Political Affairs,* March, 1946
28. *The Wage Earner,* Dec. 21, 1945.
29. *The Wage Earner,* Oct. 26, 1945.
30. *Labor Action,* April 29, 1946.

7

1. *New York Times,* Oct. 18, 1948.
2. UAW press release, March 28, 1947.
3. *Wage Earner,* April 4, 1947.
4. "How to Beat the Communists," Walter Reuther, *Collier's,* Feb. 28, 1948.
5. "A Critical Review of Party's Work in Auto." Resolution of Michigan State Committee, Communist Party, *The Daily Worker,* June 27, 1948.
6. From ACTU Articles of Federation. A large periodical literature on ACTU is accumulating. Favorable articles include: "Priests, Workers and Communists," Jules Weinberg, *Harper's Magazine,* Nov. 1948. "Nine Years of the ACTU," John C. Cort, *America,* April 6,

1946. Critical treatments include: "The Catholic Church and the Union Movement," Martin Mayer, *Labor and Nation,* March–April, 1949; "No Friend of Labor," James M. Freeman, Fulfillment Press, 1949. An interesting debate between an ACTU spokesman, Father Charles Rice, and a Marxist critic, Max Schachtman, appears in *The New International,* January, 1949.

7. Reuther speech, June 10, 1946, at caucus meeting of Reuther group for Michigan CIO convention.
8. CIO convention proceedings, Nov. 15, 1946.
9. Letter of John Brophy to Walter Reuther, Jan. 31, 1948.
10. Report of the President (Walter Reuther) to the Eleventh Convention, UAW, Nov. 9, 1947.
11. *The Daily Worker,* June 12, 1947.
12. *FDR,* Sept. 25, 1947.
13. Declaration, Circuit Court for the County of Wayne, Oct. 17, 1947.
14. UAW press release, Nov. 14, 1947.
15. *Detroit News,* Nov. 16, 1947.

8

1. *Detroit Free Press,* March 22, 1949.
2. *New York Times,* March 2, 1949.

9

1. Quoted in *Fortune,* Dec. 1940.
2. Transcript of negotiations between General Motors and UAW, pp. 185–90.

10

We are indebted in this chapter to the excellent unpublished dissertation of Lloyd Bailer, cited below. Other general sources that have been used include Gunnar Myrdhal's An American Dilemma, *previously cited; Glen Carlson's* The Negro in the Industries of Detroit, *unpublished doctoral thesis, University of Michigan, 1929; Horace Cayton's and George Mitchell's* Black Workers and the New Unions, *University of*

North Carolina, 1939; Sterling Spero's and Abram Harris' The
Black Worker, *Columbia University Press, 1931.*

*Other sources used include: UAW Fair Practices Depart-
ment files; UAW Fair Practices Fact Sheet, a bi-monthly pub-
lication;* To unite ... Regardless, *1944, UAW pamphlet;* Justice
on the Job Front, *1947, UAW pamphlet;* Fourth Annual Report, *City of Detroit's Interracial Committee, 1947;* Report,
*Emil Mazey to UAW Fair Practices Committee, 1948; reports
and speeches to UAW Fair Practices Conference, Detroit,
1948.*

1. Cayton and Mitchell; Spero and Harris, *op. cit.*
2. *Accident Rates in the Automobile Industry 1940,* National Safety
   Council, Inc.
3. *Causes of Death by Occupation,* Louis Dublin and Robert Vane,
   U.S. Bureau of Statistics, 1930.
4. *Racial Factors in American Industry,* Herman Feldman, Harper &
   Bros., 1931.
5. See "Race Discrimination in Unions," Herbert Northrop, *American
   Mercury,* July, 1945.
6. *Negro Labor in the Automobile Industry,* Lloyd H. Bailer, Unpublished doctoral dissertation. University of Michigan, 1943.
7. "Labor Tackles the Race Question," Frank Winn, *Antioch Review,*
   Fall, 1943.
8. *Ibid.*
9. Bailer, *op. cit.*
10. Quoted in *Participation of Negroes in Detroit Elections,* Thomas
    Ralph Solomon, Unpublished doctoral dissertation, University of
    Michigan, 1939.
11. "Who Owns the Negro Churches?" Horace A. White, *Christian
    Century,* Feb. 9, 1938.
12. Quoted by Bailer, *op. cit.*
13. *Ibid.*
14. *Ibid.*
15. "The Negro Automobile Worker," Lloyd Bailer, *Journal of Political
    Economy,* Oct. 1943.
16. *Detroit News,* April 12, 1943.
17. *What Caused the Detroit Riot?* Walter White and Thurgood Mar-
    shall, NAACP publication, July, 1943.
18. Quoted in testimony of Walter P. Reuther before Sub-Committee
    on Anti-Discrimination Legislation of the United States Senate
    Committee on Labor and Public Welfare, June 18, 1947.

19. *Ibid.*
20. *The Daily Worker,* June 14, 1942.
21. *UAW Convention Proceedings,* 1943.
22. Reuther testimony, *op. cit.*
23. Quoted by Roi Ottley, *New York Times Magazine,* April 20, 1947.

II

There is a paucity of material on the subjects discussed in this chapter, either with regard to the UAW in particular or trade unions in general. The article by Will Herberg cited below is probably the best on union life. We have consulted the following for material on some of the general themes of this chapter: From Max Weber: Essays in Sociology, *edited by Hans Gerth and C. Wright Mills, Oxford University Press, 1946;* Ideology and Utopia, *Karl Mannheim, Harcourt, Brace and Co., undated;* Man and Society, *Karl Mannheim, London, 1942; "The Bureaucratic Personality," by Robert Merton in* Personality in Culture and Nature, *Henry Murray and Clyde Kluckhohn, editors, Alfred A. Knopf, 1948; "Trade Union Government: A Formal Analysis," Joseph Shister,* Quarterly Journal of Economics, *Nov., 1945; "The Constitutional Power of the Chief Officer in American Labor Unions," Philip Taft,* Quarterly Journal of Economics, *May, 1948; "Bureaucracy: The Problem and Its Setting," Reinhard Bendix,* American Sociological Review, *Oct., 1947.*

1. Brief submitted by Walter Reuther to U.S. Senate Sub-Committee on Labor and Public Welfare, Feb. 21, 1947.
2. "Bureaucracy and Democracy in Labor Unions," Will Herberg. *Antioch Review,* Sept. 1943.
3. Herberg, *op. cit.*
4. "The Trade Union as a Wage-Fixing Institution," Arthur Ross, *American Economic Review,* Sept. 1947.
5. "Factions in Trade Unions," A. J. Muste, *American Labor Dynamics,* Ed. by J. B. S. Hardman, Harcourt, Brace and Co., 1928.
6. "President's Report," Walter Reuther, *United Automobile Worker,* Dec. 1948.
7. "President's Report," Ken Morris, *Voice of Local 212,* Jan. 1949.

12

For some material and ideas in the central part of this chapter we are indebted to Professor C. Wright Mills' book, cited below.

1. Radio speech, Charles Edgecomb, Oct. 16, 1945.
2. Anonymously published election leaflet.
3. "Look Forward, Labor," by Victor Reuther, *Common Sense*, Dec. 1945.
4. *United Automobile Worker*, Jan. 1948.
5. *United Automobile Worker*, April, 1948.
6. *United Automobile Worker*, Nov. 1948.
7. *Michigan CIO News*, Jan. 26, 1949.
8. *Ammunition*, Feb. 1949.
9. Conversation with B. J. Widick, March, 1949.
10. *The New Men of Power* by C. Wright Mills, Harcourt, Brace and Co., 1948.
11. *Ibid.*
12. *Proceedings*, UAW convention, Atlantic City, 1947.

Index

Note: Major UAW events listed under *UAW, UAW locals* and *UAW strikes.*